The Book of Herbs

The Book of Herbs

General Editor
Dawn Titmus

THUNDER BAY
P·R·E·S·S

Published in the United States by
Thunder Bay Press
An imprint of the Advantage Publishers Group
5880 Oberlin Drive, Suite 400
San Diego, CA 92121-4794
www.advantagebooksonline.com

Copyright © Libero Publishing Ltd, 2000
This edition produced by **Brown Partworks**
8 Chapel Place, Rivington Street
London EC2A 3DQ, England
www.brownpartworks.co.uk

Library of Congress Cataloging-in-Publication Data
The book of herbs / general editor, Dawn Titmus.
  p. cm
  ISBN 1-57145-240-0
  1. Herbs. 2. Herb gardening. 3. Herbs—Utilization. I. Titmus, Dawn.
  SB351.H5 B637 2000
  635.7—dc21   99-089560

Printed in Hong Kong

1 2 3 4 5 00 01 02 03 04

North American Edition
Managing Editor JoAnn Padgett
Associate Editor Elizabeth McNulty

Table of Contents

Introduction

Whether you want to cultivate herbs, cook with them, use them for health and beauty, or in craftmaking, *The Book of Herbs* is a comprehensive guide to all you need to know about growing and using herbs.

The **Directory of Herbs** contains information about the origin, history, cultivation, and uses of more than 30 popular herbs, helping you decide which ones you would like to grow or use in the kitchen or home. Whether you have lots of space to grow herbs or merely a small tub outside the kitchen door, **Growing Herbs** is a complete guide to cultivating herbs, from the early stages of planning a herb garden to garden chores throughout the year and growing herbs for specific uses. **Cooking with Herbs** contains more than 30 delicious recipes for all occasions, showing you how to get the best use of herbs in the kitchen, while **Herbal Beauty and Health** provides recipes for cosmetic and medicinal preparations for the whole family. Finally, **Herbs in the Home** contains instructions for using herbs in craftmaking—from potpourris and herbal displays to drawer fresheners and herbal wreaths—either to give as gifts or to decorate the home.

Chapter by chapter and step by step, *The Book of Herbs* shows you how to use herbs to improve every aspect of your life.

Directory of Herbs

This directory lists over thirty of the most popular herbs for household and culinary use. Each entry is divided into two parts. The first page describes the herb's appearance and includes information about its history, origin, and traditional uses. A ready-reference panel contains useful information about the herb's Latin name, any other common names, the parts used, its properties, and its culinary and medicinal uses, as well as any household, cosmetic, or decorative uses.

On the second page of each entry a full-page photograph enables readers to see at a glance each part of the plant and how it can be used. A column on cultivation provides all the information needed to grow, care for, harvest, and preserve the herb.

Helpful hints and caution notes are included in many of the entries, providing additional guidance and advice about the plant's properties and uses.

Basil

No other herb stands out quite like basil for its aroma—shred its leaves and the pungent smell fills the air, and it has a flavor to match. Although the plant does not like cold or wind, it grows readily in a pot placed in a sheltered corner or on a windowsill.

Basil is one of the world's major culinary herbs and its aromatic leaves are well known for the seasoning they bring to many dishes. Originally from India, the herb has long been cultivated throughout Europe and the Mediterranean. It is particularly important in Italian cooking; it is a main ingredient of pesto sauce and tastes delicious with tomatoes, garlic, and eggplants.

It also suits shellfish and can be added to omelettes. Basil flavors soups and sauces and is used to make flavored oils and marinades or basil vinegar. It is rich in Vitamin A, Vitamin C, calcium, and iron. Fresh basil is readily available to almost everyone, since it can be grown in pots indoors.

HERB TONIC

Basil has an uplifting effect on the nervous system. The essential oil is often used in aromatherapy to treat depression and negativity. As it can also ease overworked and stressed muscles, basil is popular with dancers and athletes.

Basil is good for the digestive system. An infusion of the fresh leaves will help nervous dyspepsia, or you can chew on a small leaf to ease indigestion or flatulence. The tea is said to relieve nausea.

IN THE GARDEN

There are more than 160 varieties of basil worldwide. Some look very attractive outside in the herb garden, and different varieties can look appealing when grown side by side. The purple leaves of the 'Dark Opal' or 'Purple Ruffle' varieties are an excellent counterpart

to the usual green. To add to the scent of the garden, lemon basil (*Ocimum basilicum* var. *citriodorum*) is a good choice. Although many insects are repelled by basil, it attracts butterflies and bees.

In its native India, basil was considered sacred, second only to the lotus flower. And in other countries, too, it has the reputation of being a sacred herb. It was reputedly found growing around Christ's tomb after the resurrection. In some Greek Orthodox churches it is used to prepare holy water, and pots of basil are often set below the altar and at the foot of the pulpit.

▼ Basil likes a sunny, sheltered site—it does not thrive if exposed to wind or frost. It grows to a height of 18 in. (45 cm) and sends up spikes of flowers from June to September. Flowering tops can be used to make a soothing infusion.

Harry Smith Collection

BASIL
Ocimum basilicum
Sweet basil

PARTS USED:
Leaves, stems, and flowers

PROPERTIES:
Contains vitamins A and C, and calcium and iron; the essential oil is uplifting.

USES OF THE HERB:
Culinary
Traditionally, basil should be torn with the fingers rather than chopped. It tastes delicious sprinkled over salads and is an important part of many sauces.

Medicinal
Make tea by pouring a cup of boiling water over 1 tablespoon (15 ml) of basil leaves to treat colds, flu, catarrh, and digestive upsets. (Do not take basil medicinally if you are pregnant.)

Household
Pots of basil in the kitchen will keep flies away. A fresh leaf rubbed on an insect bite reduces irritation.

CAUTION
Therapeutic doses of basil should not be used in pregnancy.

CULTIVATION

BASIL
Ocimum basilicum

LIFESPAN
Tender annual.

HEIGHT
18 in. (45 cm).

SITE
Sunny and sheltered.

SOIL
Well drained and moist.

GROWING
Basil thrives particularly well when grown in pots. Seed should be sown in late spring. Sow seed in heated greenhouse or on kitchen windowsill.

HARVESTING
Pick leaves when young. They are best picked before flowering time (June-Sep).

PRESERVING
Basil leaves can be frozen (rub olive oil on them first). Infuse fresh leaves in oils and vinegars.

HELPFUL HINT
Often grown as a companion plant in the vegetable garden—basil is said to repel aphids, mites, asparagus beetles, and tomato hornworms. It is vulnerable to slugs, whitefly, and red spider mites.

Greek Basil
Ocimum basilicum var. *minimum*
A miniature variant, also called "bush basil." Has a compact growth and very small leaves. The flavor is not so strong as some of the larger-leafed varieties, although it is ideal for pot cultivation in the kitchen.

Seeds
Small, dark brown and egg shaped. Basil is normally propagated from seeds.

Basil
Ocimum basilicum
Leafy, aromatic herb rich in a complex mixture of aromatic oils. 'Genovese,' one of many variants of this widely grown plant, favored for Italian dishes, grows to about 18 in. (45 cm).

Leaf
Naturally enhances the flavor of tomatoes, other vegetables, and pasta.

Dried leaf
Can be crushed for use in cooking or in potpourri. Infuse instead of fresh leaves as a tea that aids digestion and soothes respiratory problems.

Stem
Square, delicate stem can be chopped and used like leaves—the whole plant is edible.

Bay

The history of bay is well documented—the Ancient Greeks made wreaths out of it to crown their athletes, the Romans used it as a symbol of wisdom, and the French exploited its culinary properties. It is still used mainly for culinary purposes.

Also known as sweet bay or bay laurel, the dried leaves of this herb tree are used as a seasoning in sweet and savory cooking all over the world. Today, the essential oil is widely used in commercial condiments and sauces, meat products, and liqueurs.

TREE OF THE GODS

In ancient times, bay was sacred to the gods. The roof of Apollo's temple at Delphi was entirely made of its leaves. Bay was also dedicated to the god of medicine, and for centuries was used to ward off disease, especially in times of plague, when it was strewn around the house.

A bay wreath became a mark of excellence for athletes and poets and the Romans used it as a symbol of wisdom. The Latin for "crowned with laurel" survives in the modern "poet laureate," while the laurel wreath appears on sports trophies to this day.

ANCIENT HEALER

The tree has always served a decorative purpose and thrives on being clipped. Since the sixteenth century, bushes have been carefully trained into ornamental shapes. One traditional design is the "ball bay," which is trimmed to a globe at the top of a smooth, bare trunk. This is the traditional tree often seen on patios or beside entrances.

The bay tree is one of two small shrubs or evergreen trees in this genus. It is native to the Mediterranean region and likes full sun—although it tolerates partial shade—and a rich soil. In colder climates, clipped bushes are best grown in a tub so that they can be moved to a sheltered spot or indoors during winter.

Photos Horticultural

▲ ▼ **Bay thrives on regular clipping, traditionally into decorative "ball bays," which can be grown in tubs as a patio decoration. In the ground it can grow into a sizable tree and may reach 60 ft. (20 m).**

BAY
Laurus nobilis
Sweet bay

PARTS USED:
Leaves

PROPERTIES:
Aromatic, culinary flavoring.

USES OF THE HERB:
Culinary
Use bay leaves as part of a bouquet garni for soups, stews, and sauces. Add to stocks, marinades, and stews, curry, and poached fish. Remove leaves before serving. Place in rice jar to flavor rice. Heat in milk to flavor custards and puddings. Use to flavor vinegar.

Medicinal
Use an infusion of the leaves as a digestive stimulant. Apply infusion to scalp to relieve dandruff. Essential oil is good for massaging sprains and rheumatic pains. Make sure the oil is diluted by mixing it with a "carrier oil" such as sweet almond beforehand.

Cosmetic
Add a decoction of bay to bath water to tone the skin and relieve aches.

Decorative
Clipped and trained bay trees in tubs are an elegant and traditional decoration for doorways and house walls. Use branches in full leaf for wreaths.

Household
Crumble dried leaves into potpourri. Hang branches up to freshen the air.

Bay
Laurus nobilis
Dense, evergreen shrub
or small tree. Small
cream-yellow flowers
appear in spring.

CULTIVATION

BAY
Laurus nobilis

LIFESPAN
**Evergreen shrub or small
tree.**

HEIGHT
**To 60 ft. (20 m) tall in
Mediterranean regions.**

SITE
**Full sun or partial shade.
Protect from wind.**

SOIL
**Rich, moist and well
drained.**

GROWING
**Propagate from cuttings
and transplant when
established.**

HARVESTING
**The leaves can be picked
at any time.**

PRESERVING
**Dry the leaves. Aroma
released when leaves
crushed.**

HELPFUL HINT
**It is possible to grow
quite a large plant in a
small pot, and it will
thrive for years without
repotting.**

Leaf
Aromatic,
leathery, and
shiny dark
green with
clear veining.

Stem
Young stems are
purple-brown
becoming woody
and gray with
age.

Dried leaf
Like fresh leaves can
be used to flavor
sauces, marinades,
etc. Use freshly dried,
as flavor fades.

Bergamot (Bee balm)

The aromatic leaves and edible flowers of bergamot can be used for flavoring and decorating food. The plant also dries well, with the flowers retaining some of their color.

This North American woodland herb became a popular garden plant in Europe after explorers sent back the seeds. After the Boston Tea Party in 1773, when rioting settlers threw several hundred chests of Indian tea into Boston Harbor, bergamot was used to make a substitute tea known as Oswego tea.

Bergamot's Latin name, *Monarda*, recalls the Spanish botanist Dr. Nicholas Monardes who wrote a book about the plants of America in 1569. He named this herb "bergamot" because the scent of its leaves resembles the Italian Bergamot orange (*Citrus bergamia*), from which an essential oil is made.

The bergamot plant usually has vivid scarlet flowers, although there are varieties that bear pink, purple, mauve, and white blooms. In North America, hummingbirds are attracted to the flowers, while throughout Europe any garden featuring bergamot will attract butterflies and bees, giving rise to another popular name for bergamot—bee balm.

GARDEN BEAUTY

The plant has claw-shaped, tubular flowers that bloom from July until September, when they can be harvested whole and preserved. The leaves of the plant are strongly aromatic, particularly when the plant is young. This makes bergamot a good choice for planting along paths. As people brush past, the leaves release a delicious scent.

The edible flowers can be used to decorate salads. The leaves have a strong flavor and can be used sparingly in salads and stuffings. Dried leaves can be infused in water or milk.

An infusion drunk as tea can help with digestive problems, and Native Americans used bergamot for chest and throat complaints.

▼ **A native of North America, bergamot was introduced to Europe as a flowering garden plant.**

Harry Smith Collection

BERGAMOT
Monarda didyma
Bee balm

PARTS USED:
Leaves and flowers.

PROPERTIES:
Aromatic

USES OF THE HERB:
Decorative
Use in flower arrangements or to add scent and color to potpourri mixtures.

Culinary
Add the leaves to fruit salad and use the flowers to decorate puddings. Leaves can also be added to homemade lemonade to enhance the flavor. Add the leaves to Indian or China tea to give the flavor of Earl Grey tea. Add flowers to salads.

Medicinal
Drink an infusion for minor digestive complaints.

Household
Attracts a host of butterflies and bees to the garden.

CULTIVATION

BERGAMOT
Monarda didyma

LIFESPAN
Hardy perennial.

HEIGHT
2–3 ft. (60 cm–1 m).

SITE
Sun, or partial shade in hot climate.

SOIL
Rich, light, moist.

GROWING
Plant in late spring and early summer. Bergamot is not suitable for growing indoors.

HARVESTING
Harvest young leaves for drying before flowers form. Collect flowers in spring or summer when they are fully open. Collect whole plants for drying during flowering.

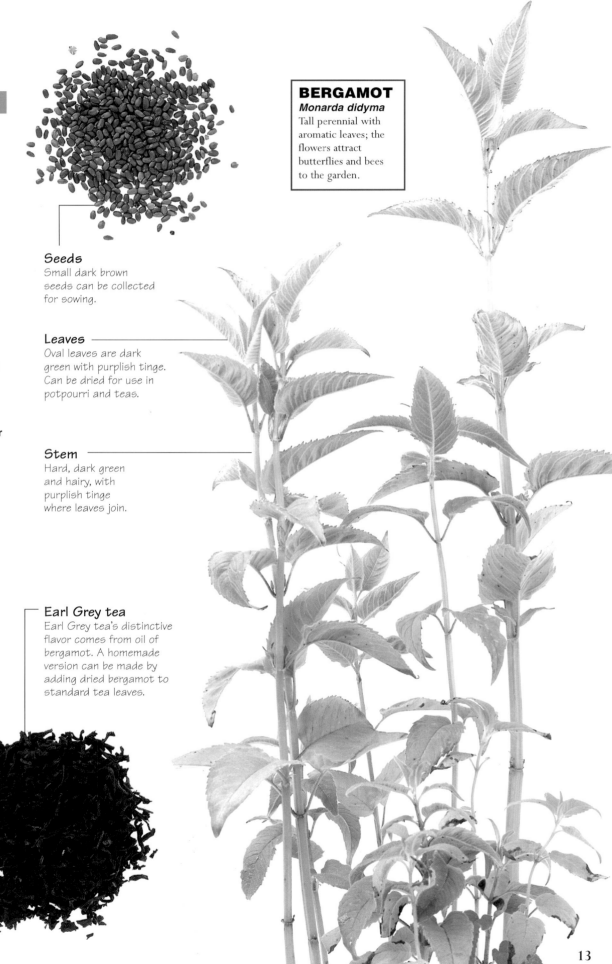

Seeds
Small dark brown seeds can be collected for sowing.

Leaves
Oval leaves are dark green with purplish tinge. Can be dried for use in potpourri and teas.

Stem
Hard, dark green and hairy, with purplish tinge where leaves join.

Earl Grey tea
Earl Grey tea's distinctive flavor comes from oil of bergamot. A homemade version can be made by adding dried bergamot to standard tea leaves.

BERGAMOT
Monarda didyma
Tall perennial with aromatic leaves; the flowers attract butterflies and bees to the garden.

Borage

This attractive herb with its colorful flowers looks good in an herbaceous border and can be put to good use in the kitchen.

Borage is an attractive, flowering plant with a wide range of culinary and medicinal uses. It is traditionally reputed to bestow both courage and happiness—the Celtic word *borrach* means courage.

In ancient times, borage was used to make herbal wine, which the Ancient Greek poet Homer is alleged to have called the wine of forgetfulness. In medieval England, borage flowers were floated on the stirrup-cups given to departing Crusader knights.

Borage flowers are edible, as are the leaves, which have a cucumber flavor. They are usually a vivid blue color, and often appear in illustrated medieval texts and tapestries. The plants may sometimes produce pink or white flowers. Once dried, borage flowers make an ideal addition to potpourri.

Traditionally, the herb is well known for its ability to calm anxiety and nervous disorders.

Recent medical research has shown that borage's high concentrations of minerals and complex compounds may work on the adrenal glands and have a stimulating effect similar to that of adrenaline.

NATIVE ROOTS

Originally a native of the Mediterranean and western Asia, and often found growing on wasteland and rough ground, this herb thrives best on rich, moist, well-drained soil.

The plants tend to have a long, robust tap root, so transplanting is seldom successful and growing plants in pots or containers is not generally advised.

The best sites for this plant are herb gardens or herbaceous borders. However, a few seeds can be sown to produce small plants for winter use, as long as they are kept indoors in a light, warm spot.

BORAGE
Borago officinalis

PARTS USED:
Leaves, flowers, seeds, oil.

PROPERTIES:
Cooling, saline, diuretic; mildly sedative and anti-depressant.

USES OF THE HERB:
Culinary
Use flowers in salads as a garnish or crystallize for cake decorations. Add young leaves to summer drinks. Chop leaves to use in ravioli stuffing.

Medicinal
Use leaves in a poultice to soothe bruises. Seed oil may be effective in treating premenstrual tension and lowering blood pressure.

Cosmetic
Add leaves to a face pack for dry skin or mix with barley and use in bath bags.

Household
Flowers attract bees to gardens. When planted near tomatoes, helps to control tomato worm.

CAUTION
May irritate the skin or cause allergies. In some countries, all members of the borage family are restricted for medicinal use as they may cause liver damage.

◄ The stunning blue star shapes of borage flowers, which attract bees, make this a lovely decorative herb. Silver hairs cover the whole plant and give it an attractive shimmering quality in bright light.

Pat Brindley

Seeds
Large, dark brown seeds remain viable for several years. Contain starflower oil that has medicinal uses.

Leaf
Although covered with prickly hairs, leaves are edible, with medicinal and cosmetic uses.

CULTIVATION

BORAGE
Borago officinalis

LIFESPAN
Hardy annual

HEIGHT
1–3 ft. (30 cm–1 m).

SITE
Full sun or partial shade in an open spot.

SOIL
Will grow in poor soil, but prefers fairly light, well-drained, and moist conditions.

GROWING
Grows best in borders and beds, but small plants will grow indoors. Plant seeds in fall for spring flowering and in spring for summer flowering. Space plants out at about 12 in. (30 cm) intervals. Will usually self-sow.

HARVESTING
Pick leaves from spring to summer, as flowering begins, and pick flowers as soon as they open.

PRESERVING
Dry leaves and dry or crystallize flowers.

HELPFUL HINT
Pick flowers by holding stamens and pulling the flower away from its sepals. Preserve promptly and do not store for too long— properties diminish quickly. Site near strawberries as the plants stimulate each other's growth.

Borage
Borago officinalis
Medium-sized hardy annual with attractive, edible flowers.

Stem
Sturdy, round stems are hollow and hairy.

15

Chamomile

Flowering varieties of this plant have culinary and medicinal uses, while the nonflowering variety makes excellent ground cover and can be cultivated to provide a fragrant lawn.

An aromatic, springy carpet of herbs makes an entrancing alternative to a conventional grass lawn. Among several herbs used for lawns, perhaps the most popular is chamomile (also known as camomile).

In fact, chamomile has been used for creating lawns since medieval times. A seventeenth-century gardener wrote that it "delights the mind and brings health to the body."

Chamomile grows well in warm, dry conditions and the plants tolerate being walked on. As the leaves are crushed underfoot, they release a pleasant perfume, reminiscent of apples. The name "chamomile" derives from the Greek word *khamaimelon*, which means "apple on the ground."

Although a chamomile lawn doesn't need mowing, it needs to be tended to prevent an invasion of weeds. It is a good idea to border the lawn with either stones or bricks.

CHOOSING VARIETIES

Chamaemelum nobile is the best type for use as a lawn because it is low growing and spreads easily. The ideal choice is the nonflowering cultivar 'Treneague,' which forms a short, dense mat about 1 in. (2.5 cm) tall and remains green without attention. However, the absence of flowers means that this variety cannot be used as a medicinal or culinary herb because it is the flowers that have these properties. Remove the flower heads from the flowering varieties from time to time.

OTHER OPTIONS

Instead of a chamomile lawn, there are other ways to make the most of this plant. Plant it in containers or in gaps in paving. It can also be used in a raised area to create an outdoor "seat." Another option is a chamomile path winding through a herb garden—the scent can be enjoyed and the leaves dried to use in potpourri and herbal pillows.

Pat Brindley

CHAMOMILE
Chamaemelum nobile
(Roman chamomile)

PARTS USED:
Whole plant, leaves, and flowers.

PROPERTIES:
A fragrant herb with culinary and medicinal uses that also provides good ground cover.

USES OF THE HERB:
Culinary
Use flowering varieties for herbal drinks.

Medicinal
The flowers can be used to make an infusion. Use as a lotion to soothe sore or irritated skin and as a mild sedative tea for insomnia.

Household
The presence of chamomile in the garden will often help to revive nearby plants that are ailing. The aromatic leaves can be used in potpourri and herbal pillows.

◀ The fragrance released by chamomile when crushed makes it the perfect choice for chamomile "seats," which are a feature of some herb gardens.

Leaf
Feathery, bright green leaves give off an apple scent when crushed.

CULTIVATION

CHAMOMILE
Chamaemelum nobile

LIFESPAN
Hardy evergreen perennial.

HEIGHT
1–6 in. (2.5–15 cm)

SITE
Full sun.

SOIL
Light and well drained. Can do well on poor soil.

GROWING
Sow in spring. Divide and plant out young plants once they are established.

HARVESTING
Pick flowers in summer, when they are fully open, and gather leaves at any time.

PRESERVING
Dry flowers and leaves. Flowers are also commercially distilled for their oil.

Chamomile
Chamaemelum nobile 'Treneague'
An apple-scented, nonflowering variety that tolerates dry conditions well and forms a fragrant carpet of leaves.

Seeds
Chamomile can be grown from seed, but the variety 'Treneague' must be propagated by division.

Chervil

Chervil has a long history—it has been used for its medicinal and culinary properties for many centuries. It also makes an attractive garden plant, and is suitable for mixed borders and containers.

This delicately aromatic herb is a perfect choice for garden containers. Enjoyed fresh in large quantities, this staple of French cuisine adds a subtle, slightly bitter aniseed flavor to a wide range of meat and vegetable dishes. The leaves are the part that is normally used, although the stem can be chopped and used in stews and casseroles. It is best used fresh as it doesn't retain its flavor well when dried.

The *Anthriscus* genus, to which chervil belongs, contains annuals, biennials, and perennials from Europe, North Africa, and Asia. Chervil is a leafy biennial that has become increasingly popular as a culinary plant in recent years.

ANCIENT CURE

The medicinal value of chervil was praised as far back as the time of ancient Rome. The herb's therapeutic uses revolve around its cleansing and expectorant properties. It can be used to ease fluid retention and relieve liver and kidney problems. It will also aid the smooth functioning of the digestive system.

Other disorders that respond to chervil include conjunctivitis, swollen eyelids, and hemorrhoids, which are treated by an external application of chervil preparations. Jaundice, rheumatism, and eczema respond well when chervil is taken internally. The leaves are also a source of vitamin C, carotene, magnesium, and iron.

Photos Horticultural

▲ Allowing some chervil plants (pictured here in a mixed border) to flower and produce seeds will ensure a self-seeding supply of the herb.

The chervil plant has a delicate, slender stem and fine, feathery leaves that take on a faint pink-purple hue during the last weeks of summer. Tiny white flowers, arranged in little clusters, appear during the late summer months. For the best results, chervil plants should be positioned in a moist, shady spot. Folklore claims that planting the herb next to radishes will give the radishes a much hotter flavor.

A fresh supply of leaves can be kept going through the warmer months by sowing seeds every few weeks through spring and summer. To keep a fresh supply going through the winter months, seeds should be sown in fall and plants raised under protection.

CHERVIL
Anthriscus cerefolium

PARTS USED:
Stems and leaves.

PROPERTIES:
A cleansing expectorant containing vitamins and minerals.

USES OF THE HERB:
Culinary
Add to salads and fish, chicken, egg, and potato dishes, as well as soups and sauces. Cooking and drying destroys the subtle flavor, so use large quantities of fresh leaves, toward the end of cooking. Chervil brings out the flavor of some other herbs very well—try cooking fish with a combination of chervil and lemon balm.

Medicinal
The herb's tonic and expectorant properties aid digestive and urinary functions—take a cup of chervil tea to cleanse the system.

Cosmetic
A chervil face mask cleanses and softens skin, while a poultice on closed eyelids refreshes tired eyes.

Decorative
Use seed heads in dried floral arrangements.

Chervil
Anthriscus cerefolium
This biennial, reminiscent of Italian parsley, thrives in cool shade and is often grown as an annual.

Leaf
Lacy, bright green leaf that resembles Italian parsley and has a hint of its flavor.

Stem
Delicate stem is hollow and ridged and can be chopped and added to various dishes.

Dried chervil
Drying chervil destroys its subtle flavor for culinary purposes, but the dried leaves are used medicinally.

Seeds
Long, thin seeds, dark in color.

CULTIVATION

CHERVIL
Anthriscus cerefolium

LIFESPAN
Hardy annual or biennial.

HEIGHT
10–24 in. (25–60 cm).

SITE
Partial shade. Avoid extreme heat or cold.

SOIL
Fertile, moist, light and well drained.

GROWING
Seedlings should be thinned to about 4 in. (10 cm) apart. Sow where plants will grow as chervil does not transplant. Sow regularly to ensure a constant supply and overwinter under protection. A good indoor plant.

HARVESTING
Collect leaves before flowering from well-established plants.

PRESERVING
Leaves can be dried, but are better used fresh. Dry seed heads to use in floral arrangements.

HELPFUL HINT
Planted alongside lettuces, chervil is said to protect them from aphids, ants, and slugs.

Chives

One of the most popular of culinary herbs, the leaves of this plant can be used in a variety of ways. The flowers are also edible, and can be used to garnish salads and other cold dishes. Chives are readily grown indoors or outside.

Chives are related to onion and garlic (all of which are members of the *Allium* genus). Most alliums are popular for both their culinary uses and health-giving properties.

The chives species grown in North America (*Allium schoenoprasum*) has pretty, pale purple flowers, and hollow, cylindrical leaves that taper to a fine point. The leaves, which are the most commonly used part of the plant, have a mild onionlike flavor that is excellent for seasoning a wide range of dishes, especially when onion itself is too strong.

While chives are not normally used as a medicinal herb, their leaves contain very large amounts of vitamins A and C, along with other vitamins and minerals.

GROWING CHIVES

Chives look delightful as an edging plant or in window boxes and pots. However, when chives are being grown primarily for cooking, rather than decoration, the flowers should be removed to prevent the plant from becoming exhausted—the flowers can be used to great effect in a range of salads.

Chives should be cut very low after flowering in order to produce fresh leaves. The leaves are best snipped or chopped and used fresh as required. Fresh leaves can be eaten in salads, soups, and sandwiches, as a garnish, or to flavor butter or soft cheeses. Chives do not dry particularly well, and dried leaves are best used in cooked dishes.

Garlic chives (*Allium tuberosum*) have a mild garlic flavor that may be enjoyed by those who prefer a less pungent form of garlic. The use of

▲ The pretty florets and green leaves of chives make it a useful decorative plant. When planted near roses, it can help to deter aphids. Remove the flowers to encourage leaf growth if chives are being grown for culinary use.

garlic chives was first recorded 4,000 years ago in China (an alternative common name is Chinese chives), and they were appreciated by the Genoan traveler Marco Polo, who helped to popularize them in the West. Medicinally, they are said to improve kidney function.

Garlic chives can be used in the same way as chives and can also be grown with ease. They have clusters of starry white flowers.

CHIVES
Allium schoenoprasum

PARTS USED:
Leaves and flowers

PROPERTIES:
Contains vitamins A and C and minerals.

USES OF THE HERB:
Culinary
Sprinkle florets or cut leaves on salads, in sandwiches and soups, and use generally as a garnish. Chives can be delicious when added to either butter or cream cheese and are especially good with potatoes and eggs. The chopped leaves are an essential ingredient of the chilled soup known as vichyssoise, and are used in remoulade sauce. Dried chives can be reconstituted with lemon juice.

Medicinal
Fresh leaves and flowers are a mild aid to digestion. Alliums are often good for the blood vessels, keeping them elastic and helping to deter premature ageing.

Household
An infusion of chives makes a spray that will remove aphids and mildew from garden plants.

CULTIVATION

CHIVES
Allium schoenoprasum

LIFESPAN
Hardy perennial.

HEIGHT
4 in.–2 ft. (10–60 cm).

SITE
Sun or partial shade. Can be grown in pots indoors.

SOIL
Fertile, moist and well drained.

GROWING
Sow seed in spring and divide in fall or spring. Cut down to the ground after flowering to produce a fresh crop of leaves. Remove dead stems in winter.

HARVESTING
Cut as early as possible in the spring. By using a cloche for protection in spring and fall, the harvesting period can be extended to about nine months.

PRESERVING
Dried leaves do not retain their flavor particularly well. Dry at a low temperature to retain color.

HELPFUL HINT
Planting chives around roses may help to prevent blackspot. They also keep aphids away.

Chives
Allium schoenoprasum
A member of the onion family, grown as a culinary flavoring and a decorative border plant.

Seeds
Small, black seeds are about ⅛ in. (3 mm) long and taste of mild onions.

Leaf
The leaves are long, grassy, and tubular. The color varies from mid- to dark green.

Flower
Chives are sometimes grown for the decorative purple florets that appear in summer. They are edible.

Dried leaf
The dried leaves do not retain their color and flavor particularly well and are best used in cooked dishes.

Cilantro

Also called fresh coriander, this aromatic herb has many culinary uses and healing properties. It is easily grown from seed, and the fresh leaves and crushed seeds can be included in a variety of dishes.

Photos Horticultural

C ilantro leaves and seeds are a well-known flavoring in many Middle Eastern and Southeast Asian dishes, such as curries and chutneys. The plant also has many healing properties.

This strong-smelling herb has been cultivated for cooking and medicinal purposes for at least 3,000 years. It was first brought to Britain and northern Europe by the Romans, who used it as part of a mixture that was rubbed into meat to help preserve it. Cilantro's preservative qualities were noted by the Chinese, who believed that it helped people live to a great age. One of cilantro's other common names is Chinese parsley.

The plant was named *koriandron* by the ancient Greeks, who thought it smelled like bugs, or *koris*. The smell of the leaves is very distinctive and not to everyone's taste. The seeds smell quite different from the plant, however, and can even be used in potpourri.

▲ Cilantro likes full sun, but when it is grown outdoors, its finely cut foliage means that it looks best planted in abundance. Although it can be grown indoors, many people find the smell unpleasant.

HEALING PROPERTIES

Like its relatives caraway, dill, and fennel, cilantro has healing properties that benefit the digestive system. It can be used instead of dill to make gripe water.

Commercially, it is used in liqueurs such as Chartreuse and Benedictine (it was originally included for its digestive properties). It can act as an appetite stimulant and is sometimes used in the treatment of anorexia nervosa.

The plant has wispy foliage and a profusion of tiny pinkish-white flowers. To create the most attractive show in the garden, plant cilantro in a drift.

CILANTRO
Coriandrum sativum
(Chinese parsley, coriander)

PARTS USED:
Leaves, seeds

PROPERTIES:
A strongly aromatic herb with preservative qualities and healing properties associated with the digestive system.

USES OF THE HERB:
Culinary
Cilantro seeds are delicious with meat, especially pork, and sweet puddings. The leaves make a welcome addition to salads and can be included in curries and stews.

Medicinal
For an infusion, pour a cup of boiling water on to 1 tsp. (5 ml) of crushed seeds and leave to infuse for five minutes. Drink before meals in order to relieve indigestion and flatulence. Cilantro is useful to relieve period pain and was once used to aid childbirth. If a breastfeeding mother drinks cilantro tea, it will help relieve colic in the child, since its anti-spasmodic effects pass readily into breast milk.

Household
Use cilantro seeds in a spicy, warm-scented potpourri.

CULTIVATION

CILANTRO
Coriandrum sativum

LIFESPAN
Hardy annual.

HEIGHT
2 ft. (60 cm).

SITE
Full sun; protect from strong winds.

SOIL
Prefers a rich, light, well-drained soil.

GROWING
Plant out or sow in late spring. Water regularly. Flowers June to July. Self-sows freely.

HARVESTING
Pick young leaves at any time. When seeds turn brown, collect by shaking them from the flower head.

PRESERVING
The seeds can be dried and stored whole or infused to make a delicious cilantro vinegar.

HELPFUL HINT
Cilantro possesses similar properties to fennel, but they should not be grown together because the fennel's seed production may suffer.

Cilantro
Coriandrum sativum
A popular and versatile herb that is easy to grow and use fresh in cooking.

Leaf
Mature, lower leaves look like parsley but have a strong scent. Upper leaves are wispy and have the same scent.

Stem
Fine, round stems may become straggly and branching. Can be chopped and used in soups and stews.

Seeds
Small, round and light brown. Seeds can be collected by shaking the seed head after they gain full color. Strong-scented, the seeds are also ground and used in powder form. more commonly known as coriander. Flavor matures in storage.

23

Comfrey

Comfrey has fallen out of favor as a culinary herb as it is thought to be toxic. However, it is still widely used medicinally, and has practical uses in the garden as well.

Comfrey has long been used externally and is known for its impressive ability to heal wounds. Its properties are due to the presence of allantoin, a chemical that stimulates cell division.

Comfrey's genus name, *Symphytum*, is also the name of a homeopathic remedy. The name comes from the Greek for "unite" and thus recognizes the plant's claimed ability to knit together broken bones. One of the old-fashioned folklore names for comfrey is "knitbone," and in the days before plaster casts, comfrey root was prepared and placed over an injury in a compress, where it would provide valuable support.

The flowering tops of comfrey contain vitamin B^{12}, and the plant also contains calcium, potassium, and phosphorus. Traditionally, young leaves were eaten as vegetables, either raw or steamed like spinach. However, recent studies suggest that comfrey may be harmful if consumed in large quantities.

There are as many as twenty varieties of comfrey worldwide. Some are cultivated as fodder— pigs are especially partial to it, and it is also given to race horses.

IN THE GARDEN
Comfrey is a dense, hairy plant with purple, pink, or white flowers. Apart from its medicinal qualities, comfrey is certainly decorative enough to include in any herbaceous border.

Choose comfrey's position carefully. It is a deep-rooted plant and hard to move once established. However, its long taproots can help to raise moisture and valuable minerals to the upper soil levels. Organic gardeners use it to energize the compost heap.

Pick leaves for drying in spring. Both the roots and the leaves can be used to treat external bruises, wounds, and sores.

Lyndon Parker

COMFREY
Symphytum officinale

PARTS USED:
Leaves and roots.

PROPERTIES:
Astringent, expectorant; soothes and heals, and reduces inflammation.

USES OF THE HERB:
Medicinal
Apply comfrey root as a poultice over bruises, sores, or minor fractures that the doctor has decided not to set in plaster. Comfrey ointment is good for skin inflammation and other disorders including eczema. You can add an infusion of the leaves, or tincture, to the bath water. Comfrey is also used as a homeopathic remedy, *Symphytum*, for the same purposes.

CAUTION
Recent testing shows that comfrey contains alkaloids that, in very large doses, have been found to cause liver damage in animals. Although all comfrey preparations are considered perfectly safe for external use, except on broken skin, while tests continue, it is advised that comfrey is not taken internally over long periods. Comfrey is subject to legal restrictions in some countries.

◀ **With its mauve, bell-shaped flowers, comfrey adds color to the garden from late spring. The plants enjoy full sun, but position them carefully as comfrey is invasive and deep-rooted.**

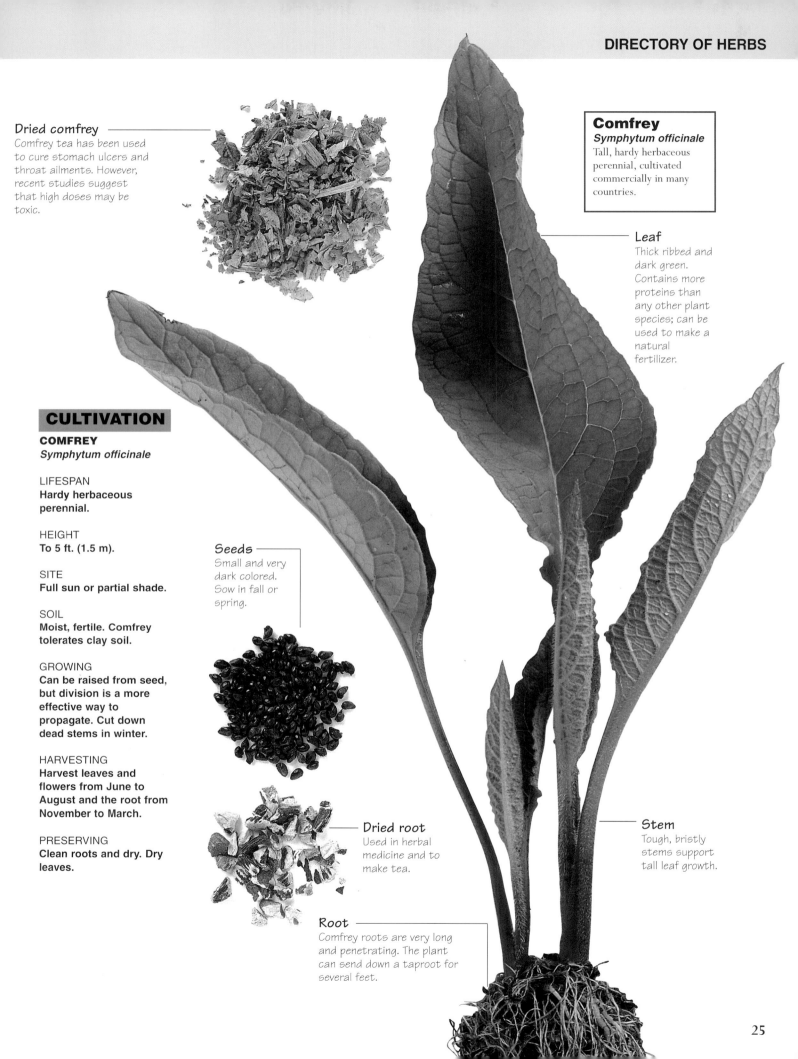

Dried comfrey
Comfrey tea has been used to cure stomach ulcers and throat ailments. However, recent studies suggest that high doses may be toxic.

Comfrey
Symphytum officinale
Tall, hardy herbaceous perennial, cultivated commercially in many countries.

Leaf
Thick ribbed and dark green. Contains more proteins than any other plant species; can be used to make a natural fertilizer.

CULTIVATION

COMFREY
Symphytum officinale

LIFESPAN
Hardy herbaceous perennial.

HEIGHT
To 5 ft. (1.5 m).

SITE
Full sun or partial shade.

SOIL
Moist, fertile. Comfrey tolerates clay soil.

GROWING
Can be raised from seed, but division is a more effective way to propagate. Cut down dead stems in winter.

HARVESTING
Harvest leaves and flowers from June to August and the root from November to March.

PRESERVING
Clean roots and dry. Dry leaves.

Seeds
Small and very dark colored. Sow in fall or spring.

Dried root
Used in herbal medicine and to make tea.

Stem
Tough, bristly stems support tall leaf growth.

Root
Comfrey roots are very long and penetrating. The plant can send down a taproot for several feet.

Dill

Dill has a long and varied history—the ancient Greeks used it to cure hiccups, and since then it has been used to ward off evil and to make love potions, among other things. Today the leaves and seeds feature as a culinary ingredient—it's particularly suited as a flavoring ingredient with fish dishes. It is also used medicinally.

An herb garden without dill is almost unthinkable. It is so versatile in cooking and so easy to grow that it is an ideal choice for any garden.

Dill also has many medicinal benefits. Its common name comes from the Saxon word *dilla,* meaning "to lull," and the seeds have gentle tranquilizing properties. The ancient Greeks found that dill cured hiccups, and the tradition of using it in preparations for infant colic has been passed down through the ages.

Its uses have been recorded throughout history, from the Roman writer Pliny to the famous Elizabethan herbalist Nicholas Culpeper. Among more fanciful ideas, it was used to protect against witchcraft, and it has also been used for centuries as an ingredient of love potions.

CULTIVATION

The plant has wispy, feathery leaves, and in midsummer puts out tiny, highly aromatic yellow blooms arranged in clusters. Dill looks very attractive when planted against a backdrop of marigolds and evening primrose, and has the advantage of attracting insects that are beneficial to the garden.

VERSATILE PROPERTIES

Dill leaves contain magnesium, iron, calcium, and vitamin C, so it is beneficial to use them in salads, soups, and grilled meats. The seeds make an aromatic and pungent flavoring for pickles. Dill is particularly compatible with fish dishes—it is, for example, a main ingredient of the Scandinavian dish gravadlax and of dill mayonnaise for fish salads.

Ardea London Ltd

◄ **Dill's branching, umbrella-shaped flower heads are similar to those of parsley, an indication that the two are related. Large clusters of tiny, aromatic blooms appear in midsummer and have a stronger flavor than the leaf.**

DILL
Anethum graveolens

PARTS USED:
Leaves, flowers, and seeds.

PROPERTIES:
Pungent, aromatic with cooling and diuretic effects.

USES OF THE HERB:
Decorative
Dill flowers look pretty when used as a filler in floral arrangements. The different varieties, such as 'Bouquet' and 'Fernleaf,' look similar.

Culinary
Use the seeds in soups, fish dishes, pickles, dill butter, and bread. You can add the flowering tops to a jar of homemade pickled gherkins, cucumbers, or cauliflowers. The leaves can be boiled with new potatoes and added to egg and salmon dishes.

Medicinal
Useful in a salt-free diet as it is rich in mineral salts. Dill water is good for indigestion, flatulence, and colic. Make by steeping a teaspoon of seeds in a cup of hot water, strain and drink. Breastfeeding mothers can drink dill tea to pass the soothing properties on to their baby.

Cosmetic
Chewing dill seeds can help to clear up bad breath.

CULTIVATION

DILL
Anethum graveolens

LIFESPAN
Hardy annual.

HEIGHT
2–5 ft. (60 cm–1.5m).

SITE
Full sun, protected position.

SOIL
Rich and well drained.

GROWING
Self-seeds freely. Sow seed in spring. In mild areas, fall sowing produces earlier plants. For a succession of young leaves, sow regularly every two weeks throughout early and midsummer.

HARVESTING
Harvest the leaves just before the plant comes into bloom (July–August), and pick the flowers just before the fruits begin to form. Collect the seeds after the flowering heads turn brown. Hang the plant over a cloth so that the seeds fall into it, and let them dry naturally.

HELPFUL HINT
Useful in companion planting with cabbages as it attracts insects that prey on aphids. Avoid planting near fennel as the two may produce unwanted hybrids. Does not like poor soil or overcrowding.

Dill weed
Dried dill leaves are sold commercially as dill weed. The flavor is milder than leaves gathered fresh from a growing plant.

Dill
Anethum graveolens
Important culinary and medicinal herb that forms a thick mass of fine leaves.

Leaf
Delicate, feathery and blue-green. Has an aromatic scent.

Seeds
Flat oval seeds can be gathered in summer and used to flavor savory dishes. Also infused to make dill water.

Stem
Normally only one stem per plant, grows tall and branching in maturity, with umbrella-shaped flowers at top.

Echinacea

Widely cultivated in gardens for its attractive flowers, this plant also has extensive medicinal applications. One of its most important properties is that it stimulates the immune system.

Echinacea, or the coneflower, is one of the most important and striking medicinal herbs of North America. Its common name comes from the flower's central cone, while the botanical name *Echinacea* is derived from *echinos*, the Greek word for "hedgehog," an allusion to the cone's prickly scales.

Along with its close relatives—*Echinacea angustifolia* and *E. pallida*—*E. purpurea* has been shown to stimulate the body's immune system to combat all kinds of viral and bacterial infection, encourage healing, and aid digestion. An extract of the roots and rhizomes is taken for a long list of complaints, including eczema, blood poisoning, boils, fungal infections, infections of the upper respiratory tract, colds and flu, fever, and venereal disease. A mouthwash or gargle can be useful for sore throat, tonsillitis, and gum disease, while external applications include herpes, acne, psoriasis, and infected wounds.

Echinacea is not toxic but excessive use can lead to throat irritation. Because of its dramatic effect on the immune system, it is now under scrutiny in the search for a cure for AIDS.

CURE FOR SNAKEBITE
The peoples of the North American plains used echinacea roots for their antiseptic and painkilling qualities, often to treat wounds and snake- and spider bites. After the root was chewed, the pulp was made into a poultice to lay on the wound once it had been lanced and the venom sucked out. By the late 19th century, the herb was well known in American medicine as a blood purifier. Modern science has since confirmed many of its powers, and there are now more than two hundred pharmaceutical preparations made from echinacea plants in Germany alone.

BORDER PLANT
The three most widely used species—*Echinacea purpurea*, *E. angustifolia,* and *E. pallida*—range in color from white to pink and purple. Their daisylike blooms make a stunning feature for a summer border, as well as being ideal as cut flowers. Flowers of *E. purpurea* have a sweet scent, rather like honey.

◀ The large daisy blooms cause plants to droop unless they are staked before flowering. The cultivar *E. purpurea* 'Robert Bloom' has especially striking, magenta-colored flowers.

Deni Bown

CONEFLOWER
Echinacea spp.

PARTS USED:
Roots, rhizomes.

PROPERTIES:
Bitter, slightly aromatic, antibacterial and antiviral; stimulates the immune system and promotes healing.

USES OF THE HERB:
Medicinal
Stimulates immune system to fight all kinds of infection and inflammation—currently being studied for possible use in AIDS treatment. Antiviral and antibacterial, promotes healing and aids digestion. Taken internally for skin diseases, blood poisoning, boils, abscesses, fungal infections, infections of the upper respiratory tract, venereal diseases. Externally to treat herpes, acne, psoriasis, infected wounds. Gargle or mouthwash for throat infections. Key ingredient of Native American medicine—used for wounds and bites.

CAUTION
Excessive use can cause throat irritation.

▼ The remarkable power of the coneflower to stimulate the body's immune system has led to a large number of *Echinacea* products.

Coneflower
Echinacea spp.
Hardy, rhizomatous
perennial, native to parts
of America—Michigan,
south to Virginia,
Louisiana, and Georgia.
Likes dry grasslands and
open woodland.

CULTIVATION

Coneflower
Echinacea spp.

LIFESPAN
Hardy perennial.

HEIGHT
2–4 ft. (60 cm–1.2 m).

SITE
Prefers full sun.

SOIL
Rich and well drained.

GROWING
**Sow seed in spring or
take root cuttings in late
winter. Alternatively, by
division while dormant.
Dig in plenty of rich
compost in spring.**

HARVESTING
**Rhizomes and roots
gathered in fall.**

Leaf
Slender, oval,
tapering to a
point. Toothed,
with rough surface.

Flower
Scaly, orange-
brown central
cone and long,
narrow, drooping
petals—white,
pink, or purple in
color.

Dried
coneflower
Used to make
infusions,
decoctions, and
tinctures.

Roots
Dense and
brown with
slender
rhizomes.

Stem
Erect and
sparsely
branched.

29

Fennel

The various forms of fennel have a range of culinary and medicinal uses. Most parts of the plant—including the seeds, widely used as a flavoring—are edible.

Fennel is one of the most familiar kitchen herbs. A well-known digestive aid, its strongly aniseed flavor and aroma add a unique feature to all kinds of fish dishes, salads, sauces, soups, and breads.

The species *Foeniculum vulgare* has several forms. The variety *F. vulgare* var. *dulce*, otherwise known as Florence fennel, sweet fennel, or *finocchio*, is a native of Italy and the Mediterranean. With its distinctive bulbous base, it is cultivated all over the world and is especially popular in Italy, where it is often eaten raw as a snack, simply dipped in olive oil. The cultivar *F. vulgare* 'Purpureum,' known as bronze fennel, is an attractive shade of brown and is slightly hardier than the usual green-leaved kind.

MEDICINAL QUALITIES

Fennel seeds can relieve colic, flatulence, and an irritated bowel, and extracts are included in laxatives and babies' gripe water. The root is particularly useful for urinary disorders, and the plant also relieves sore throats and gum disease. This potent herb should not be used during pregnancy.

Fennel oil is used in perfumes, food flavorings, and soaps, while an infusion—of sweet fennel only—makes a refreshing face wash. With its feathery leaves and yellow flowers, fennel is also attractive enough to be cultivated purely as a garden ornamental, and makes a fine focal point for a mixed or herbaceous border.

HERB OF VIGOR

Fennel spread throughout central and northern Europe on the instigation of the Emperor Charlemagne (742–814). Said to be an aphrodisiac, with the power to bestow courage, strength, and longevity, it was eaten by Roman warriors and was one of nine herbs held sacred by the Anglo-Saxons as having the ability to ward off evil. In medieval times, the seeds were eaten during the Lent fast to ward off hunger. Fennel was also said to keep fleas away if left in kennels and stables.

Lyndon Parker

FENNEL
Foeniculum vulgare

PARTS USED:
Leaves, stems, roots, seeds, and oil.

PROPERTIES:
Aromatic, diuretic; relieves digestive problems, relaxes spasms, reduces inflammation and increases milk flow.

USES OF THE HERB:
Culinary
All parts used variously in fish and vegetable dishes, salads, curries, pies, breads, soups, and sauces. Also used to flavor the Italian salami, *finocchiona*, and the French liqueur, *fenouillette*. Crushed seeds infused for tea.

Medicinal
Digestive aid, diuretic, boosts lactation (but not to be taken during pregnancy), relaxes spasms, anti-inflammatory. Seeds combat flatulence and stomach disturbances; root effective for urinary complaints. Use as mouthwash, eye bath, and rub for bronchial congestion.

Cosmetic
Infused crushed seeds make a cleansing face wash. Add a few drops of essential oil to skin lotions.

Household
Add to potpourri.

CAUTION
Not to be taken during pregnancy.

◀ With its yellow flowers and feathery foliage, fennel is an attractive garden plant. It attracts insects such as hoverflies and parasitic wasps, which eat common garden pests.

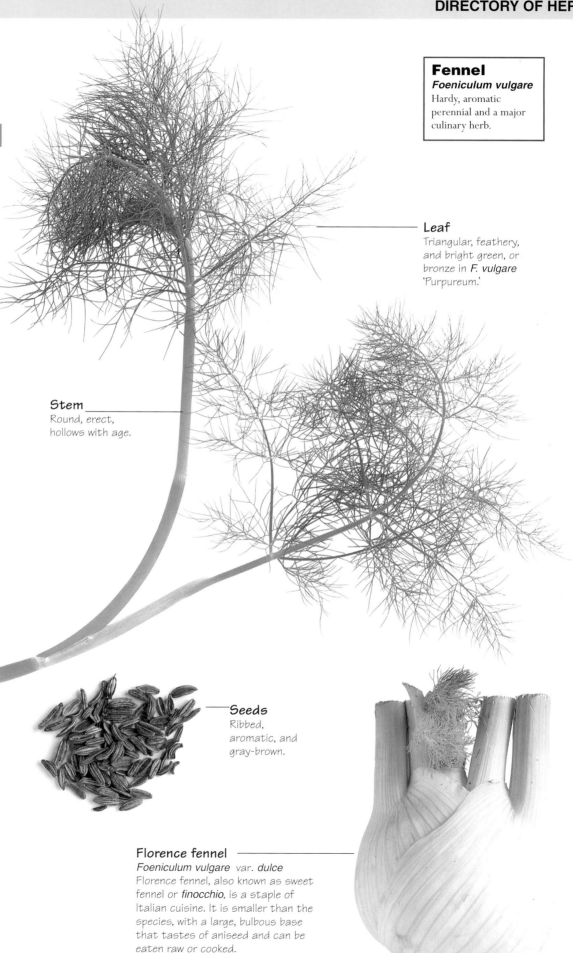

CULTIVATION

FENNEL
Foeniculum vulgare

LIFESPAN
Hardy perennial.

HEIGHT
Up to 6 ft. (2 m).

SITE
Full sun.

SOIL
Well drained (rich, moist and light for var. *dulce*).

GROWING
Sow seed in spring or fall, divide in spring. Usually self-seeds freely.

HARVESTING
Pick leaves and stems when tender. Lift roots in fall. Collect unripe seeds in summer to use fresh.

PRESERVING
Cut seed heads to collect ripe seeds before they fall, and dry in a paper bag. Use whole, ground or distilled for oil. Dry roots for use in decoctions.

HELPFUL HINT
Do not plant near beans, tomatoes, or coriander, as it is thought to stunt their growth, and keep away from its close relative, dill, to avoid hybridization.

Fennel
Foeniculum vulgare
Hardy, aromatic perennial and a major culinary herb.

Leaf
Triangular, feathery, and bright green, or bronze in *F. vulgare* 'Purpureum.'

Stem
Round, erect, hollows with age.

Seeds
Ribbed, aromatic, and gray-brown.

Florence fennel
Foeniculum vulgare var. *dulce*
Florence fennel, also known as sweet fennel or *finocchio*, is a staple of Italian cuisine. It is smaller than the species, with a large, bulbous base that tastes of aniseed and can be eaten raw or cooked.

Feverfew

Two thousand years ago this herb was prescribed for the treatment of headaches, and it is still used effectively for migraines to this day. It is of limited culinary use, but can be decorative in the home.

A strongly aromatic herb that originated in the Balkan region, feverfew has been grown for centuries in Europe as a medicinal and ornamental plant.

Feverfew's common name derives from its reputation for healing. English herbalists of four centuries ago described it as good for aches and pains in the head. In fact, feverfew was being prescribed for these ailments by the ancient Greeks almost 2,000 years ago.

Modern science has proved that the ancient lore was right. In 1985, a study of the effectiveness of feverfew affirmed its place in modern healthcare, especially in treating migraine. It is particularly effective with the type of migraines that are eased by applying warmth to the head.

Feverfew (either in leaf or concentrated form) also has a strong anti-inflammatory action. This can make it useful in the

▲ Golden feverfew (*T. parthenium* 'Aureum') has bushy, yellow-green leaves, which provide year-round color. Relatively low-growing, it puts out single, daisylike flowers in summer.

treatment of painful arthritis. Because it reduces muscle spasm, it can also help in the case of painful periods. Feverfew has also been effective in conjunction with other herbs (such as black cohosh and golden seal) in the treatment of tinnitus.

GARDEN PLANTS

Feverfew is a pretty, daisylike plant, with soft, green serrated leaves and stems that are sprinkled with small white flowers throughout the summer and fall. It can look particularly decorative sown along walls and between paving stones or grown in clumps against darker green foliage.

FEVERFEW
Tanacetum parthenium

PARTS USED:
Whole plant, leaves

PROPERTIES:
Bitter, aromatic, pungent smell and nauseating taste.

USES OF THE HERB:
Culinary
Feverfew is very bitter so its main uses are medicinal rather than culinary. But adding a few leaves to greasy foods will freshen them.

Medicinal
Eat one or two fresh leaves daily in a salad or sandwich, over a period of a couple of months to help with migraine or period pain. Its effect is direct, but also preventative, so better results are seen over a period of time. Take also for hot flushes during the menopause.

Decorative
Golden feverfew makes an attractive year round plant for the garden. Use feverfew in pretty herbal wreaths and posies.

Household
Feverfew is an effective moth repellent. Place dried flowers and leaves in sachets. An infusion of the flower heads dabbed on to the skin will ease the pain of bites and keep other insects away.

CAUTION
Fresh feverfew can sometimes cause mouth ulcers. If this happens try frying the leaf first. It is also a uterine stimulant and should be avoided in pregnancy. It should not be taken by people with a sensitivity to the daisy family. Lastly, it should not be taken by anyone on blood-thinning drugs, since it affects clotting rates.

CULTIVATION

FEVERFEW
Tanacetum parthenium

LIFESPAN
Hardy perennial.

HEIGHT
To 2 ft. (60 cm).

SITE
Full sun.

SOIL
Dry and well drained.

GROWING
Sow in spring or fall. The plants self-seed freely once established.

HARVESTING
Leaves can be harvested all year, although just before flowering is best.

PRESERVING
Use fresh. You can also freeze the leaves if required. They are strongly aromatic and should be kept away from other stored herbs.

Leaf
Aromatic, divided leaves vary in color from yellowish to bright green. Attractive foliage makes it a useful border plant.

Feverfew
Tanacetum parthenium
A member of the daisy family. There are several ornamental varieties.

Stem
Fine, branching stems give bushy growth from which long flower stems grow in spring.

Feverfew tablets
In some patients, feverfew has demonstrated a better ability to reduce or cure migraine than any synthesized drug.

Garlic

This member of the onion family has a long history and is known to have been regarded as a sacred herb by the Ancient Egyptians. Apart from its culinary uses, it has also been recognized as being of medicinal value, especially benefiting the cardiovascular system.

GARLIC
Allium sativum

PARTS USED:
Bulbs

PROPERTIES:
Expectorant, cleansing, antibacterial, antifungal.

USES OF THE HERB:
Culinary
Garlic adds a classic touch to all kinds of foods—vegetables, meat, and fish—and is used widely in dips, sauces, and salad dressings, such as the traditional Mediterranean aïoli (garlic mayonnaise).

Medicinal
Used to relieve colds, flu, bronchitis, gastro-enteritis, infectious diseases such as typhoid, and skin problems such as acne. Also an effective antifungal agent and a treatment for sore joints and rheumatism.

Cosmetic
A garlic hair rinse can ease dandruff. Apply in the evening and wash out the following morning to remove the smell.

CAUTION
Garlic can irritate sensitive skin.

Garlic is one of about 700 species of *Allium*, or onion, grown all over the world for their culinary and medicinal value.

Garlic's distinctive, pungent aroma and flavor have made it one of the most popular culinary herbs. It is widely used in oriental and Mediterranean-style dishes. It is used raw in salads and dressings, and cooked in casseroles, stews, and roast joints of meat and poultry. It is also sometimes used with seafood.

Garlic is rich in strong-smelling sulfur compounds that have a potent detoxifying effect on the body. It acts as an expectorant and, more importantly, has antibiotic and anti-fungal effects, and benefits the cardiovascular system. It is ideal for combating colds and other infections, as well as helping to treat circulatory and bronchial disorders.

ASIAN ORIGINS
The long story of garlic is thought to have begun in Central Asia, and it was cultivated in Mediterranean countries in ancient times. The Romans and the Greeks enjoyed garlic, while the Egyptians considered it to be a sacred herb—their slaves ate it allegedly to give them the strength to build the pyramids.

Garlic appeared in English herbals from the 900s onward—the name comes from the Anglo-Saxon words *gar* and *leac*, meaning "spear" and "leek," referring to the leaf shape.

During the nineteenth century, much research was done to analyze garlic's healing properties, and certain active constituents were isolated. The herb was used as an antiseptic and to relieve dysentery during World War I.

GROWING YOUR OWN
Although native to warm climes, garlic can be grown in cooler regions. The outer cloves should be planted in fertile, well-drained soil and new bulbs harvested after the leaves have died. Dry bulbs in the sun and store in a cool, frost-free place.

▶ For those who want to enjoy the benefits of garlic without any lingering smell, odorless tablets are widely available.

Garlic cloves
The bulb consists of 5–18 bulblets, or cloves. It is widely used for culinary purposes.

CULTIVATION

GARLIC
Allium sativum

LIFESPAN
Hardy perennial.

HEIGHT
1–3 ft. (30–90 cm).

SITE
Sunny.

SOIL
Rich and well drained, preferably sandy.

GROWING
Plant cloves or whole bulbs in spring, fall or winter (or early spring in cold areas), about 8 in. (20 cm) apart.

HARVESTING
Gather when the leaves are dying down.

PRESERVING
Dry bulbs in the sun before storing at about 39°F (4°C).

HELPFUL HINT
Garlic is generally effective as an insect repellent. Planting garlic among roses will help to deter greenfly.

Garlic
Allium sativum
Garlic is a hardy perennial with cleansing and antibacterial properties. Its main active constituents are sulfur compounds.

Leaf
Narrow, flat leaves are gray-green in color and measure up to 2 ft. (60 cm) in length.

Commercial growing
Once widely used medicinally, garlic is now mainly used as a culinary ingredient and is grown commercially in vast quantities.

Stem
Long, delicate, and erect stems produce clusters of flowers in summer.

Bulb
The garlic bulb is encased in a papery white or pink-flushed skin, with a clump of fine roots at the bottom similar to those of other onion species.

Photos Horticultural

Ginger

Ginger is a warming herb with a pungent aroma and flavor. It enhances all kinds of foods—from confectionery and cakes to savory dishes. It is widely used in the cuisines of the Far East, especially in curries and stir-fries.

The Greek word for ginger—*zingiberis*—has given this perennial its name. The distinctive, branched rhizomes (commonly called ginger root) have all kinds of uses, both fresh and dried, and oil can also be distilled from them and used in various ways.

This herb has just as wide a range of effects on the body—ginger has the ability to stimulate blood circulation; promote perspiration; relieve pain and cramp; calm muscle spasm, nausea, vomiting, and coughing; boost the digestive system; and relieve colds and flu. It has a proven track record in helping to control travel sickness.

Ginger features prominently in Chinese medicine as a cure for conditions associated with "cold," such as colds and bronchial congestion, and with digestive upsets linked with spleen "deficiency."

FRESH, DRIED, AND GROUND

Taking a cup of ground or fresh ginger infusion is an excellent way to purify the system and combat indigestion, while chewing ginger rhizome can soothe a sore throat. Use sliced or grated fresh ginger in curry dishes and ground ginger in cakes and biscuits. Ground ginger is also delicious in mulled wine and with melon, thanks to its sweet, pungent flavor.

CULTIVATION TIPS

There are about 100 species within the *Zingiber* genus, all of which have aromatic rhizomes. *Zingiber officinale* has long, pointed leaves and, rarely, fragrant yellow-green flowers streaked with purple.

Ginger plants should be treated as annuals or biennials as a reasonable length of time is required to produce good rhizomes. Remove the older ones when new plant shoots appear. Ginger rhizomes may be unearthed partway through the growing cycle if specimens need to be nonfibrous.

Deni Bown

◄ **A native of the world's warmer regions, ginger can also be grown as an attractive, exotic pot plant.**

GINGER
Zingiber officinale
Ginger root

PARTS USED:
Rhizomes, oil.

PROPERTIES:
Pungent, aromatic; expectorant; controls nausea; aids digestion and liver function; relieves pain; stimulates circulation.

USES OF THE HERB:
Culinary
Dried, ground ginger is used in cakes, biscuits and various sauces, and commercially in sweets, soft drinks and condiments (the oil is also used as a flavoring), while the rhizomes appear in all kinds of meat and vegetable dishes, including curries, marinades and chutneys. Pickled, ginger appears in Japanese cuisine, while green ginger (young rhizomes) are often preserved and candied.

Medicinal
Ginger's anti-spasmodic, warming, circulation-boosting and pain-relieving properties make it ideal for a wide range of problems, including nausea and travel sickness, rheumatism, sprains, colds and flu.

Cosmetic
Ginger oil is used in some perfumes.

CAUTION
Avoid in cases of high temperature, inflamed skin, or ulcers of the stomach or intestines.

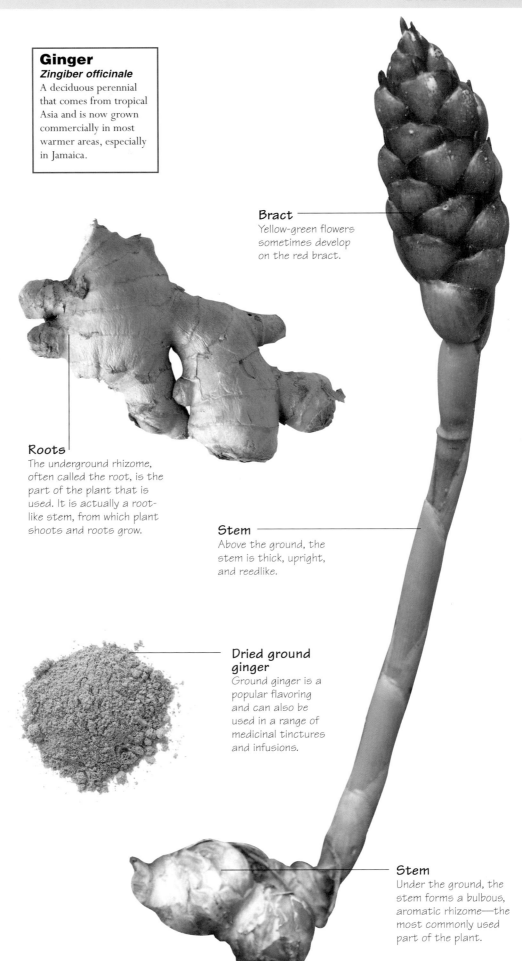

Ginger
Zingiber officinale
A deciduous perennial that comes from tropical Asia and is now grown commercially in most warmer areas, especially in Jamaica.

CULTIVATION

GINGER
Zingiber officinale

LIFESPAN
Tender, deciduous perennial.

HEIGHT
3–4 ft. (90 cm–1.2 m).

SITE
Tropical conditions— warm, humid with partial shade.

SOIL
Well drained and fertile.

GROWING
Grow as an annual or biennial. Propagate by division in late spring or take root cuttings.

HARVESTING
Pick young rhizomes at about seven months for using fresh and gather dormant specimens for drying.

PRESERVING
Young, fresh rhizomes ("green ginger") are less fibrous than older, dormant ones; they keep for two months in cool, dry conditions. They may be preserved in syrup to form "crystallized ginger." The older specimens can be stored peeled, unpeeled, or pickled.

Bract
Yellow-green flowers sometimes develop on the red bract.

Roots
The underground rhizome, often called the root, is the part of the plant that is used. It is actually a root-like stem, from which plant shoots and roots grow.

Stem
Above the ground, the stem is thick, upright, and reedlike.

Dried ground ginger
Ground ginger is a popular flavoring and can also be used in a range of medicinal tinctures and infusions.

Stem
Under the ground, the stem forms a bulbous, aromatic rhizome—the most commonly used part of the plant.

37

Lavender

No garden is complete without lavender. A traditional cottage garden plant, it has always been appreciated for its sweet perfume, silver-gray foliage, and flowers in a variety of colors.

The ancient Romans used lavender for cosmetic purposes, and its name comes from the Latin *lavare*, meaning to wash. It has long been valued for its fragrance and insect-repellent qualities. Centuries ago, lavender flowers were strewn on the floor to keep rooms freshly scented.

Lavender has also long been recognized as beneficial to the nervous system. Three hundred years ago, it was described as especially good for all forms of headache. Today, taken as an infusion, it will help relieve headaches and minor mental depression. It can be used to treat bruises, bites, and aches and will lower blood pressure and calm palpitations. It is also antiseptic.

To cure a migraine attack, draw a hot bath and add 15–20 drops of lavender essential oil to it. Lie still in the bath for 10 minutes, keeping the water hot. Then lie in a darkened room and try to sleep. When you wake, the pain should have gone. A few drops of essential oil in the bath water will banish fatigue, while a drop on the pillow of a restless child will help them to sleep.

DIFFERENT VARIETIES

There are many species and hybrids of lavender. Colors vary from purple to white. English lavender (*Lavandula angustifolia*) is used in expensive perfumes since it yields a very high-quality essential oil. A hybrid, lavendin (*L.* x *intermedia*), is widely grown for perfumery and as a garden plant. French or fringed lavender (*L. dentata*) is also used in perfume. Spike lavender (*L. latifolia*), also known as Italian or Spanish lavender, is native to the Mediterranean and is the species most often used in cleaning products. It yields a very good oil for masking unpleasant smells.

ENGLISH
LAVENDER
Lavandula angustifolia

PARTS USED:
Flowers, oil

PROPERTIES:
Aromatic, antiseptic, tonic; sweet smelling.

USES OF THE HERB:
Culinary
Crystallize the flowers as decorations for cakes and puddings. Fresh flowers can also be added to jam or ice cream.

Medicinal
Take a weak infusion of the flowers for headaches and to lower blood pressure. Add lavender oil to a warm bath to help cure a migraine or aches and pains. The oil is an antiseptic and painkiller for bites and stings.

Cosmetic
Lavender mouthwash will help cure bad breath.

Household
Lavender is an insect repellent. Sachets of dried lavender will keep away insects and also scent clothes. Useful in pot pourri.

Decorative
Use in dried arrangements. Growing plants make a decorative hedge.

CAUTION
Do not use lavender if taking insulin for diabetes. Avoid in pregnancy.

◀ **Lavender is grown on a commercial scale and the essential oil is extracted for use in perfume and toiletries. Flowerheads are also gathered and dried.**

Photos Horticultural

Dried flowers
Retain their clean, sweet scent for long periods.

Seeds
Gather small, dark brown seeds from the flower heads.

CULTIVATION

ENGLISH LAVENDER
Lavandula angustifolia

LIFESPAN
Best replaced every 3 to 4 years.

HEIGHT
2–3 ft. (60–90 cm).

SITE
Sunny and open.

SOIL
Prefers light, well-drained sandy soil, but tolerates other types.

GROWING
Sow from seed in summer and fall or take cuttings.

HARVESTING
Harvest as the first flowers open. Dry in small bunches, hanging over paper bags opened out to collect the florets as they fall.

PRESERVING
Dry flowering stems by laying on open trays or hanging in small bunches.

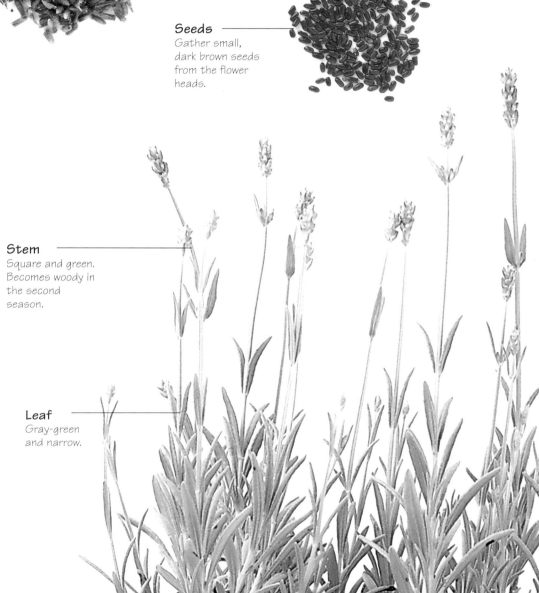

Stem
Square and green. Becomes woody in the second season.

Leaf
Gray-green and narrow.

Lemon balm

This fragrant garden plant releases its scent when brushed against. It is also widely used in the kitchen and for its medicinal effects.

Photos Horticultural

Lemon balm should be a first choice for the herb garden as it is both decorative and useful. Its pleasant, lemon-scented leaves should be placed where they can be brushed against, releasing their delightful fragrance.

The plant takes its name from the Greek word for honeybee—*melissa*—and is highly attractive to bees, which were believed never to leave any garden in which lemon balm was grown. In days gone by, before sugar was widely available, honey was highly prized, which made lemon balm a valuable plant.

During the Middle Ages, lemon balm was widely used for strewing on floors, since it possessed the important qualities of smelling pleasant and driving insects away.

CHEERING SPIRITS

Lemon balm has long been established as one of the most effective herbs in banishing depression. Five hundred years ago, it was called "the elixir of life," and during the

▲ **Although lemon balm likes bright sunlight, it grows best when shaded from the full midday sun. It is grown commercially as a source of essential oil, although this may be mixed with oil extracted from citrus trees.**

eighteenth century, it was taken to renew vigor. Lemon-balm tea was claimed to have been drunk by several people who lived to be over one hundred years old.

An infusion of lemon balm is excellent for calming nerves, and a cup of the tea taken at bedtime will aid sleep. It is also good for menstrual cramps. Lemon-balm tea is much more effective if it is made from fresh, rather than dried, leaves.

Lemon-balm flowers are insignificant, and the plant is grown primarily for its foliage. The ornamental cultivars can look marvelous in a flower bed. They include the variegated 'Aurea,' with a splash of yellow, and the 'All Gold' cultivar, which is entirely yellow.

LEMON BALM
Melissa officinalis

PARTS USED:
Whole plant, leaves, and oil.

PROPERTIES:
An aromatic, cooling, and sedative herb; lowers fever and relaxes spasms; also antibacterial and antiviral, and acts as an insect repellent.

USES OF THE HERB:
Culinary
Chop the leaves into salad. Add to fruit salads, jelly, ice cream, and custard. Add to blended vinegars. Try serving as an iced tea. The leaves can be crystallized and added to cold puddings and cakes. Can also be added to game and fish.

Cosmetic
Infuse as a hair rinse or add to bath water to give a delicious scent.

Decorative
Use the leaves in potpourri.

Medicinal
Good for feverish colds, nervousness, and depression, including postnatal depression. Add a cupful of infusion to a bath for a fretful baby or hyperactive child. Good remedy for childhood infections and chronic bronchitis. Use lemon-balm oil externally on cold sores.

Household
Crush fresh leaves and rub onto bee or wasp stings for a soothing and healing effect. You can make lemon- balm tinctures and ointments for year-round use. Put a few drops of the essential oil in an oil burner to repel insects. Oil can be added to furniture polish for a sweet smell.

Lemon balm
Melissa officinalis
Hardy ornamental
perennial. Strongly
aromatic. There is a cultivar
with variegated leaves.

Dried leaf
Dried lemon balm
loses some of its
scent and medicinal
properties.

CULTIVATION

LEMON BALM
Melissa officinalis

LIFESPAN
Hardy perennial.

HEIGHT
3 ft. (90 cm).

SITE
**Light, cool shade. The
scent becomes weaker if
the plant is grown in too
strong sun.**

SOIL
Fertile and moist.

GROWING
**Flowering season is June
to August. Grows easily
from seed. Sow in spring.
Cut back plants after
flowering. Divide clumps
in spring or fall.**

HARVESTING
**Use the leaves fresh as
required. Drying the
leaves reduces their
medicinal qualities and
scent.**

PRESERVING
**Pick leaves at any time,
but ideally just before
flowering. Dry slowly or
add fresh to flavor
vinegar.**

Leaf
Deep-veined leaves
have a strong lemon
scent. They prefer
light shade—full sun
may turn them
yellow and reduce
their scent.

Stem
Fine, round stems can
become straggly and
branching. Can be
chopped and used in
soups and stews.

Lemongrass

This fragrant herb is a versatile one—it is widely used as a flavoring ingredient in Southeast Asian dishes and has a range of medicinal applications as well.

Wherever you site lemongrass plants, make sure that they are in a place where you can press the long, vivid green leaves as you walk past. This will release the fresh lemon scent for which this herb is famous and which adds so much fragrance and flavor to products as diverse as fish dishes, perfume, potpourri, and confectionery.

There are more than 50 species in this genus of scented grasses, native to tropical and temperate regions of the world and to the grassy plains of Sri Lanka and southern India. Plants can be grown outdoors in warmer areas and will happily survive the warmer months outside in cool areas, as long as they are brought indoors when the temperature falls below 45°F (7°C).

Cymbopogon grasses either contain citral, which is a lemon fragrance, as in *C. citratus*, or geraniol, which gives a rose scent, as in the species *C. martinii*.

Usually found growing in distinctive clumps, the long, thin leaves can reach great lengths in the right conditions. The plant seldom produces flowers.

A VARIETY OF USES
This is a bitter herb with cooling and calming properties. The leaves, stem, and oil are the valuable parts of the plant. Only the lower 4 in. (10 cm) of the leaves are suitable for use—fresh or dried, in teas and Oriental or Asian cookery.

To use the stems, cut them off above ground level and use either fresh or dried. The stems are also a rich source of an aromatic oil, which is commercially extracted.

The oil finds is used in all kinds of household and cosmetic products, lending them a highly distinctive fragrance, and features as a popular flavoring in a variety of foods. The "lemongrass oil" sold for flavoring is extracted from the species *C. flexuosus* (East Indian lemongrass).

LEMONGRASS
Cymbopogon citratus

PARTS USED:
Leaves, stems, and oil.

PROPERTIES:
Aromatic, bitter, calming, and cooling; antifungal and antibacterial.

USES OF THE HERB:
Culinary
The fresh or dried leaf bases create a piquant, refreshing lemon tea or add a distinctive character to Southeast Asian fish and meat dishes. Chop young stems into salads. Can also be used in *sereh* powder form.

Medicinal
This herb's antibacterial and antifungal properties help combat conditions such as athlete's foot; its cooling, calming properties relieve fever by promoting perspiration. Can also help children's digestive upsets.

Household
Add to scented sachets and potpourri.

Cosmetic
Lemongrass oil is used in cosmetics, soap, and perfume—use it to cleanse oily skin or add to a bath.

Decorative
This aromatic herb gives a refreshing boost to potpourri.

◀ **A popular culinary herb in the floating markets and market stalls of Thailand and other Southeast Asian countries, lemongrass has found favor in Western countries as well. It is available from large supermarkets.**

Photos Horticultural

Lemongrass
Cymbopogon citratus
This perennial forms clumps that can reach 6 ft. (1.8 m) in height in warmer, fertile climes.

Leaf
Long, thin, light green leaves release a fresh lemon scent.

Stem

Strong stem is reminiscent of cane. Base of stem is sliced and used for culinary purposes.

Adding zest
Lemongrass features strongly in Thai cooking, its sharp fresh flavor predominating in dishes such as fragrant rice and red and green curries.

CULTIVATION

LEMONGRASS
Cymbopogon citratus

LIFESPAN
Tender perennial grass.

HEIGHT
5 ft. (1.5 m).

SITE
Full sun.

SOIL
Prefers fertile, well-drained soil in mild or warm conditions; overwinter indoors in cooler climates.

GROWING
Propagate by division in spring.

HARVESTING
Use the bottom part of the leaf blade as a fresh herb and the fresh stem for infusions and for extracting oil.

PRESERVING
Dried stems can be powdered or used in infusions.

Lemon verbena

This fragrant herb is an attractive feature in a mixed border. It is indispensable in the kitchen—in teas and as an accompaniment for meat dishes—and is used medicinally and in cosmetics.

As its name suggests, lemon verbena is best known for the strong citrus aroma of its leaves. South American in origin, it is relatively easy to grow and is widely cultivated in many other regions for its foliage. It is a source of essential oil, which has antibacterial and insecticidal properties.

Lemon verbena was traditionally used to treat conditions such as flatulence and indigestion. Aromatherapists use its essential oil to treat digestive problems and nervous complaints, and the plant's astringent qualities to combat acne, boils, and cysts. Leaf infusions can be good for colds and fever and act as a gentle sedative and antispasmodic.

Lemon-verbena leaves are picked in summer and used fresh in herbal teas and in syrups, salads, or stuffing for meat and poultry. They can also be chopped and sprinkled over drinks and fruit puddings. When dried, they hold their fragrance for several years—making them ideal for potpourri or herbal sachets. A strained infusion of the leaves or flowers also makes a refreshing final rinse for laundry, or may be added to a warm bath to produce an invigorating effect.

HOUSEHOLD SCENT

Lemon verbena was introduced to Europe at the end of the eighteenth century. The genus, *Aloysia*, was named after the Italian princess Maria Louisa of Parma, who died in 1819. In Victorian England, *A. triphylla* was known simply as "the lemon plant," and its sharp fragrance made it very popular around the home. It was heavily cultivated by the Spanish for its valuable oil, much used by perfumiers.

This use later declined after evidence that the herb sensitized the skin to sunlight.

CULTIVATION

This herb is common in fields and on grass verges in Argentina and Chile. When cultivated in cooler climates, it is normally frost-hardy, but prefers a warm, sheltered spot. It produces pale purple flowers, but its main feature is its aromatic foliage.

Deni Bown

CULTIVATION

LEMON VERBENA
Aloysia triphylla

LIFESPAN
Frost-hardy deciduous shrub.

HEIGHT
Up to 10 ft. (3 m).

SITE
Sun.

SOIL
Light and well drained.

GROWING
Take heel cuttings in spring at 64°F (18°C) or softwood cuttings in summer. Trim main stems back to 1 ft. (30 cm) in spring, and also trim offshoots right back or remove dead wood at the start of summer.

HARVESTING
Pick leaves in summer to use fresh or to extract essential oil.

PRESERVING
Dried leaves used in medicinal infusions or potpourris and herbal sachets.

Lemon verbena
Aloysia triphylla
Frost-hardy, deciduous shrub with citrus-scented foliage. Easily cultivated for its flavor and fragrance.

Stem
Round and ridged. Green but later turns reddish and woody.

Leaf
Long and pointed, with a strong lemony scent, especially when crushed.

Flower
Loose spikes of tiny white or pale purple flowers appear in summer.

Dried leaves
The dried leaves retain their fragrance well, making them ideal for potpourris.

45

Lovage

This single species occurs naturally in the eastern Mediterranean region. The new, celery-scented growth appears in early spring when few other herbs are available, making it useful in the kitchen.

This well-loved plant, commonly known as lovage, is a traditional feature of the English cottage garden. It is, in fact, a native of Iran, and flourishes in warm Balkan and Mediterranean regions.

A tall and leafy plant, with a powerful aroma and sweetish flavor that is strongly reminiscent of celery, lovage was once popular in the kitchen but fell out of favor as a culinary herb.

Lovage is now gaining popularity once again. All parts of the plant can be used. Fresh, young leaves and seeds can be added to salads, while young stems and shoots can be used like celery—cooked as a vegetable or as an ingredient in soups, casseroles, and stews.

The aromatic properties of lovage give it a host of other uses, too. The fragrant seeds can be added to potpourri—harvest the seeds when the fruits begin to pop open. The leafy stems look attractive and smell pleasant as a part of floral arrangements.

Medicinally, lovage eases spasms and has a diuretic effect. An infusion, especially of the roots but also of the leaves and seeds, can be drunk as a pleasant tea or taken to ease a range of problems, especially indigestion, wind, stomach ache, and urinary disorders such as cystitis.

Lovage extracts and oil are used commercially to flavor foods and drinks, and the oil is used in perfumery.

COUNTRY LORE

Historically, it seems that there is no folklore attached to lovage, but it is known that it was a popular therapeutic plant in medieval times and was later recommended by the English herbalist Nicholas Culpeper.

CULTIVATION

This species—the only one in its genus—is extremely hardy and robust and so is a good choice for most gardens when grown in fertile, moist soil. It should not be confused with plants in the genus *Ligusticum*, which are commonly referred to as various types of lovage. For example, *Ligusticum scoticum*, or Scots lovage, also has a celerylike aroma and taste and similar properties and uses to *Levisticum officinale*. Harvest the leaves as needed, or bunch foliage and stems together and hang to dry in fall.

Pat Brindley

LOVAGE
Levisticum officinale

PARTS USED:
Leaves, seeds, stems, roots.

PROPERTIES:
Aromatic, bitter-sweet, diuretic, expectorant, and sedative; aids digestion, increases perspiration, and relaxes spasms.

USES OF THE HERB:
Culinary
Cook stems and roots as a vegetable; use stems, roots, and leaves in soups and casseroles. Add young leaves, seeds, and grated root to salads.

Medicinal
Relaxes digestive system and helps to relieve cystitis, bronchitis, mouth ulcers, and menstrual cramps.

Cosmetic
Use an infusion of seeds, leaves, or roots as a deodorant, facial wash, or cleansing addition to the bath.

DECORATIVE
Use leafy stems in flower arrangements.

CAUTION
Do not use in pregnancy; not to be taken by those with kidney problems.

◄ Leave plenty of space for this very tall plant to grow, placing it at the back of borders, so it will not swamp smaller species.

CULTIVATION

LOVAGE
Levisticum officinale

LIFESPAN
Hardy perennial.

HEIGHT
Up to 6 ft. 6 in. (2 m).

SITE
Sun or partial shade.

SOIL
Moist and loamy.

GROWING
Sow seed in autumn or spring, in situ or indoors, planting out seedlings. Take root cuttings from established plants.

HARVESTING
Gather leaves before flowering, young stems in spring, seeds when ripe and roots from mature plants.

PRESERVING
Use fresh or dried. Oil is extracted from foliage.

HELPFUL HINT
Keep soil well-watered and enriched with compost.

Lovage
Levisticum officinale
The leaves, seeds, stems and roots of this tall, aromatic and leafy plant can all be put to various uses.

Leaf
The large leaves resemble those of the celery plant, and also taste and smell similar to celery.

Dried leaves
The dried leaves can be used to make a pleasant celery-flavored herbal tea to ease indigestion.

Deni Bown

Stem
Round, hollow, and ridged stems are celerylike and branch toward the top.

Seeds
Brown, crescent-shaped seeds have a celerylike aroma.

Marigold

As well as its vibrant flowers, which can be seen in gardens for most of the summer, this plant has many other uses—both culinary and medicinal, including the treatment of skin conditions.

More often cultivated for its eyecatching flowers than for its practical uses, this colorful herb blooms almost continuously. The decorative flowers are a bright yellow-orange, bringing year-round sunshine and life to the garden. The Romans believed that the marigold could be found in flower on the first of every month and called it *calendula*, Latin for calendar.

Planted in the garden, marigold will keep many insect pests away from other flowers. It also has many practical uses in the kitchen and home, as well as in medicine.

POWERFUL MEDICINE

Marigold can be eaten or drunk in teas. Five hundred years ago, it was a great favorite of King Henry VIII of England, who mixed it with sorrel, feverfew, snapdragon, and rue, believing it would combat the plague.

Herbalists of King Henry's time used it in the treatment of smallpox, but while it may have helped, its main uses are to reduce inflammation and accelerate healing.

During World War I, marigold was used extensively in the trenches in order to prevent sepsis and to clean filthy wounds. It proved to be invaluable when there was a shortage of medical supplies. There is also evidence that marigold was used by surgeons during the American Civil War.

Nowadays it is available as an ointment or tincture and as a homeopathic remedy. It benefits most skin problems, including acne, eczema, bruising, diaper rash, and minor burns.

Photos Horticultural

MARIGOLD
Calendula officinalis

PARTS USED:
Flower petals.

PROPERTIES:
Stimulates the uterus, gall bladder, and liver; clears infections and is beneficial to the skin.

USES OF THE HERB:
Culinary
Use marigold leaves in salads and stews. Add the petals to fish dishes and salads. Marigold can also be used as coloring for rice.

Medicinal
Drink an infusion to heal wounds in the digestive tract such as ulcers and colitis. It also helps the lymphatic system and can aid swollen glands. Use it for viral and fungal infections such as thrush and athlete's foot. An infusion in the bath will help heal and clean an injury.

Household
Use to add color to potpourri.

Cosmetic
Infuse as a face wash and a hair rinse for auburn hair. Use as an eyebath to soothe tired, itchy eyes.

CAUTION
Do not confuse the plant with wild marsh marigold, which is mildly poisonous, or with French marigold (*Tagetes*), which has different uses. Do not drink infusions in pregnancy or when breastfeeding.

◀ **Marigold can be grown in most soils except where the ground is heavy and waterlogged. It needs a sunny position and will flower almost continuously.**

Dried marigold petals
Dried marigold is sold for making infusions, coloring and flavoring food, and for medicinal uses.

Marigold
Calendula officinalis
Popular as a garden flower, it grows 1–2 ft. (30–60 cm) tall and has many herbal uses.

CULTIVATION

MARIGOLD
Calendula officinalis

LIFESPAN
Hardy annual.

HEIGHT
1–2 ft. (30–60 cm).

SITE
Full sun.

SOIL
Tolerates poor soil but likes well-drained loam.

GROWING
Grow from seed sown in fall for early flowers and in spring for late flowers.

HARVESTING
Harvest either the whole flower or the petals between June and September (but use only the petals).

PRESERVING
Strip and dry the flower petals.

Flower
Measures 2–3 in. (5–7.5 cm) across, with daisylike, radiating petals. Can be used to color and flavor many foods.

Leaf
Mid-green and fleshy. Occasionally used in salads and stews.

Seeds
About ¼ in. (6 mm) long and C-shaped. Light to mid-brown when ripe.

Marjoram and Oregano

These herbs, with their culinary and medicinal properties, have a history dating back to the Ancient Egyptians. They are two of the few herbs that retain their flavor and aroma when dried.

There are about twenty species of *Origanum*. Among these many species are the herbs commonly known as oregano and marjoram. Hybrids between cultivated species abound, which can often make precise identification difficult.

Confusingly, true oregano (*Origanum vulgare*) is also known as wild marjoram, while the classic marjoram herb is either sweet marjoram (*O. majorana*) or pot marjoram (*O. onites*). Commercial dried oregano (used for culinary purposes) is produced from several different species.

AROMATIC PROPERTIES

Oregano is well known for its aromatic properties—in summer, it covers hillsides across Europe and central Asia and fills the air with its sweet, distinctive scent. This fragrance is preserved by drying, and the herb is used to great effect in products such as scented sachets and potpourri.

PLANT OF THE ANCIENTS

Oregano has been famed for its wide-ranging medicinal properties since the days of Ancient Egypt. The warming, slightly antiseptic nature of oregano gives it an excellent reputation for calming fevers, nervous headaches, and irritability and helping the digestive system.

GARDEN FAVORITE

Fragrant and easy to cultivate, oregano looks attractive wherever it grows, with its pink-purple flowers dotted against dark green leaves. Other variations have entirely golden or gold-dipped leaves, and the flowers can be white in color. Low-growing, golden varieties of oregano make attractive, aromatic edging plants. However, they are a great favorite with insects, too, so think about where you plant this herb if bees bother you.

◀ **Oregano forms bushy plants up to 20 in. (50 cm) tall. Divide older plants or take cuttings to keep them looking attractive.**

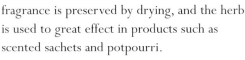

MARJORAM AND OREGANO

Origanum spp.

PARTS USED:
Leaves, flowers, and stems

PROPERTIES:
Aromatic, antiseptic

USES OF THE HERB:
Culinary
Mainly used in dried form, both herbs provide a strong flavoring that complements ingredients such as chile, garlic, tomato, onion, and wine. Oregano oil is used in many commercially branded foods and sauces.

MEDICINAL
Tea made from the leaves and flowers is good for coughs, colds, and flu, indigestion and period pain. Steam inhalation is used for bronchitis and asthma. Compresses can be applied for arthritis and muscular pain. Oil is used in aromatherapy to treat these conditions.

Cosmetic
Oil is used in toiletries and perfumes.

Decorative
Golden marjoram is a popular garden plant for its colored leaves, which fade as flowering begins and scorch in sunlight. Dry leaves and flowers for potpourri.

CAUTION
Avoid during pregnancy. May irritate the skin if used externally.

Oregano
Origanum vulgare
(Wild marjoram)
Hardy perennial, grown ornamentally as well as for use. Dislikes damp and cold.

CULTIVATION

MARJORAM AND OREGANO
Origanum spp.

LIFESPAN
Perennial.

HEIGHT
Marjoram: to 2 ft. (60 cm). Oregano: 12–30 in. (30–75 cm).

SITE
Sunny position. Although oregano is hardy, it does best in warm spots.

SOIL
Prefers well drained.

GROWING
Best grown in beds. Plant seeds or divide plants in spring or fall and grow from cuttings in summer. Trim plants after flowering to encourage new growth.

HARVESTING
Best harvested between June and August, although young leaves can be picked at any time. Pick plants as flowers appear.

PRESERVING
Freeze or dry leaves and dry flowers. Infuse leaves in vinegar or oil.

Leaf
The whole plant, including leaves, stems, and flowers, can be dried for use in cooking and for medicinal and cosmetic purposes.

Seeds
Used to propagate the plant in spring or fall.

Culinary delights
Whether infused as tea, added to salads, or sprinkled over pizza, the herb has an unmistakable flavor. The name comes from the Greek origanon, meaning "bitter herb."

Dried oregano
The dried, crushed leaves are used as a flavoring ingredient in many dishes, especially pizzas.

Variegated Oregano
O. vulgare 'Country Cream'
One of the many cultivars of this perennial.

Mint

There are many species of mint, and all have a distinctive but not identical smell and appearance. The common garden mint is perhaps the most widely appreciated as it can be put to so many varied uses.

It has been said that mint is the most popular flavoring in the world, appearing in so many foodstuffs and medicines that it is often barely given a second thought.

There are many species of mint, but the one that appears in the majority of gardens is *Mentha spicata,* also known as spearmint—the taste that is commonly associated with chewing gum and toothpaste.

The different types of mint are rich sources of various volatile oils, but all contain menthol and it is this that provides the characteristic smell and taste.

Spearmint—which is milder in taste and aroma than peppermint (*M.* x *piperita*), the other highly popular mint—is a stimulating herb that is both cooling and warming. Drunk as a pleasant herbal tea, it can be extremely effective in easing spasms, hiccups, indigestion, and wind. Spearmint is also recommended for lowering certain fevers.

As a culinary herb, spearmint is well known as the mint used in mint sauce and jelly to accompany classic lamb dishes. It is also traditionally used in tabbouleh, a Middle Eastern dish of vegetables and burgul (cracked wheat), and in Greek tzatziki, with yogurt and garlic. Commercially, it is used to flavor confectionery and oral hygiene products.

HERBAL WISDOM

Spearmint, which represents wisdom in country folklore, has been valued as a culinary herb since the days of Ancient Rome. It is now an important commercial crop, grown for its leaves and oil.

This hardy, creeping perennial can easily become rampant, so restrict its growth by planting it in a container (which can be sunk beneath the surface of the soil). It should be divided and repotted each year when dormant, and dead stems cut back in the fall.

Spikes of tiny flowers appear during the summer and early fall. Mint species can be grown from seed or cuttings, and grow best in moist soil. They prefer partial shade, rather than full sun.

▲ **Mint grows profusely, and you may want to limit its spread in your border by growing it in pots sunk into the ground.**

MINT
Mentha spicata
Spearmint

PARTS USED:
Whole plant, leaves.

PROPERTIES:
A stimulating herb, both cooling and warming; contains volatile oils, including menthol.

USES OF THE HERB:
Culinary
Use spearmint in classic mint sauces and jellies and to accompany lamb; add to salads and cold summer drinks and punches, and use as an attractive garnish on desserts such as fruit flans.

Medicinal
The cooling, warming, and stimulating effects of this herb make it effective in relieving digestive problems and soothing fevers.

Household
Added to scented candles, it produces a stimulating aroma with hints of caraway, which comes from a substance found in spearmint called carvone .

Decorative
Include in floral arrangements and wreaths to produce a clean, fresh scent.

New potatoes
Served with fresh mint, a culinary classic that combines well with meat dishes.

Spearmint
Mentha spicata
Spearmint is the most commonly grown mint and is widely considered to be the best choice for cooking purposes.

Leaves
Bright green, lance-shaped leaves have a spearmint aroma, little or no stalk, strongly marked veins, and toothed edges.

CULTIVATION

SPEARMINT
Mentha spicata

LIFESPAN
Hardy perennial.

HEIGHT
1–3 ft. (30–90 cm).

SITE
Full sun. Protect from strong winds.

SOIL
Prefers partial shade but will tolerate full sun.

GROWING
Try to contain spread by planting in containers or in a small space. Propagate by cuttings during the growing season or division in spring or fall.

HARVESTING
Gather whole plants as flowers appear, and leaves only during the growing seson.

PRESERVING
The leaves can be dried for use in various forms. Oil is distilled commercially from the leaves.

Chopped fresh mint
Freshly chopped mint is used extensively as a flavoring ingredient in the kitchen—it is particularly popular with lamb and potato dishes.

Nasturtium

Popular in the garden for its colorful flowers, the nasturtium plant has a variety of culinary and medicinal applications—it is diuretic and antiseptic and helps treat some skin problems.

This highly popular plant, with its many brightly hued varieties, brings a bold splash of South American color to any herb garden. These natives of Peru were brought to Europe during the 1500s by the Spanish conquistadors.

Nicknamed "Indian cress" during its early days in Europe, the leaves of this plant have a strong, watercresslike flavor that can be used to great effect in salads, along with the flowers as edible decoration. Nasturtium's botanical name, *Tropaeolum*, comes from the Greek word for trophy—a reference to the shieldlike form of the large, round leaves and the helmet shape of the delicately scented flowers.

Close relations within the genus may be either trailing or climbing annuals or smaller, more compact perennials that are suited to herbaceous borders and container gardening. Interesting cultivars of *Tropaeolum majus*, the classic garden nasturtium, include 'Alaska,' with its creamy-white variegated leaves and bushy form, and 'Empress of India,' with violet-tinged leaves and rich crimson blooms.

RICHER AND POORER

The nasturtium grows and spreads very readily and will actually flourish on relatively poor soil. Rich, overwatered soil will tend to produce a mass of leaves but few flowers.

Nasturtiums are used extensively in organic pest control—hoverflies, which prey on aphids, are attracted to them. For this reason, nasturtiums are good plants to site next to flowering plants or vegetables that you want to protect from these garden pests.

BLOOD TONIC

This tonic plant is said to purify the blood and may even act as an aphrodisiac. It is recommended for easing infections in both the respiratory and genito-urinary systems. The leaves have a high Vitamin C content and, when eaten as a salad herb, they may be helpful in relieving the symptoms of a cold.

◀ **This rapidly growing trailing plant needs regular thinning out to keep it under control. It is an excellent ground- and trellis cover.**

Pat Brindley

NASTURTIUM
Tropaeolum majus
Indian cress

PARTS USED:
Leaves, flowers, seeds, whole plant.

PROPERTIES:
Bitter, antiseptic, diuretic; tonic herb with expectorant effects; controls bacterial and fungal infections.

USES OF THE HERB:
Culinary
The beautiful, bright colors of the edible flowers add the perfect touch to summer salads, as do the peppery leaves. The leaves can also be chopped and added to soft cheeses. Pickle unripe seeds and use as you would capers and make a delicate nasturtium vinegar from the flowers.

Medicinal
Taken internally, nasturtium tea combats breathing problems and urinary infections. It has antiseptic and diuretic qualities, helping with the flow of urine. The plant contains a substance that reacts with water to give a type of antibiotic. External use helps combat skin problems and heal minor injuries.

Cosmetic
Can help improve the condition of poor hair, and so is included as an ingredient in hair lotions. The high sulphur content of this plant helps combat baldness.

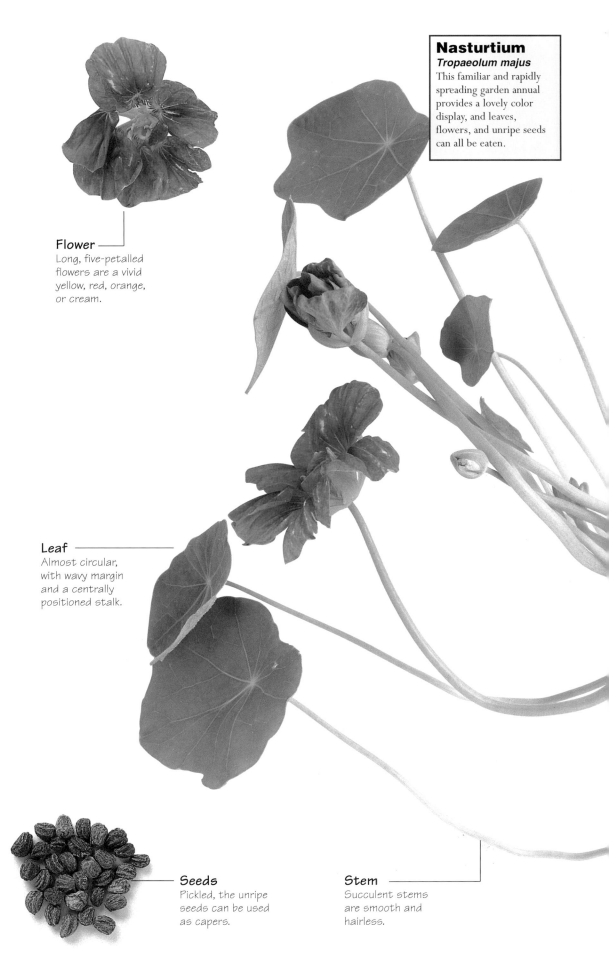

CULTIVATION

NASTURTIUM
Tropaeolum majus

LIFESPAN
Hardy annual.

HEIGHT
10 ft. (3 m).

SITE
Full sun.

SOIL
Any soil, but not too fertile or overwatered; does best in fairly poor, well-drained conditions.

GROWING
Sow seeds late spring or early summer. Often self-sows.

HARVESTING
Gather all parts during the summer and use fresh; juice can also be extracted.

PRESERVING
Pickle unripe seeds and use flowers to flavor vinegar.

HELPFUL HINT
Nasturtiums are prone to caterpillars, so remove any affected leaves as soon as they appear, to avoid having to spray edible plants with poisonous insecticides.

Nasturtium
Tropaeolum majus
This familiar and rapidly spreading garden annual provides a lovely color display, and leaves, flowers, and unripe seeds can all be eaten.

Flower
Long, five-petalled flowers are a vivid yellow, red, orange, or cream.

Leaf
Almost circular, with wavy margin and a centrally positioned stalk.

Seeds
Pickled, the unripe seeds can be used as capers.

Stem
Succulent stems are smooth and hairless.

Parsley

Probably the most widely used of all culinary herbs, fresh parsley provides flavor to cooked and uncooked food, and also makes an attractive garnish. It is suitable for planting in the garden as well as in containers.

Parsley was originally native to southern Europe, but it is now grown throughout the world. Spread across Europe by the Romans, it gained huge popularity as a culinary herb. Its dark green curly leaves contain vitamins A and C, as well as plenty of minerals and iron.

GROWING PARSLEY

Three main types of parsley can easily be grown in the garden. The first is the curled, or garden, parsley that makes a wonderful garnish for soups and salads. It is also a common ingredient of bouquet garni.

Other varieties include Italian, or French, parsley, which has flatter leaves and a stronger flavor. An infusion of this herb is said to revive the appetite.

The third type—the large turnip-root, or Hamburg, parsley—is less widely grown. It is used either as a root vegetable or as a tea to aid rheumatism.

Parsley is a biennial but is best grown annually. It has tiny flowers in the second year, but this means that it is past its best and should be discarded.

By sowing at regular intervals, you should be able to pick parsley all year round—especially if you protect it from frost with a cloche. It can be transplanted or sown on site. The seed can be slow to germinate, but

Pat Brindley

▲ **As an important culinary herb, parsley can conveniently be grown in pots or other containers near to the kitchen.**

usually succeeds if the ground is warm and moist. Soaking seeds in warm water for two hours before sowing may speed germination.

MEDICINAL AID

Parsley tea has a very beneficial effect on the urinary system and is an excellent treatment for kidney and bladder complaints. Chew on parsley to sweeten the breath, and in particular to counter the smell of garlic.

PARSLEY
Petroselinum crispum
'Moss Curled'

PARTS USED:
Leaves and stems; the root of Hamburg parsley is also used.

PROPERTIES:
Contains vitamins, minerals, and iron; diuretic.

USES OF THE HERB:
Culinary
Add raw parsley to salads. Finely chop and sprinkle in sandwiches, soups, and egg, fish, and potato dishes. It is an ingredient of many classic sauces.

Medicinal
Make an infusion of parsley leaves to aid digestion. It has a diuretic action and can be taken by those suffering from fluid retention and for helping with arthritis and osteoarthritis. Drink 1 tsp. (5 ml) of leaves in a cup of boiling water three times daily.

CAUTION
Parsley should not be taken in medicinal doses by pregnant women or those with stomach ulcers. A poisonous weed, *Aethusa cynapium* (known as 'fool's parsley'), resembles flat-leaved Italian parsley, so do not pick this plant in the wild.

Parsley
Petroselinum crispum
'Moss Curled'
A bushy cultivar with a complex leaf structure, widely grown as both a commercial and garden herb.

CULTIVATION

PARSLEY
Petroselinum crispum

LIFESPAN
Hardy biennial (better treated as an annual).

HEIGHT
2 ft. (60 cm).

SITE
Full sun. Light shade.

SOIL
Rich and moist. Slightly alkaline and well drained.

GROWING
Sow from spring to late summer. Water well. Cover with a cloche in winter. Can be grown indoors.

HARVESTING
Pick leaves as required.

PRESERVING
Dry or freeze leaves. Dry seeds for infusions.

HELPFUL HINT
Prone to suffer from leafspot and viral diseases that can damage the leaves. Seeds can be slow to germinate (up to six weeks), but soaking seeds for two hours in lukewarm water may help speed the process.

Seeds
Small, grayish-brown seeds can be toxic if taken in excess.

Leaf
Curly, with a saw-toothed edge. Bright green and fresh-tasting, the leaves are an important source of vitamins and minerals.

Stem
Strong, edible stems have more flavor than the leaves.

Dried parsley leaves
Parsley leaves retain their flavor well when dried, but are best added late in the cooking process.

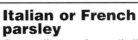

Italian or French parsley
Petroselinum crispum 'Italian'
This flat-leaved parsley has a stronger flavor than the curly type. The stems are succulent and finer than other varieties.

Rosemary

A versatile herb, rosemary has many culinary and medicinal applications. It grows readily in warm, dry conditions, is evergreen, and produces flowers in the early spring.

This distinctive herb has a wonderful and instantly identifiable aroma that has made it popular in cooking and medicine for many centuries.

Today, rosemary is best known as a culinary herb. It is generally used to flavor roast meats—lamb and sometimes pork—and to add flavor and aroma to herb oils and vinegars. Rosemary grows into a sizable bush, covered with needlelike leaves that, when crushed, release the volatile oil and scent. But it is also a valuable garden plant.

It has many varieties, with flowers varying in color from white, through pink to blue. It is also fast-growing, while its height and density make it possible to use it as a garden hedge. Four hundred years ago, rosemary was used for just this purpose, often trimmed into fanciful shapes. It was also used in weddings to deck the church and make bridal wreaths.

FOLK REMEDIES

Rosemary's history is rich in folklore going back to biblical times. One tale has it as the bush that shielded the Virgin Mary as she fled to Egypt. Its flowers were originally white, but, so the story goes, turned blue to match the color of her cloak.

Most of the stories concern rosemary's aromatic properties. Its scent was believed to ward off disease and was often used to purify the air in sick chambers. It was carried during plagues, to be sniffed while passing through areas of possible infection. In ancient times, scholars wore rosemary garlands to strengthen the memory. Thus the plant came to be associated with fidelity.

◀ Rosemary sprigs can be steeped in vinegar or olive oil to provide a distinctive flavor.

ROSEMARY
Rosmarinus officinalis

PARTS USED:
Leaves and stems.

PROPERTIES:
Stimulating and aromatic, this herb contains a volatile oil used for a variety of medicinal treatments and culinary applications.

USES OF THE HERB:
Culinary
Use fresh or dried leaves or sprigs of the herb to flavor meat, particularly lamb, while roasting. Use fresh sprigs to flavor herb oils and vinegars, and fresh leaves sparingly in herb butters. Fresh rosemary is delicious in salads. Burn branches on a barbecue to flavor meat.

Medicinal
Rosemary is a very good all-round tonic. It stimulates circulation and increases blood supply, and has been used as a remedy for hardening of the arteries. Take as an infusion three times daily. Rosemary can also lift mild depression and is good for treating headaches and migraines.

Cosmetic
Use the essential oil in eau-de-cologne. Use fresh or dried leaves in a facial steam to stimulate circulation. Infuse leaves as a rinse for dark hair.

CAUTION
Not recommended for epileptics. Avoid during pregnancy and while breast-feeding. Don't take rosemary to excess at any time.

◀ Rosemary likes sheltered areas and dislikes cold, wet winters. It grows into quite a large shrub, particularly if it is well pruned after flowering to encourage branching growth.

Seeds
Mid-brown seeds are tiny and oily. They do not have a practical use other than propagating the plant.

Rosemary
Rosmarinus officinalis
Aromatic shrub that is a staple of any herb garden. There are many decorative varieties.

CULTIVATION

ROSEMARY
Rosmarinus officinalis

LIFESPAN
Hardy evergreen shrub.

HEIGHT
To 6 ft. (2 m).

SITE
Dry, sunny sites protected from cold wind. Rosemary can be transplanted and kept indoors during a frosty winter.

SOIL
Rosemary needs excellent drainage. It is more fragrant in limy soil. You can add garden lime or crushed egg shells to the soil. Can be container grown, indoors or outside.

GROWING
Propagate from cuttings and transplant when established.

HARVESTING
Leaves can be harvested in small amounts all year but are best before flowering time.

PRESERVING
Dry the sprigs and branches and strip the leaves off before storing. Crush the leaf just before use to release the aroma.

Leaf
Tough, needle-like leaves release their aromatic oil when crushed.

Stem
Tough and woody by the second year. Branches can be burned to release aromatic smoke, but strip away all leaves to discourage flaring.

Provençal herbs
Rosemary is a major ingredient of the classic mix of dried Provençal herbs, used to flavor dishes from this region of France.

Dried leaf
A basic of many flavorings, dried leaves retain their flavor well in storage.

Sage

This low-growing aromatic herb has a reputation for its healing properties as well as its culinary value. Taller and more colorful varieties are also grown as ornamentals.

Sage is among the most versatile kitchen herbs—but as it has a strong flavor, it is best used on its own rather than together with other herbs. It combines well with rich and fatty foods, breaking them down as an aid to digestion. Sage is often used with meats such as pork, duck, and sausage, and is a classic companion to liver.

Sage contains powerful medicinal properties, and has been credited throughout history with promoting a long life and restoring memory in the elderly.

SACRED HERB
Sage's Latin name, *Salvia,* comes from a word meaning to "cure" or "save." The Romans gathered the herb with great ceremony, treating it as sacred. They used infusions of the leaves to treat fevers and to stimulate the nervous system. The herb was said to stem bleeding, and the juice from the leaves was used to treat snakebites.

▲ **Sage is a decorative plant, and its flowers are very attractive to bees. It tends to grow sparse with age, when it should be replaced.**

Sage originates from the Mediterranean region but happily survives colder climates. Grown in the garden, its soft, evergreen, gray-green leaves make an ideal contrast to darker, spiky herbs such as rosemary, while giving off a delightful and distinctive aroma.

Sage flowers are small and usually mauve in color, although white and pink forms are found. Bees love the blooms, and in hot climates such as Greece, where the plants flower prolifically, sage honey is much sought after and commands high prices.

There are many species and cultivars, with leaves ranging in color from gold to purple, some of which are variegated. Purple sage (*Salvia officinalis* 'Purpurea') has attractive reddish-purple leaves and can be used in the kitchen like common sage.

SAGE
Salvia officinalis

PARTS USED:
Leaves, seeds.

PROPERTIES:
Aromatic, healing.

USES OF THE HERB:
Culinary
Use fresh or dried leaves to make sage and onion stuffing, and to flavor duck, pork, liver, or sausage meat. Blend the chopped herb into cheese or butter, and use in cream sauces. Use to flavor oils and vinegars. Eat purple sage with pork, veal, and game.

Medicinal
Purple sage can be drunk as an infusion at the first sign of any respiratory infections. It soothes inflammations of the mouth and throat and is an effective gargle. Pour boiling water on to 1–2 teaspoonfuls of the dried leaves and leave to infuse for 10 minutes.

Household
Burn dried leaves or boil in water to neutralize cooking or animal odors in a room. Dried sage in potpourri or sachets among clothes discourages insects.

CAUTION
Although small amounts are quite safe when cooking, pregnant and breastfeeding women should not take therapeutic doses. Sage contains thujone, which can trigger fits in epileptics.

Common sage
Salvia officinalis
An aromatic shrub with many uses. Has decorative leaves and flowers that attract bees to the garden.

CULTIVATION

SAGE
Salvia officinalis

LIFESPAN
Hardy evergreen.

HEIGHT
2–3 ft. (60–90 cm).

SITE
Plant in borders or pots in full sun.

SOIL
The shrub prefers a light, well-drained alkaline soil but is generally quite tolerant.

GROWING
Plant 18–24 in. (45–60 cm) apart to allow for spreading. Prune in early spring to encourage new shoots and cut back after flowering. Plants become woody with age—replace every 4 to 5 years. Grow colored and variegated species and cultivars from cuttings rather than seed.

HARVESTING
Fresh leaves are at their best just before the flowers appear.

PRESERVING
Air-dry the leaves slowly to preserve their flavor.

HELPFUL HINT
Use sage as a companion plant in the vegetable garden—when grown with cabbage, it will stop the cabbage white butterfly from attacking. Traditionally, it was grown side by side with rue to keep away toads.

Leaf
Gray-green, thick, and downy with heavily veined underside. Can be dried for cooking, medicinal, and cosmetic purposes.

Stem
Square and covered with fine hairs. The stems become woody by the second year.

Seeds
Tiny, dark brown and egg-shaped.

Purple sage
Salvia officinalis
'Purpurea'
A decorative form with strongly flavored leaves.

61

St. John's Wort

This flowering perennial is part of folklore and has a long history as a healing plant. New scientific research substantiates its medicinal properties and is finding more and more ways of using it.

This cheery, golden-flowered perennial is native to the hedgerows and woodlands of Europe and temperate Asia. Prized as a healing herb since ancient times, it contains a powerful substance called hypericin, now being investigated by scientists looking for help in treating AIDS. Hypericin is also a well-established anti-depressant, although it is not suitable for those suffering from chronic depression.

HEALING QUALITIES

St. John's wort sometimes causes dermatitis, especially on skin exposed to direct sunlight, and the raw plant can be harmful if eaten. But it has a host of healing qualities—it acts as a local antiseptic and painkiller, soothes jittery nerves, speeds natural healing, and reduces inflammation. It is good for toothache, shooting pains, and hemorrhoids. Taken internally, this herb can relieve shingles, sciatica, premenstrual tension, and menopausal problems as well as fibrosis, and may also be of help to children who wet the bed at night.

EXTERNAL USE

Used externally, St. John's wort relieves skin sores, minor burns, bruises, cramp, sprains, and other injuries involving damage to the nerves, such as tennis elbow. The plant also features in various guises in homeopathic and traditional Indian Ayurvedic remedies.

MAGICAL PROPERTIES

Hypericin, a bright red pigment, leaks from the crushed flowers of this herb rather like blood—one reason for the ancient belief in its magical properties. The name *Hypericum* probably derives from the Greek *hyper*, meaning "above," and *eikon*, "picture," because the flowers were hung above religious icons to ward off evil on St. John's Day (June 24). The common name comes from St. John the Baptist, beheaded at the request of Salome, King Herod's stepdaughter. The red pigment from the crushed flowers is said to symbolize his blood.

The plant has been used in medicine since ancient times—the Greek scholar Galen described it as the antidote to intestinal worms, and it was later used in treatments for tumors. Today, the whole plant is usually harvested just as it is flowering and used fresh or dried.

Deni Bown

ST. JOHN'S WORT
Hypericum perforatum

PARTS USED:
Whole plant.

PROPERTIES:
Astringent, bitter, cooling herb; reduces inflammation, promotes healing, and calms nerves; local antiseptic and painkiller.

USES OF THE HERB:

Medicinal
Tackles inflammation, nerve pain, and injury. Promotes healing. Internally for bed-wetting in children, anxiety, premenstrual syndrome, menopausal problems, sciatica, fibrosis, and shingles. Good for toothache, shooting pains, neuralgia, concussion, nausea, hemorrhoids. Externally for burns, bruises, sprains, cramp, tennis elbow, and any kind of nerve damage. Used in homeopathy and Ayurvedic medicine. Formerly for diarrhea, dysentery, tumors.

CAUTION
Should not be given to patients with chronic depression. Can be harmful if eaten raw. May cause dermatitis, especially in direct sunlight.

◄ Commonly found in its native habitats growing in woodland or along hedgerows, St. John's wort is now cultivated the world over for its medicinal qualities.

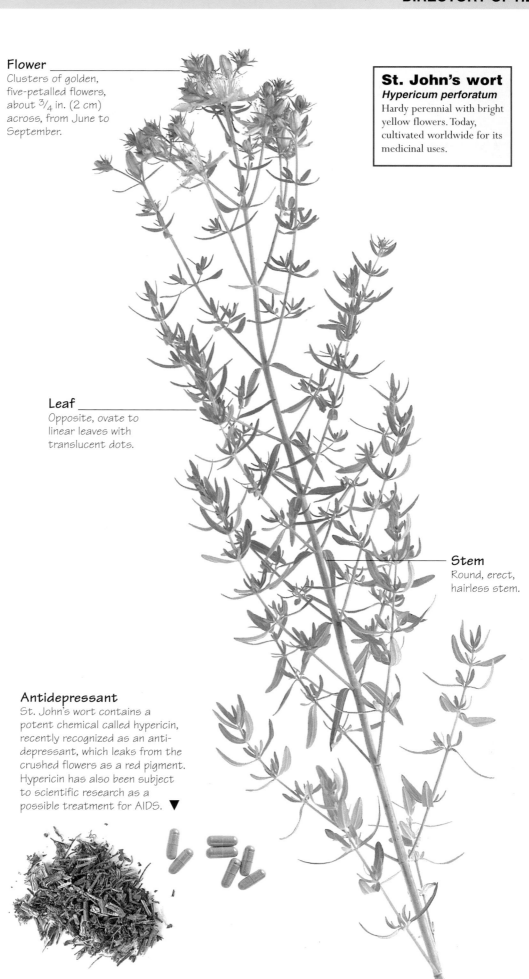

Flower
Clusters of golden, five-petalled flowers, about ¾ in. (2 cm) across, from June to September.

St. John's wort
Hypericum perforatum
Hardy perennial with bright yellow flowers. Today, cultivated worldwide for its medicinal uses.

CULTIVATION

ST. JOHN'S WORT
Hypericum perforatum

LIFESPAN
Hardy perennial.

HEIGHT
2–4 ft. (60–105 cm).

SITE
Sunny or partly shady.

SOIL
Well-drained or dry soil.

GROWING
Sow seed or propagate by division in spring or fall. (Controlled as a weed in Australia and other countries.)

HARVESTING
Cut plants just as they are flowering.

PRESERVING
Plants used fresh or dried for use in tinctures, infusions, commercial creams, oils, and liquid extracts.

Leaf
Opposite, ovate to linear leaves with translucent dots.

Stem
Round, erect, hairless stem.

Antidepressant
St. John's wort contains a potent chemical called hypericin, recently recognized as an anti-depressant, which leaks from the crushed flowers as a red pigment. Hypericin has also been subject to scientific research as a possible treatment for AIDS. ▼

Savory

Winter and summer savory have many similarities and are almost interchangeable. Although summer savory is more subtly flavored than winter savory, it is medicinally more potent.

Winter and summer savory (*Satureja montana* and *S. hortensis*) are two of the oldest staples of the kitchen spice rack and herbal medicine cabinet. These herbs contain volatile oils with a strong aroma and a variety of therapeutic effects, although they are most usually cultivated for culinary use.

Many of their properties, both culinary and medicinal, are interchangeable. The two species are similar in appearance, but summer savory has a rather more delicate flavor than winter savory. Cultivation differs slightly in that winter savory is an evergreen perennial and summer savory is an annual. Neither herb should be taken medicinally by pregnant women as they stimulate the uterus.

The leaves of both plants add a peppery flavor to sausage and other meat dishes, stuffings, and pulses. They counter flatulence when cooked with beans, and are sometimes made into jelly with grape juice. In former times, dried winter savory was powdered and mixed with finely grated bread crumbs for coating meat or fish.

DIGESTIVE TONIC

Antiseptic, astringent, and warming, summer savory and, to a lesser extent, winter savory have long been used as a tonic for digestive and gastric complaints.

Both herbs relieve diarrhea and nausea, clear bronchial congestion with their expectorant effect, and stimulate the nervous system and uterus, making them useful for treating menstrual disorders. They soothe sore throats, taken internally or as a gargle, and a fresh sprig rubbed on a bee or wasp sting provides instant relief. The flowering tops make a cleansing facial steam for oily skin.

Winter and summer savories have a reputation as aphrodisiacs—which might explain the genus name, *Satureja*, possibly derived from "satyr." They were much in demand as seasoning among the Romans, and were used liberally in sauces and vinegars. The Romans introduced the herbs to northern Europe, where they were taken for colic and strewn on the floor as a disinfectant.

HEDGING

Nowadays, winter savory is sometimes planted to create a dwarf hedge, being hardy and able to tolerate occasional clipping. It also makes a pretty container plant.

Deni Bown

SAVORY
Satureja montana
Winter savory
Satureja hortensis
Summer savory

PARTS USED:
Leaves, shoots.

PROPERTIES:
Astringent, antiseptic, expectorant, and warming; increases perspiration, improves digestion, stimulates the uterus and the nervous system; reputed to be an aphrodisiac.

USES OF THE HERB:
Medicinal
Tonic for digestive and gastric complaints; relieves nausea and diarrhea; helps menstrual disorders; loosens bronchial congestion; antiseptic—ease sore throat by gargling with an infusion. Apply fresh sprig to wasp and bee stings.

Culinary
Dried leaves crumbled as peppery seasoning, added to meat and bean dishes, stuffing, sauces, vinegars. Used to make grape jelly.

Cosmetic
Try using flowering tops as astringent facial steam for oily skin.

Cosmetic
Oil once used to remove facial blemishes.

CAUTION...
Not for medicinal use during pregnancy.

◄ Because of its hardy, evergreen nature and ability to withstand occasional clipping, winter savory makes an effective informal dwarf hedge.

CULTIVATION

WINTER SAVORY
Satureja montana

LIFESPAN
Hardy evergreen perennial.

HEIGHT
Up to 16 in. (40 cm).

SITE
Sunny.

SOIL
Dry or well-drained, and neutral to alkaline.

GROWING
Sow seed or layer in spring, or propagate by division in autumn or spring; take softwood cuttings in summer.

HARVESTING
Pick leaves in growing season, flowering tops in summer.

PRESERVING
Leaves and flowering tops used fresh or dried for use in infusions and oil extraction.

SUMMER SAVORY
Satureja hortensis

LIFESPAN
Annual; sow seeds in spring; can be grown in containers.

An infusion made with the leaves can be used for treating sore throats. ▼

Deni Bown

Flower
Sparse clusters of sky-blue blooms appear in summer.

Leaf
Stalkless, narrow, and usually pointed. Spotted with glands. Pungent aroma.

Stem
Hairy, square, green turning to reddish-brown.

Winter savory
Satureja montana
Hardy, evergreen perennial found growing wild in the Mediterranean region. Long appreciated for its culinary and medicinal qualities. ▶

Summer savory
Satureja hortensis
Similar in appearance and uses to winter savory but annual in growth; has a slightly less pungent flavor. ◀

Sorrel

In the past, this plant was used medicinally—the ancient Romans used it to cure scurvy—but nowadays, it is mainly used for its tangy flavor in salads and soups or cooked with other leafy vegetables.

This hardy perennial belongs to a large genus of about 200 plants and is found across northern temperate areas.

The use of common sorrel dates back many centuries, to the days of the Roman empire, when it is said that soldiers took a particular species to cure themselves of scurvy.

As a plant, garden sorrel (*Rumex acetosa*), also known as sour dock, falls somewhere between a herb and a vegetable and is grown for its docklike leaves, which add a very tangy flavor to soups, sauces, and salads. Sorrel should be used in small quantities as it has an acidic flavor.

Sorrel is less well known as a medicinal plant, but it does have various therapeutic uses, thanks to its astringent, cooling, and diuretic effects. Tea made from the leaves can be used to lower fevers and treat liver and kidney problems, while leaf poultices ease certain skin complaints. However, many *Rumex* species contain oxalates, which are highly acidic and possibly poisonous if taken in large amounts. The concentrated juice of *R. acetosa* is used in preparations designed to bleach and remove difficult stains such as rust and mold.

CLOSE RELATIONS

Closely related is *R. scutatus*, French sorrel, which has a slightly milder flavor than garden sorrel. Dock species, such as *R. crispus*, are also members of this genus, but are generally less palatable than sorrel.

Garden sorrel has a distinctive appearance. As well as its docklike leaves, it produces spikes of rust-colored flowers in summer and tiny fruits shortly afterward. It has deep roots, and once established, can spread like a weed. For this reason, it is a good idea to grow it as an annual—especially as the young leaves have a less astringent flavor than those on more mature perennial specimens.

Plants should be propagated by sowing seeds during spring and by dividing plants in spring or fall. Leaves should be picked when young and used fresh.

Michael Leach/Oxford Scientific Films

GARDEN SORREL

Rumex acetosa

PARTS USED:
Leaves.

PROPERTIES:
Cooling, astingent, acidic herb; diuretic effects.

USES OF THE HERB:
Culinary
Add fresh leaves to salads, soups, and sauces and some egg dishes. Chopped or puréed leaves may be mixed in with soft cheese or mayonnaise.

Medicinal
Not commonly used medicinally, but its diuretic effects can help with certain kidney and liver complaints; applied externally, its cooling properties may ease skin complaints such as boils and acne.

Household
Used in stain removers and may be used as a green and yellow vegetable dye.

Decorative
The seed heads are attractive in herbal arrangements and wreaths.

CAUTION
May be harmful if consumed in large quantities.

◄ Sorrel will grow freely in moist soil and sun or partial shade. Remove flowerbuds to keep a good supply of young, tender leaves.

CULTIVATION

GARDEN SORREL
Rumex acetosa

LIFESPAN
Hardy perennial.

HEIGHT
Up to 3 ft. (90 cm) when flowering.

SITE
In sun or partial shade.

SOIL
Fertile and moist.

GROWING
Sow seeds in spring, where the plants will grow, and then thin out seedlings to about 1 ft. (30 cm) apart. Divide plants in spring or fall. To ensure a winter supply of the herb, protect pots of sorrel from frost by keeping under glass.

HARVESTING
Pick leaves when young before the plant flowers and use them fresh.

▼ **This astringent and cooling perennial has a range of culinary uses—it should be eaten in small quantities.**

Garden sorrel
Rumex acetosa
The slightly sharp flavor of sorrel combines well with other green leaves to add zest to salads. It can also be combined with spinach. It is not commonly used medicinally.

Leaf
Bright green, docklike leaves have a distinct lemony scent.

Stem
Ridged stem is tinged with red.

Photos Horticultural

Seeds
Small brown seeds are pointed in shape.

Tarragon

Well known as a culinary herb, this plant is also used medicinally. The leaves contain vitamin A, minerals, and trace elements. It is easily cultivated and is at its best used fresh.

The unique flavor of this aromatic and versatile herb has long made it popular among cooks, and it is a classic element of French cuisine. It is one of the more important ingredients of *fines herbes* (mixed herbs) and a number of sauces. The leaves contain vitamin A, niacin, calcium, and iron.

Originally from Central Asia, tarragon was probably introduced to Europe during the Moorish occupation of Spain in the 1500s.

The *Artemisia* genus, of which tarragon is a member, includes some very bitter herbs indeed. Among these is wormwood, which is used to treat worms and also to stimulate the digestive system. Tarragon is the only herb in the genus that is not too bitter to be used in cooking, and it can be used quite generously.

The species name for tarragon is *dracunculus*—meaning "little dragon," which may refer to the plant's supposed ability to cure poisonous bites.

GROWING TARRAGON

Tarragon is a creeping perennial, and its narrow, aromatic leaves contrast well with other foliage in the herb garden. It can also be grown outdoors in large pots and moved to a cold frame in fall to give protection.

Small, green flowers appear in early to midsummer and should be pinched out to encourage leafy growth. In colder areas, the plant may not flower at all.

Photos Horticultural

▲ **Tarragon is a perennial and is hardy enough to withstand a few degrees of frost. It is grown in commercial quantities for dried leaves and an oil used in flavorings and perfumes.**

Two kinds of tarragon are commonly cultivated—French tarragon (*A. dracunculus*) and Russian tarragon (*A. dracunculoides*). The French is infinitely superior to the Russian, which is not as highly flavored.

Tarragon sold as seed is almost always Russian tarragon. When buying plants, note that Russian tarragon has thinner, paler leaves than its French counterpart. If in any doubt, bruise the leaves and smell them—French tarragon smells rather like aniseed.

TARRAGON
Artemisia dracunculus
French tarragon

PARTS USED:
Leaves.

PROPERTIES:
Aromatic, diuretic.

USES OF THE HERB:
Culinary
Use the leaves with chicken and egg dishes, soups, stuffings, sauces for fish. A classic ingredient of *fines herbes* (with chervil and parsley), tarragon vinegar, herb butter, and sauce béarnaise and hollandaise. Good with many cream sauces. Very compatible with asparagus. Use to season strong flavored fish, liver, and roast duck.

Medicinal
Medicinal uses are limited although it is good for digestion and can help delayed menstruation. Destroys intestinal worms and acts as a diuretic.

CAUTION
Do not take in medicinal quantity during pregnancy, but culinary use is fine.

CULTIVATION

FRENCH TARRAGON
Artemisia dracunculus

LIFESPAN
Hardy perennial.

HEIGHT
2–3 ft. (60–90 cm).

SITE
Sunny.

SOIL
Well drained, neutral to slightly alkaline.

GROWING
Cuttings or division. Remove the flower heads to encourage leafy growth. Divide and replant after 3 or 4 years to maintain flavor. Protect in cold winters. Tarragon is suitable for growing indoors.

HARVESTING
Use fresh from early summer to fall.

PRESERVING
Dry leaves carefully to retain some flavor. Freezing retains flavor better. Sprigs of tarragon can also be infused in oil or vinegar. Oil is extracted commercially.

HELPFUL HINT
Protect with straw or mulch in hard winters— especially when grown in pots or containers. Foliage is prone to attack by rust.

Flavored vinegar
A sprig of fresh tarragon can be used to flavor vinegar for use in salad dressings and in mayonnaise.

Dried leaf
Contains far less flavor than the fresh leaf and may lose this with age.

Leaf
Narrow, glossy green leaves release aromatic oils from their underside when lightly pressed.

Stem
Round and branching, can become brown and woody near the base of the plant.

Root
Dense and fine. Has been used to cure toothache.

French tarragon
Artemisia dracunculus
This straggling, bushy herb has important culinary uses. Its aniseed flavor goes well with chicken and egg dishes.

69

Thyme

Every part of this sweet-smelling, flowering herb is used—the leaves, fresh or dried, are widely used in the kitchen, and infusions and extracts from the rest of the plant have medicinal uses. Thyme also looks attractive in the garden.

Common thyme is a small, aromatic herb with a bushy habit. It is a member of a large genus with a range of uses. The leaves of the different species may be green, gray, golden, or variegated, and the flowers can be lilac, white, or one of many shades of pink. There are several other useful forms of thyme, including lemon thyme (*Thymus* x *citriodorus*).

Garden, or common, thyme (*T. vulgaris*) has wide-ranging culinary and medicinal properties. It has a reputation for aiding the digestion of rich foods, and is used to flavor stocks, stuffings, and soups. It blends well with wine in sauces for poultry, fish, and pork. Thyme has been used since Roman times to flavor liqueurs.

Thyme has a powerful antibacterial effect, stimulating the immune system. It can be used to medicate surgical dressings as it does not irritate the skin, as an insect repellent, and as an inhalation to ease breathing problems. An extract, thymol, is used in many toothpastes and mouthwashes, and the essential oil is used for aches, pains, and skin disorders.

HEAVEN SCENT

Thyme grows wild around the Mediterranean region, where its fragrance scents the hillsides. The Greeks called it *thymus*, which means 'courage.' They used it for massage oil, and Roman soldiers are reputed to have bathed in thyme water before battle. Its antiseptic and preservative qualities were recognized by the Ancient Egyptians, who used it in embalming fluid and burned it to fumigate rooms.

Thyme grows well in colder climates, provided the soil is well drained. It makes a good ground-cover in borders or rockeries, and the flowers attract bees.

◀ **Thyme forms a low-growing aromatic bush that spreads widely, especially if trimmed lightly after it has flowered. All parts of the plant are useful, including the flowers.**

THYME
Thymus vulgaris

PARTS USED:
Whole plant, leaves, flowering tops, oil.

PROPERTIES:
Aromatic, astringent, expectorant, antiseptic and anti-fungal.

USES OF THE HERB:
Culinary
Dry the leaf, chop finely and use to make bouquet garni with parsley and bay. Use the fresh leaf to flavour white wine sauces, stuffings, stocks and soups and to cook chicken, fish and shellfish. Use sprigs of the fresh herb in cooking oils and vinegars, and in mulled red wine.

Medicinal
An infusion of thyme leaves will aid digestion. Combine with honey for troublesome coughs and sore throats and deep-seated chest infections. It can also help to clear asthma, catarrh, laryngitis and bronchitis but should not be taken for longer than three weeks at a time.

Cosmetic
Use fresh or dried herbs in facial steams to cleanse the skin.

Decorative
Use flowering sprigs in summer posy arrangements.

Household
Use essential oil mixed with alcohol to spray on paper and pressed flower specimens as a mold inhibitor. Make up a decoction to use as a mild disinfectant.

CAUTION
Avoid therapeutic doses during pregnancy.

CULTIVATION

GARDEN THYME
Thymus vulgaris

LIFESPAN
Low evergreen shrub.

HEIGHT
To 1 ft. (30 cm).

SITE
Full sun. Dislikes winter wet.

SOIL
Light, well-drained, alkaline soil suits thyme perfectly.

GROWING
Grow from cuttings, layers, or seeds. Not very successful indoors unless light conditions are extremely good.

HARVESTING
Pick leaves or sprigs at any time during the growing season. Flowering branches can be collected between June and August on a sunny day.

PRESERVING
Discard the stems and preserve the leaves and flowers.

HELPFUL HINT
Grow as a companion plant in the vegetable garden—when grown with cabbage, it will keep away a variety of cabbage pests.

Garden Thyme
Thymus vulgaris
Pink to mauve-flowered, it grows into a small bushy plant. Has a host of culinary and medicinal uses.

Culinary favorite
This herb is easily grown in well-drained soil in full sun. It is also suitable for containers and combines well with other culinary herbs.

Leaf
Aromatic and pointed, mid-green, with rolled edges and fine hairs underneath.

Seeds
Shiny brown, tiny, and spherical.

Stem
Greenish-brown, becoming woody with age.

Dried leaf
Used to flavor sauces and stocks. Retains strong flavor.

Root
Thyme forms a fine, dense mat of thin, brown roots.

Growing Herbs

Whether you have a large backyard with plenty of space, or a small balcony with room for only a few container plants, growing herbs has never been easier. Most garden stores stock a wide range of plants, and you can grow herbs from seed, seedlings, or cuttings.

Before you start planting, think about the type of herb garden you would like to create. Do you want herbs for use in the kitchen, for their medicinal properties, for cosmetic preparations, or for use in herbal crafts around the home? Alternatively, perhaps you would prefer to create an herb garden that looks attractive all year-round with little maintenance, in which case you should concentrate on perennials rather than annuals and biennials. Another way to plan an herb garden is to focus on plants that have attractive and constrasting foliage—planting the soft grays and greens of sage next to the darker green, spikier leaves of rosemary, for instance, for dramatic effect.

Whatever kind of herb garden you want to create, this chapter will give you the information you need to plan, plant, and maintain your garden, from sowing seed and selecting plants for dry areas, to garden chores throughout the year and growing plants for specific purposes..

Herb Categories

Herbs fall into one of four main plant categories that may need slightly different treatments in their planting and positioning.

PLANT TYPES

WOODY TREES OR SHRUBS

Taller plants, such as bay, berberis, and rosemary, form the backbone of a bed or border. Since these are the most permanent plants in the scheme, it is important that they are positioned in the right place where they will look effective as they grow and not crowd other plants.

PERENNIALS

These die down in the fall or winter, but grow again every year in the spring. They include chives, fennel, marjoram, mint, and tarragon. They can be used to bulk out beds and borders, and provide seasonal interest with flowers and foliage.

ANNUALS AND BIENNIALS

These grow and die off within one or two years, and should be dug up as they die off at the end of their growing season. They include herbs, such as basil and parsley, and cottage flowers such as marigolds, nasturtiums, foxgloves, and pansies, which form the mainstay of seasonal color.

SUBSHRUBS

These are low plants, shrubby in growth and appearance, such as common thyme, lavender, and sage. They make excellent edgings for borders, but they are not always long lived and are best renewed every few years by taking cuttings in summer, which can be planted the following year when they have formed new rooted plants.

Woody trees and shrubs
These are the more imposing plants and include shrubs such as berberis.

Perennials
Plants such as edible chrysanthemums add color to beds and borders.

Annuals and biennials
Among the many herbs in this category is winter savory. These herbs, which include many flowering species, provide plenty of color.

Subshrubs
Plants such as lavender are ideal in herbaceous borders.

Making the Most of the Four Categories

▼ Mixing different categories of herbs will provide a colorful border during the summer months.

If you are starting your garden from scratch, spend a little time planning to provide shape, color, and seasonal interest so that your herb border looks good all year round. Include a mixture of plants from all four categories. If your border is established, be prepared to thin, cut back, or even move plants for best effect.

PLANNING AND PLANTING

Establishing priorities and order of work

- As woody trees and shrubs are permanent and include many evergreens, they should be considered first. Use them for winter interest, when the other plants have generally little foliage or color.
- Subshrubs, several of which are evergreen, generally make good mid-border plants. Do allow for access.
- Perennials need to be planted where there is space between shrubs, allowing for size, shape, and color.
- Use annuals and biennials to fill gaps in the front of borders; some self-seed and may have to be weeded out.

PLANT TYPE	INTEREST	SEASON	REQUIREMENTS
WOODY TREES AND SHRUBS			
Camellia	evergreen leaves flowers	all year early–late spring	needs neutral to acid soil, not too dry
Lemon verbena	scented leaves mauve flowers	summer–fall summer	only hardy to about 23°F (-5°C), new growth may not show until early summer
Juniper	aromatic evergreen flowers	all year summer	needs good drainage
SUB SHRUBS			
Curry plant	aromatic gray foliage yellow flowers	all year summer	sun and good drainage
Lavender	flowers	summer	sun and good drainage
Sage	semi-evergreen flowers	all year summer	sun and good drainage
ANNUALS AND BIENNIALS			
Angelica	foliage and flowers	spring–summer	sow seeds in situ
Purple basil	foliage and flowers	summer	temperatures above 59°F (15°C)
Viola	flowers	winter–spring	part shade
PERENNIALS			
Bronze fennel	foliage and flowers	spring–fall	most perennials require
Chives	flowers	summer	well-drained soil
Columbine	flowers	spring–summer	and sun; apply a general
Lily of the valley (note: poisonous)	flowers	spring	feed during the
Variegated marjoram	foliage and flowers	spring–fall	growing season

Planning a Small Herb Garden

The traditional enclosed kitchen garden provided excellent conditions for growing herbs, retaining heat and sheltering plants from the wind. Such gardens are no longer practical, but similar conditions can be achieved by siting an herb patch in a sunny sheltered corner.

PLANTING PLAN
The plan is for a site measuring about 11 x 5 ft. (3.3 x 1.5 m), with north and south as indicated at the top and bottom. Place taller plants in such a position that they don't shade smaller, sun-loving plants.

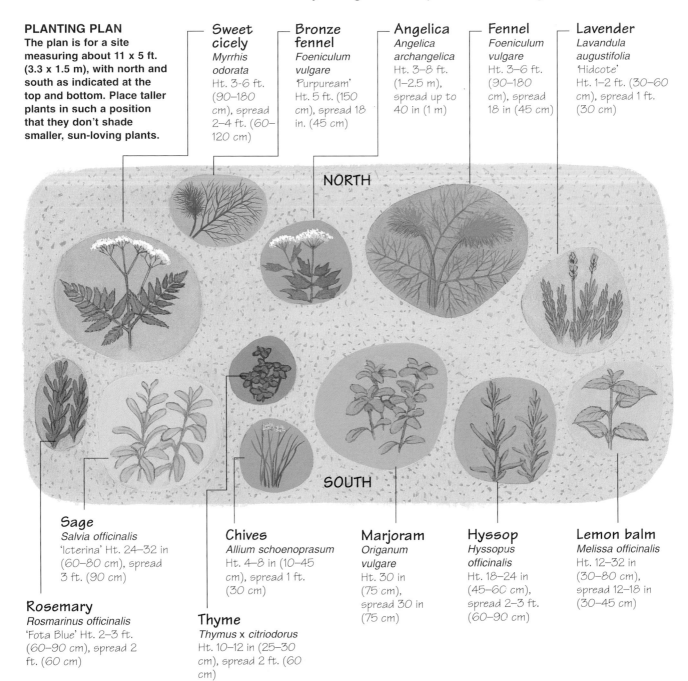

Sweet cicely
Myrrhis odorata
Ht. 3–6 ft. (90–180 cm), spread 2–4 ft. (60–120 cm)

Bronze fennel
Foeniculum vulgare 'Purpuream'
Ht. 5 ft. (150 cm), spread 18 in. (45 cm)

Angelica
Angelica archangelica
Ht. 3–8 ft. (1–2.5 m), spread up to 40 in (1 m)

Fennel
Foeniculum vulgare
Ht. 3–6 ft. (90–180 cm), spread 18 in (45 cm)

Lavender
Lavandula augustifolia 'Hidcote'
Ht. 1–2 ft. (30–60 cm), spread 1 ft. (30 cm)

NORTH

SOUTH

Sage
Salvia officinalis 'Icterina' Ht. 24–32 in (60–80 cm), spread 3 ft. (90 cm)

Rosemary
Rosmarinus officinalis 'Fota Blue' Ht. 2–3 ft. (60–90 cm), spread 2 ft. (60 cm)

Chives
Allium schoenoprasum
Ht. 4–8 in (10–45 cm), spread 1 ft. (30 cm)

Thyme
Thymus x citriodorus
Ht. 10–12 in (25–30 cm), spread 2 ft. (60 cm)

Marjoram
Origanum vulgare
Ht. 30 in (75 cm), spread 30 in (75 cm)

Hyssop
Hyssopus officinalis
Ht. 18–24 in (45–60 cm), spread 2–3 ft. (60–90 cm)

Lemon balm
Melissa officinalis
Ht. 12–32 in (30–80 cm), spread 12–18 in (30–45 cm)

What to Plant Where

EDGINGS

The following won't detract from taller plants. Use them for beds and edgings. Catmint, chervil, chives, feverfew, hyssop, marigold, marjoram, parsley, thyme.

HEDGES

The following plants can be cut back to form hedges and to provide shelter for some of the less robust plants.
Bay, lavender, rosemary, wormwood.

FILLERS

Low-growing herbs can be used between paving stones and along path edges. Chamomile, creeping savory, creeping thyme, pennyroyal, woodruff.

SPECIAL NEEDS

Some plants do better out of full sun. The following can be planted in the more shady area of a herb patch:
Angelica, arugula (rocket), bergamot, chervil, dill, lamb's lettuce, lemon balm, lovage, mint, parsley, sorrel, sweet cicely, woodruff.

HEIGHT AND SPREAD

It's tempting to place seedlings or young plants close together to cover bare patches of ground, but avoid doing this as the plants will spread in a matter of weeks, given the right conditions.

Allow sufficient space between plants—approximately 12–18 in. (30–45 cm)—to avoid overcrowding and provide for spreading growth. A planting plan, drawn to scale, will help.

CONTAINED HERBS

Some herbs, like this species of thyme, require more specialized treatment whereby they can be grown in pots and given protection from winter wet.

Photos Horticultural

SPREADING HERBS

Some herbs are invasive and are best contained to prevent excessive seeding or roots spreading and affecting other plants. Plant the following in containers sunk in the ground: comfrey, mint, soapwort, tansy, and tarragon.

Some tender herbs can be given the same treatment—it makes it easy to lift them in winter and to repot them.

Harry Smith Collection

MAIN TYPES OF HERBS

To plan a herb patch, bear in mind the following categories:

- larger shrubby herbs or tall perennials— bay, lavender, rosemary, sage, and fennel. Plant these at the back of a bed or where they will not block the sun from low-growing species.

- smaller perennial herbs—chives, marjoram, and thyme. These need plenty of light; place them near the edges of borders, handy for picking.

- annual and biennial herbs—basil, borage, chervil, cilantro, dill, marigold, parsley, and arugula (rocket). Place these in convenient gaps for picking, but remember there will be gaps again when they are removed at the end of the growing season.

Preparing Soil for an Herb Garden

Like ordinary gardens, a successful herb patch depends on well-prepared soil for year-on-year results. Once this basic chore is complete, success is virtually guaranteed and the herbs will grow readily without a great deal of attention.

SOIL TESTING

In urban areas, the chances are that the soil is neutral to alkaline, which suits most herbs. If in doubt, test your soil type with one of the several testing kits now available from garden centers and mail-order companies. Most of these use a color system to indicate soil types—blue or green for acid soils (6pH or less), red, orange, or brown for alkaline soils (8pH or higher).

• If you have acid soil, it can be made more suitable for herbs by the addition of garden lime forked into the soil in the early spring and/or fall.

There are many different types of soil, which can be divided into five categories, each with its own characteristics.

Sandy soil is grainy and loose, and drains quickly, making it ideal for Mediterranean herbs; it benefits from compost.

Clay is heavy when wet, and hard and solid when dry, making it difficult to dig. Digging in compost and farmyard manure will improve it; the soil also benefits by the addition of lime.

Loam is dark and crumbly, retains moisture, and is the ideal soil; it benefits from mulching.

Chalk and limestone soils need organic material on a regular basis; also potash and nitrogen.

Peaty soil doesn't drain well, tends to be acidic and needs lime added.

Preparation

The best time to prepare soil for a herb garden is in late fall, early winter, or early spring. If you are growing herbs from seed, you can sow them indoors in early spring so they can be planted out toward the end of May.

Harry Smith Collection

Clay is often thought of as being difficult soil to use as it tends to be solid and restricts root growth. The solution is to dig in as much compost as deeply as you can to make it lighter and to improve drainage. Add crushed limestone every second year. Mulch can be used on the surface in the fall, and left until spring before being dug into the clay. Growing plants in the clay will also improve it.

1 Mark out the area of your herb bed. Dig up the soil and remove any vegetation, making sure the patch is thoroughly weeded and free of roots. ▲

2 Once the site is cleared, dig the whole patch to a depth of the spade length, breaking down any large clods of earth as you go. A light dressing of organic fertilizer, such as fish, blood and bone, or chicken pellets, will give good results if forked into the soil before planting. ▶

Photos Horticultural

SITE AND SUN

The site for a herb patch needs to be sunny, meaning that it should get sun for more than half the day. This is ideal for most herbs, but there are exceptions. A few herbs prefer a position that does not become too hot and dry. These include mint, chervil, dill, parsley, sorrel, and salad herbs, such as arugula (rocket) and lamb's lettuce. Plant these in a moisture-retentive spot that receives dappled shade or sun for less than half the day.

Photos Horticultural

FEEDING

Fall/winter: a dressing of compost forked into the soil is good practice.

Spring: use a general balanced fertilizer, such as Miracle Gro.

Summer: some annual herbs grow better with monthly liquid feeds, but don't over-feed Mediterranean herbs, such as thyme and rosemary.

Liquid feed Use a measuring spoon to make up the liquid feed according to the size of your watering can. ◀

Sowing the Seeds for an Early Crop

Sowing seeds indoors in a propagator in the depths of winter will give you a headstart for an early crop of herbs. It is also more economical than buying individually potted herbs.

S eed companies now produce a wide variety of herb seeds that can be obtained from good garden centers or by mail order. For the potting compost, John Innes No. 1 mixed with a little peat is ideal. To get the seeds started, you need to keep them at a temperature between 50 and 60°F (10 and 16°C). A sunny porch, windowsill, or greenhouse is ideal. A propagator, although not essential, helps keep the seeds at a constant temperature, retains moisture, and protects them from drafts of cold air. Some of the seeds will take longer than others to germinate. Basil, being more tender than most, is the one herb that can be difficult to sow early.

HERBS SUITABLE FOR EARLY SOWING

Chervil
Anthriscus cerefolium
Chives
Allium schoenoprasum
Cilantro
Coriandrum sativum
Dill
Peucedanum graveolens
Fennel
Foeniculum vulgare
Parsley—curly
Carum petroselinum crispum
Arugula/rocket
Eruca vesicaria sativa
Sage
Salvia officinalis
Sweet marjoram
Origanum majorana
Thyme
Thymus

Sowing Seeds for an Early Crop

If using very small containers, transplant the seedlings into slightly bigger pots once they are established. When the plant reaches about 3 in. (7.5 cm) in height, start feeding it weekly with a diluted liquid feed. The leaves can be picked as soon as the plants become bushy. Any spare seedlings can be planted outdoors in late May, when there is less risk of frost.

Materials: *A selection of herb seeds • Water sprayer • Plant propagator, seed trays, or shallow pots, about 2–3 in. (5–7.5 cm) deep • Soil-based compost*

1 Fill the containers with the compost and press it down lightly so that it is about ½ in. (12 mm) below the rim of the container. ◄

2 Sprinkle the seeds lightly on top of the soil-based compost, using a different container for each type of herb. ▶

3 Cover the seeds with a little compost no more than ¼ in. (6 mm) deep. Smooth the compost with your fingers to level it. ◄

4 Spray with water, being careful not to soak the compost. Place in propagator, if using, and leave in a warm area—on a windowsill, for example. The seedlings usually appear within one to two weeks. ▲

Taking Cuttings

Once you have a few herbs established, you can sustain stocks by taking cuttings. Plants that can be grown this way include culinary staples such as marjoram, rosemary, sage, and tarragon. Cuttings are usually taken in the spring or summer, and will grow to resemble the parent plant—unlike plants from seed, which tend to be more variable.

▼ Trays are useful when you are taking a lot of cuttings. They are also easier to water than individual pots. Use gardening tags to label the plants for easy identification.

Preparing the Cuttings

Cuttings must be prepared to encourage root growth and planted in loose, fertile soil. They can be grown outdoors in sheltered open soil, or in containers indoors or out. Placing containers on a heating mat will encourage root growth. Once established, the cuttings can be transferred into individual pots.

There are three types of cuttings: softwood, semiripe (semihardwood), and hardwood. Their names describe the shoot's growth on the parent plant.

• **Softwood cuttings** are new shoots with soft green stems and leaves, usually taken in spring. Many herbs can be propagated by either softwood or semiripe cuttings, depending on the time of year.

• **Semiripe cuttings** are usually taken in mid- to late summer, when the shoots have started to harden at the base where they join the parent plant. Shrubby herbs such as myrtle and rosemary grow well from semiripe cuttings.

• **Hardwood cuttings** are taken from woody shrubs and trees in fall and winter.

Softwood cuttings should be quite small: 2–4 in. (5–10 cm), while later, semiripe cuttings should be about 4–6 in. (10–15 cm).

Hardwood cuttings can be from 6 to 14 in. (15 to 35 cm) in length.

The method is similar for all three types. With hardwood cuttings, remove any soft shoots or buds from the top to encourage vigorous growth.

1 Take a healthy shoot with plenty of leaves but no flower bud. Cut cleanly through the stem with a sharp knife, just below where the leaves join. Make the cut at an angle to give more surface area for root growth. ▶

2 Cut away excess leaves from the stems, leaving about two pairs plus the central leaf tips. If there are more, the cutting will have to work to support the leaves, rather than to grow roots. ◀

3 Dip the cut end of the stem into hormone rooting powder and shake off any excess. Most cuttings will take without the powder, but it gives them a head start. ▶

4 Insert the cuttings into pots of gritty compost, with the lower leaves almost level with the soil. Firm them in and don't overcrowd the pot. Keep the cuttings moist—drying out is the main cause of failure. To maintain humidity and create a mini-greenhouse, set sticks in the pot to support a polythene bag, secured around the base. ◀

◀ A number of cuttings from the same species can be placed in one pot. Once they have taken, they can be planted on outside or in separate containers.

Layering and Dividing

Layering and dividing are two basic techniques to use when you want to make new plants. You can use your own herb-garden plants and increase your stock of plants at no cost.

HERBS FOR DIVIDING

Divide plants in spring, except tansy and soapwort—divide these in fall.

- Bergamot *Monarda didyma*
- Catnip *Nepeta cataria*
- Chives *Allium schoenoprasum*
- Comfrey *Symphytum officinale*
- Elecampane *Inula helenium*
- Fennel *Foeniculum vulgare*
- Feverfew *Tanacetum parthenium*
- Lemon balm *Melissa officinalis*
- Lovage *Levisticum officinale*
- Marjoram *Origanum majorana*
- Mint *Mentha*
- Mugwort *Artemisia vulgaris*
- Sage *Salvia officinalis*
- Soapwort *Saponaria officinalis*
- Tansy *Tanacetum vulgare*
- Tarragon *Artemisia dracunculus*
- Thyme *Thymus vulgaris*
- Woodruff *Galium odoratum*

HERBS FOR LAYERING

The following can be layered throughout the growing season.

- Bay *Laurus nobilis*
- Cotton lavender *Santolina chamaecyparissus*
- Honeysuckle *Lonicera japonica*
- Hyssop *Hyssopus officinalis*
- Marjoram *Origanum majorana*
- Rosemary *Rosmarinus officinalis*
- Sage *Salvia officinalis*
- Thyme *Thymus vulgaris*
- Winter savory *Satureja montana*

Louis Jordaan

Once plants start to crowd each other, divide large clumps such as lemon balm, thyme, and chives, and layer herbs such as rosemary. ▲

83

Layering

Layering is done by selecting a low-level stem from an existing plant in the herb garden and securing it in the ground while it is still attached to the parent plant. You can use wire bent into hairpin shapes to hold the stem down or simply put a large stone or half-brick on the stem to weight it down.

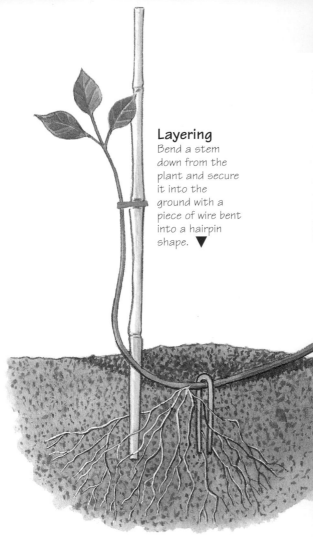

Layering
Bend a stem down from the plant and secure it into the ground with a piece of wire bent into a hairpin shape. ▼

GETTING IT RIGHT

- Prepare the soil with compost and make a small hole.
- Gently pull the stem down, cover with soil and peg it in place over the prepared hole.
- Water it well and don't allow to dry out.
- Leave until the stem has taken then sever and leave in place or replant as required.

You can layer plants all through the growing season, but the earlier you start, the sooner you will have healthy, strong-growing new ones. Either leave the new plants in place until the following spring or sever them in fall. You can replant them immediately or pot them up to overwinter in a container until you are ready to plant them out in spring.

Division

Division is one of the most satisfying and cheapest forms of increasing your plant stocks. Many herbs such as chives, mint, lovage, and tarragon spread to form large clumps. If the clump is too thick, the plant will lose vigor and it will benefit from division. Many plants, including chives, fennel, and lovage, need to be divided every three to four years to ensure good growth.

If clumps of herbs such as comfrey, soapwort, and tansy have spread too far, you can reduce their size by division.

The best time to divide plants is in spring when they begin to grow well, or in the fall when the new plants can get established before winter sets in.

If the clump is very congested you may need to use two forks back to back to prise it apart. Move the new sections into different areas of the garden or plant them in containers if you need to overwinter them.

SUCCESSFUL DIVIDING

- Lift the clumps out of the bed and then carefully work the roots free from the soil.
- Depending on the size of the clump, separate it into two or more sections. With large, established clumps, work the sections free from the outside and discard the center, which, being the oldest part of the plant, may be past its best.
- Discard any damaged or diseased parts of the clump.
- Replant the sections in soil that has been prepared with compost and water in well.

Dividing
Use two garden forks, back to back, and pull the handles together to loosen the roots, then pull the handles apart. ▲

Companion Planting

Many herbs have a natural ability to protect other plants from insect pests, while others stimulate the growth of certain plant species. When grown as "companion plants," such herbs can help keep the garden fruitful and healthy.

▼ Aphids and whitefly are partial to tomato plants, but growing marigolds nearby helps to deter them—and also attracts hoverflies, which feed on aphids.

Choosing Companion Plants

This table shows which herbs to plant where. Some deter insect pests with their scent or attract certain beneficial insects. Others enrich the soil and help bring minerals and nutrients to the surface. For companion planting to work well, you have to combine vegetable and flower gardens, such as growing chives among roses to deter the aphids.

Stephen Dalton/Oxford Scientific Films

◄ The flowers of borage are particularly attractive to bees, which help to pollinate nearby plants, encouraging them to fruit.

HERB	WHERE	WHY
Borage	Near strawberries and tomatoes	Attracts bees, which help to improve crop yield by pollinating plants.
Chamomile	Near sick plants	Acts as a tonic and encourages growth.
Comfrey	Flower borders and vegetable garden	Deep taproots help bring minerals to the surface of the soil.
Dill and fennel	Among vegetables	Attract hoverflies, which then eat aphids.
Garlic and chives	Under roses	Keeps away aphids and leaf spot.
Nasturtium	Among vegetables	Attracts aphids away from the vegetables. Also repels ants and whitefly.
Sage	Among cabbages	Repels cabbage white butterfly.
Summer savory	Among vegetables and roses	Deters blackfly.
Tagetes (African and French marigolds)	Among tomatoes and vegetables	Deters aphids and whitefly through scent and by attracting hoverflies. Roots secrete chemicals that kill ground elder and bindweed. The roots also stop eelworm from recognizing their host plants, which include potatoes, tulips, and roses.
Valerian	Amongst vegetables	Stimulates earthworms, which help aerate the soil and boost plant growth.
Wormwood, hyssop, and rue	Vegetable gardens and flower borders	Act as insect deterrents.

Plants for Dry Areas

A difficult dry spot devoid of shade in the garden need not be a problem. Many herbs are sun-lovers, preferring well-drained, even dry, and hot conditions.

By choosing the right plants for your conditions, you can create a beautiful border out of an unpromising site. Dry areas can be a problem, especially during dry spells when you may need to conserve water. It will help if you make sure that the area for planting is well dug, free of roots and rubble, and has compost or humus forked into the soil. Providing ground cover will help retain some moisture. When selecting plants, include some for their fragrance—choose from lavender and cotton lavender, rosemary, and wall germander.

TOP CHOICES

These plants will succeed in dry soil, providing interest from flower color in spring and summer:

- **Annual clary**
  Salvia viridis Ht. 12–20 in. (30–50 cm); a colorful annual grown from seed, available in shades of purple, mauve, pink, and white
- **Cotton lavender**
  Santolina chamaecyparissus Ht. 10–32 in. (25–50 cm); yellow button-head flowers on a dense, gray-leafed shrubby plant
- **French lavender**
  Lavandula dentata Ht. 28–32 in. (70–80 cm); bright purple bracts top the flowers on an upright bush
- **Periwinkle** *(right)*
  Vinca major Ht. 8–16 in. (20–40 cm); spreads vigorously to form a loose ground cover; tolerates partial shade
- **Rosemary**
  Rosmarinus Ht. variable up to 6 ft. (1.8 m); available in a selection of blue-flowered cultivars, such as *R.* 'Sissinghurst Blue'
- **Tansy**
  Tanacetum vulgare Ht. 18–24 in. (45–60 cm); yellow heads and green, ferny foliage
- **Wall germander**
  Teucrium chamaedrys Ht. 4–10 in. (10–25 cm); low, shrubby edging plant with rosy mauve flowers.

Deni Bown

Harry Smith Collection

▲ The aromatic silver-gray foliage of artemisia is set off to good effect against a background of mauve flowers provided by clary sage. Both these plants thrive in dry spots and can be included in mixed borders.

Practical and Ornamental Plants

By growing herbs that thrive in dry, sunny spots, you can ensure that your plants remain healthy for picking and also provide ornamental value from foliage and flowers.

Low-growing shrubby herbs, such as some varieties of sage, lavender, artemisia, and common thyme, make attractive front-of-border plants with a long season of interest. Taller herbs such as clary sage, fennel, and rosemary should be placed farther back in the border. Bear in mind that evergreens, such as rosemary, bay, and boxwood, will provide foliage in winter when annuals have died off. Myrtle is another evergreen suited to a dry spot, but it needs the protection of a warm wall in winter if it is to produce a good display of flowers. Perennials such as the curry plant and annuals such as French or African marigolds will also provide colorful stopgaps.

Harry Smith Collection

COLORFUL FOLIAGE

• ARTEMISIA
A. ludoviciana 'Silver Queen': artemisias are renowned for their ability to withstand dry conditions. They are grown primarily for the beauty of the silvery-gray foliage, which makes a pretty foil for other herbs with blue, mauve, pink, or purple flowers such as hyssop, sage, or lavender. Some artemisias are hardy perennials that spread in light soil; be prepared to thin them out or reduce clumps of the more vigorous species and cultivars in fall or early spring.

• CREEPING THYME
Thymus x *citriodorus* 'Silver Queen' makes a good edging plant with its low, neat habit of growth, and pink, mauve, or purple flowers from early to late summer. In addition to their aromatic foliage, some cultivars such as *T. vulgaris* 'Silver Posie' and *T.* x *citriodorus* 'Golden King' provide the additional bonus of silver or yellow variegated leaves.

• GIANT CLARY
Salvia sclarea var. *turkestanica* has imposing flower heads in harmonious shades of mauve, pink, and white rising from a large clump of basal leaves, making it a stunning plant for a large patch. Because it grows to about 40–52 in. (1–1.3 m) tall, it is best placed at the center or back of a border. Several planted in a group make even more impact. As it is usually a biennial, seeds should be sown each year to ensure a succession of plants.

• PURPLE SAGE
Salvia officinalis 'Purpurea,' with its soft, mauve-tinted leaves, is more decorative than culinary sage. Other cultivars with colored foliage, such as 'Icterina' (yellow and green) and 'Tricolor' (gray, white, and pink), also make colorful border plants. Trim sages in early spring; young leaves need to be protected from slugs and aphids.

◀ Purple and mauve creeping thyme provides ground cover and a colorful display of flowers, complemented by purple sage at back.

Using Water Wisely

With summers tending to be dry, it's important to use good watering techniques if your garden is to thrive. The secret is to water wisely so that plants get the most out of the minimum amount of water.

Much can be done to keep your herb patch or mixed border growing happily despite the restrictions on water. A number of factors need to be taken into account in a "dry" garden. For instance, you need to know your soil type, as some are more moisture-retentive than others and each type needs to be treated differently to improve it.

EFFICIENT USAGE

Watering techniques also matter—the aim should be to get as much water as possible directly to the roots of plants rather than simply sprinkling the garden in a random fashion. Collecting rainwater and using suitable domestic water are also helpful in dealing with periods of drought. Bear in mind, too, that some plants need less water than others, so if you have lost plants to drought or have bare patches that need filling, choose plants that do not need a plentiful supply of water.

▶ A water barrel attached to a downpipe on the side of the house is the most efficient way of collecting rainwater. The barrels are usually cask-shaped and some have a flat back (with the tap on the opposite side) to fit closer to the wall. Plastic barrels, available from garden centers, are not particularly attractive to look at, but they can be hidden from view with trellises and climbing plants. In small gardens or where space is limited, wall-mounted barrels are the most practical option.

Conserving Water

Apart from storing water, there are other things you can do to save water. Apply the following guidelines before resorting to the garden tap:

- use drought-resistant plants where possible in planting schemes—many herbs, being Mediterranean in origin, will tolerate a dry period

- mulch beds that are prone to drying out with a layer of compost or chipped bark

- depending on the size of your garden and the space available, consider installing a plastic or metal water-storage tank

- use cold bath or washing-up water for the garden as long as it doesn't contain strong detergents or bleach

- use a short length of hose to feed water directly to shrub roots to avoid evaporation from the soil surface

- use plastic (rather than timber) water barrels connected to downpipes from gutters. Ensure that the base of the barrel is sufficiently raised on bricks to allow a watering can underneath the tap

Sink a 14–18 in. (35–45 cm) length of plastic tubing or hosepipe to the bottom of a hole when planting key shrubs or climbers that need good moisture. This will allow efficient watering to the roots and prevent waste through surface evaporation. ◄

PLANTS FOR DRY SPOTS

Use these plants if your site is sunny, exposed, and well drained:

bay, bearded iris, box, broom, eucalyptus, golden rod, lavender, male fern, oregano, rock rose, rosemary, sage, sunrose, tansy, thyme, viburnum tinus, yarrow.

DO	DON'T
• water thoroughly but infrequently	• mix plants that are drought tolerant in the same area as those that are drought prone
• concentrate on watering newly established plants and drought-prone annuals	• sprinkle soil lightly with water; fine sprays are less effective than a solid water flow
• water the planting hole thoroughly before filling it with soil	• water indiscriminately and cause 'puddling,' which results in water running off and being wasted
• water in the evening or early morning	• water in the hottest part of the day
• plant deeply, making a slight depression around the plant that will retain water	• leave plant rootballs exposed above the soil when planting

TYPE OF SOIL	RETENTIVE QUALITY	HOW TO IMPROVE
CLAY SOIL	retains water but becomes solid, compacted, and poorly drained	dig in compost and fine gravel to improve soil, structure, and drainage
SANDY OR GRAVELLY SOIL	water drains away quickly or runs off the top	dig in plenty of humus and compost to improve absorption and retention
LOAM SOILS	contains a good balance of coarse and fine particles	only mulching may be necessary in fertile loam soils

Gardening in the Shade

Although many herbs are sun-lovers, a shady garden need not be without herbs. Several plants classed as herbs will succeed in shade, particularly if the ground is well prepared with plenty of moisture-retaining compost in the soil.

Trees
Use birch for its bark, and evergreens, such as upright yew and variegated holly, for their foliage.

Difficult areas of dry shade at the base of trees or walls can be made to look attractive—it is a matter of matching the right plant to the right spot. ▼

Climbers
Ivy and honeysuckle provide a backdrop to a planting scheme.

Shrubs
Butcher's broom, cherry laurel, fern-leaved elder, and hydrangea provide a mix of foliage and flowers.

Perennials
Use plants such as lily of the valley, primrose, and wood spurge for their flowers.

Groundcover
Gaps between larger plants can be planted with bugle, white deadnettle, and woodruff.

Culinary herbs
Chervil, parsley, and mint will grow in moist soil. Several members of the borage family (but not annual borage), all with blue-purple flowers, will form large clumps in difficult shady areas: comfrey, dyer's bugloss, hound's tongue, and lungwort.

SPECIMEN PLANTS

- **Bugle**
  Ajuga reptans 'Atropurpurea'
  Ht. 8 in. (20 cm); low-spreading perennial with purple-brown leaves and spikes of violet-blue flowers

- **Fern-leaved elder**
  Sambucus nigra laciniata
  Ht. 16 ft. (4.8 m); deciduous tall shrub with finely ornamental leaves and clusters of white flowers followed by edible black berries

- **Foxglove**
  Digitalis purpurea 'Alba'
  Ht. 4 ft. (1.2 m): biennial, flowering in its second year with tapering spires of white flowers in late spring

- **Lungwort**
  Pulmonaria officinale
  Ht. 12 in. (30 cm); clump-forming perennial with silvery spotted leaves and clusters of mauve-pink to blue flowers in early spring; needs moisture-retentive soil

- **Male fern**
  Dryopteris filix-mas
  Ht. 30 in. (75 cm); hardy, deciduous perennial fern, drought-tolerant when established, with graceful crown of rich green foliage

- **Primrose**
  Primula vulgaris
  Ht. 6 in. (15 cm); clump-forming perennial with clusters of soft yellow flowers from late winter to late spring

- **Silver birch**
  Betula pendula
  Ht. 26 ft. (7.8 m); a graceful white-barked deciduous tree of semicreeping habit

- **Solomon's seal**
  Polygonatum odoratum
  Ht. 34 in. (85 cm); perennial plant spreading by underground rhizomes with elegant green-tipped white flowers on arching stems

- **Variegated holly**
  Ilex aquifolium 'Madame Briot'
  Ht. 26 ft. (7.8 m): evergreen slow-growing tree with bold yellow-margined leaves

Gardening in the Shade

Since few annual flowering plants succeed in shade, it is better to choose shrubs and perennials that will grow in shady spots. Plant them in bold groups so that they spread to form solid, lush groundcover. Remember to position taller shrubs and perennials toward the back of borders and boundaries, and use honeysuckle, ivy, and climbing hydrangea to cover shaded walls or fences. Some species of clematis will also succeed in shade.

Reg Page

GETTING IT RIGHT

- Make sure plants requiring moisture-retentive soil are grouped together and watered in dry spells.

- Prune or thin large trees to allow sunlight to filter through in winter and spring.

- Prepare ground for planting thoroughly, working in compost and mulches to enrich the soil and help retain moisture.

- Plant sun-loving culinary herbs in pots so they can be moved to follow the sun.

- Replace, or heavily trim, evergreen shrubs that are too large.

A shady patch requires more planning than a sunny site if the plants are to thrive. It need not be without flowers—one shade-lover is the spring-flowering Solomon's seal (*Polygonatum odoratum*). ▲

CATEGORY	COMMON NAME	LATIN NAME	FEATURES
TREES	Silver birch	*Betula pendula* 'Tristis'	elegant weeping form; deciduous
	Upright yew	*Taxus baccata* 'Fastigiata'	slow-growing, dark green columnar; evergreen
	Variegated holly	*Ilex aquifolium* 'Mme Briot'	yellow variegated leaves; evergreen
SHRUBS	Butcher's broom	*Ruscus aculeatus*	dark green leaves, occasional red berries; evergreen
	Cherry laurel	*Prunus laurocerasus* 'Otto Luyken'	shiny green leaves, white flowers; evergreen
	Fern-leaved elder	*Sambucus nigra laciniata*	foliage and flowers; deciduous
	Hydrangea	*Hydrangea arborescens* 'Annabelle'	large white flowers in summer, deciduous
CLIMBERS	Honeysuckle	*Lonicera japonica*	twining, scented cream flowers; semideciduous
	Ivy	*Hedera helix* 'Goldheart'	yellow variegated leaves, evergreen, self-clinging
PERENNIALS & BIENNIALS	Foxglove	*Digitalis purpurea*	purple, pink, or white flowers
	Lily of the valley	*Convallaria majalis*	white flowers
	Primrose	*Primula vulgaris*	pale yellow flowers
	Solomon's seal	*Polygonatum odoratum*	green-tipped white flowers
	Wood spurge	*Euphorbia robbiae*	fresh lime-yellow flowers
GROUND COVER	Bugle	*Ajuga reptans*	violet-blue flowers
	Periwinkle	*Vinca major, V. minor*	blue-purple flowers
	White deadnettle	*Lamium maculatum* 'White Nancy'	white flowers, silvery foliage
	Woodruff	*Galium odoratum*	white flowers

Early Spring in the Herb Garden

The garden starts losing its winter drabness as new growth begins to appear and early bulbs come into flower to add a touch of color. ▼

As early spring arrives, time and the weather are the factors that determine how well prepared you are for the frenzy of activity that will take you from early spring through to late summer.

• PLANNER

Containers

If you don't have sufficient space for a herb garden, use containers. Group them near the kitchen or back door for easy access. Choose herbs that you use regularly in cooking such as chives, parsley, rosemary, sage, and thyme. You can grow them in individual containers, or combine some of them in the same pot. Basil needs a sunny site—wait until all danger of frost is past before planting it out.

Watering

Water container plants regularly and use a liquid feed once every two to three weeks. Cover the soil surface of the container with a layer of gravel for a more ornamental look—this will also help conserve water.

Seed sowing

Sow indoor and outdoor seeds to make sure you have all the herbs you want for the summer. The indoor seeds will provide earlier harvests, as the seedlings can be planted out as soon as the soil warms up sufficiently.

Cleaning

Cleanliness is the key to success when growing from seeds. Always use clean pots or propagating trays and fresh sowing compost.

Early spring is the time to buy from specialized herb nurseries and it is also the best time to start planting out hardy herbs if the soil is sufficiently warm. Check the plants well before you buy them to see that they are strong-growing and healthy. If there is a mass of root showing at the base of the pot, choose another specimen, as once a plant is potbound, it will not start growing strongly or quickly when planted out.

Avoid plants with dead or damaged stems or foliage, and if you see any insect damage on foliage, check the underside of leaves or soil surface for the culprits.

Early Spring Chores

Continue with outdoor soil preparation and indoor seed sowing. Pot up seedlings as they grow, and toward the end of the season, harden them off before planting them out. Buy new plants from garden centers, and plan and plant your container herb garden. Finish cutting back and checking on plants as part of the postwinter maintenance program.

BUYING AND PLANTING HERBS

Check the plants to be sure of healthy strong-growing specimens:

- no weeds on soil surface of pots
- good root system
- not potbound
- bushy, compact shape.

Plant the bought herbs into the ground as soon as you can. Meanwhile, keep them in a warm, sheltered spot until you are ready to plant them out. Water regularly until the plants are established, then water only during dry seasons.

SEED SOWING

Fill the seed trays with fresh, sterilized seed-sowing compost. Firm the surface using a flat board, then water, using a watering can with a fine rose. You can also stand the tray in water, which is absorbed through the compost. Leave the tray to stand so that excess water drains off, then sow seed. Fine seed is sown as evenly as possible on to the surface, while large seed is placed at regular intervals on the surface.

Lightly cover large seeds with a thin layer of compost. Cover the trays with a piece of glass or clear plastic such as clingfilm, then put the tray into a dark area in the greenhouse, or on a windowsill covered with a sheet of newspaper. As soon as the seeds germinate, remove the newspaper and put the tray in a lighter area that is sheltered from the cold.

SEEDS THAT NEED A COLD START

Some seeds need a period of cold before they will germinate. This is their mechanism to prevent them from germinating too early and being damaged by severe weather conditions. The following need a cold start:

- Angelica
- Juniper
- Soapwort
- Sweet cicely
- Sweet violet
- Sweet woodruff

Juniper

Use clean trays or pots when propagating seeds and fresh, soil-based compost. Water well and leave to drain excess water. Sow the seeds and then cover with glass or clear plastic. ◄

• CHECKLIST

 SOWING

Indoors
Aniseed
Anise
Borage
Caraway
Chives
Chives
Cilantro
Hyssop
Lemon verbena
Marjoram
Pinks
Pot marigold
Salad burnet
Sorrel
Summer savory

Borage

Salad burnet

 PLANTING OUT

Box
Chives
Pinks
Sage
Sorrel
Spearmint
Sweet cicely
Tarragon
Winter savory

Pink

Winter savory

 CUTTINGS

Take heel cuttings of rosemary and thyme; you can also take cuttings of winter savory or layer the stems.

 DIVIDING

Anise
Chives
Salad burnet
Sorrel
Spearmint

Spearmint

Late Spring in the Herb Garden

In late spring there is much to do in the herb garden—seed sowing and planting are the main activities, plus other chores such as staking tall plants.

With spring in the air, plants come to life and bring an abundance of fresh, new colors provided by foliage and a variety of blossoms. ▶

Harry Smith Collection

• PLANNER

Height in the garden

Whether in the herb or ornamental garden, height is important to give balance and visual variation. Most herbs are low-growing, sprawling plants, but there are some taller ones that will provide height.

Angelica, bay, fennel, lovage, and verbena, when well established, are among the giants. All except bay are herbaceous perennials that die down in winter, so the height they provide is seasonal, but nonetheless effective.

For more permanent high points you will need to put in place suitable statuary, such as bird baths and sundials. Old chimney pots can perform the same function, as can a stylish, attractively painted wooden or iron obelisk that will support plants in season.

Support for plants

Support for some of the sprawling plants, as well as for the taller growing ones, is sometimes necessary. Twigs or hazel poles offer a rustic style, as do bamboo canes.

A tepee shape made from bamboo canes, set into the ground and tied together at the top, will be a good support for sweet peas, and for golden hop to twine around if taller poles are used. Hops are very vigorous growers and may need stronger support than the canes.

Toward the end of spring, you can start most seeds off in a seedbed outside or sow directly into their growing sites. Basil will need a warmer start in the greenhouse and shouldn't be planted out until early to late summer, depending on the weather conditions.

Seedlings that have been sown indoors are ready to pot up and, if the weather is good enough, to harden off. A cold frame is useful for this purpose. Put the seedlings in their individual pots into the cold frame, with pot bases directly on the soil. Keep the frame open during the day. Water the seedlings regularly, especially in warmer weather.

Late Spring Chores

Herbs are generally pest- and disease-free, but if they are growing in crowded conditions or become stressed through lack of water or light, they may succumb to the insect and disease problems that affect gardens through the seasons. In a wet spring, always remove any slushy, rotting leaves to prevent mildew and other fungal infections affecting the herbs.

Aphids and blackfly affect basil seedlings and nasturtiums outdoors. You may need to spray the plants with an insecticidal soapy solution. Do this out of full sun, so that the leaves are not scorched.

Encouraging some wildlife, especially birds, into your garden is one way of deterring the insect invasion, as the birds will feed themselves and their young on the insects.

A hoe makes light work of weeding. With a long handle, it also means you do not have to tramp through the planted flower beds. ▲

WEEDING

Weeding helps to keep the herb garden healthy. Weeds may harbor insect pests and will compete with your plants for space, light, nutrients, and water, so should be removed by hoeing off or by hand.

COMPANION PLANTING

Some plants that appear to protect others from insect and disease are described as companion plants. Many of the combinations have not been researched and the way they work is not fully understood. Their effects have been observed by gardeners over time, and in recent years, the organic gardening movement has begun formal research into companion-plant properties.

Chives, tagetes, and pyrethrum are among the plants that have such attributes.

Tagetes seems to deter certain soil pests and are often planted in greenhouses alongside tomatoes. Chives seem to prevent aphid build-up on roses, while summer savory, often called the "bean herb," is planted with broad beans to deter blackfly. Aromatic herbs including dill, fennel, hyssop, and thyme attract many beneficial insects including bees and butterflies that are important for pollination. These plants, when in flower, will be alive with hoverflies, which feed on aphids.

• CHECKLIST

 SOWING

Indoors
Basil
Outdoors
Aniseed
Chervil
Dill
Fennel
Heartsease
Lemon balm
Orach
Pot marigold

Chervil

 PLANTING OUT

Perilla
Sunflower
   (hardened off first)

Sunflower

 HARVEST

Bay
Fennel
Flowers
   from heartsease
Lemon balm
Rosebuds
   for potpourri
Sage
Winter savory

Lemon balm

 PROPAGATE

Hops   *Hops*
Lavender
Marsh mallow

 LAYER

Madder
Sage   *Madder*
Upright thyme

Cut comfrey for the compost heap or to lay on the soil surface around plants.

Early Summer in the Herb Garden

In early summer the herb garden resembles a green and fragrant oasis with a variety of plants providing exuberant blooms and abundant foliage. Enjoy the garden scents, as well as the flavors in the kitchen.

Some plants start flowering, especially if spring comes early. Tall plants may need stakes to protect them from the wind. ▼

Tim Shepherd/Oxford Scientific Films

● PLANNER

Seed sowing
Think ahead and make new sowings of landcress, parsley, and purslane, so that you have more of their leaves to harvest later in the year.

Propagation
Increase your stock of herbs such as tarragon, lemon verbena, and myrtle by taking softwood cuttings from them. Take the cuttings from nonflowering stems and remove the lower leaves on each stem. You can dip the stem ends into hormone rooting powder, but this is not necessary if you plant them up straight away.

Place the cuttings into a cuttings compost around the edge of a pot—about four to each pot. Cover the pots and cuttings with a polythene bag, tied at the top or under the pot. Each day remove the bag and turn it inside out. Condensation inside the bag will provide sufficient moisture for the plants. Turning the bags prevents overmoist conditions that could lead to disease.

When you see fresh leaves developing, remove the plastic and check the base of the cuttings for roots. Pot up the individual new plants and keep them in a cold frame or, in the case of myrtle and lemon verbena, in the greenhouse, until you are ready to plant them out the following spring.

Although it is a little early for the garden to have reached its full glory, there are plenty of attractive and colorful plants to provide interest. Water the garden during dry spells and make sure newly planted herbs do not dry out. Feed the plants once or twice a month, and look out for any signs of pests and disease. Pinch out shoots coming into blossom on basil, fennel, lemon balm, lovage, mint, and sage to encourage more foliage.

Despite it being so early in the season, it is time to think of taking cuttings to overwinter and to increase herb stocks. You should also be able to enjoy some fresh herbs from the garden.

Early Summer Harvest

Harvest leaves from all leafy herbs as you need them. Pick the flowers of lady's mantle, borage, chives, pinks, foxgloves, hyssop, lavender, nasturtium, roses, thyme, and arugula (rocket). Some can be put to use in the kitchen, and others, such as foxgloves and roses, can be used for ornamental purposes, either fresh or dried in potpourri and fragrant sachets.

Herbs such as lavender—now in flower—can be harvested for drying. Tie the flowering stems into bunches and store them in a dry area. Don't allow the bunches to touch each other. ▼

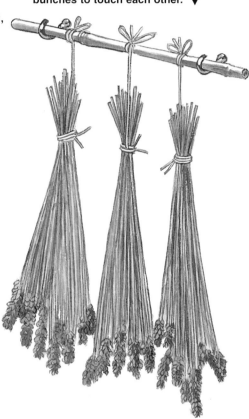

HARVESTING HERBS

At the beginning of summer, you can harvest leaves and flowers to use immediately or to dry, freeze, or preserve in other ways for later use.

You want the plants to continue to look attractive in the garden and to grow into well-shaped plants. Over-cutting will be counter-productive, as you will not have enough material left on the plant for it to grow on well. It is a busy period and you should never pick more material than you have time to work with at any one session.

- Pick on a warm day and cut from plants in an even way, so that they do not end up lopsided or untidy.

- Always use a sharp, clean pair of scissors and place a gardening basket in the shade to collect the cut material.

- Don't heap the cut herbs into the basket, or you may damage and bruise the leaves.

- Pick flowers just as they open or when they are in bud. Handle them carefully so they are not damaged or bruised.

DRYING HERBS

You need warmth, air circulation, and darkness or shade to dry the herbs efficiently. Small quantities can be dried on absorbent kitchen paper laid out on trays and placed in a warm site, such as an airing cupboard. You might consider making a herb-drying frame if you plan to dry material on a larger scale.

You can also dry herbs such as sweet-smelling lavender in small bunches. Lay the stems down, tie them into bunches, and hang them upside down from a hanger or a bamboo cane suspended from a pair of hooks. Depending on the warmth of your site, the herbs will take up to two weeks to dry well.

Late Summer in the Herb Garden

It is time to harvest and dry herbs for the winter. Seed heads can be dried for floral displays or the seeds can be collected for propagating a new crop. ▼

This is a busy time in the garden, turning your herb harvests into produce to use now or later. Most plants have reached their peak, producing seeds for you to dry for kitchen use or for future crops.

• PLANNER

Toward the end of summer you can take semiripe cuttings from slightly older growth on stems rather than of softwood cuttings. You can also layer plants such as sage and pinks.

Cuttings
Take softwood cuttings from: catnip, curry plant, rosemary, southernwood, tarragon, thyme, and wormwood.
　　Take semiripe cuttings from: bay, cotton lavender, hyssop, lavender, lemon verbena, rosemary, sage, thyme, and winter savory.

Harvest
Check plants and remove any dead or damaged shoots and flowers.
　　Flowers for drying: pick anise hyssop, cotton lavender, hyssop, lavender, roses, and scented pelargonium.
　　Seeds: use nasturtium seeds to make into nasturium "capers."

Potting up
Pot up new sage, thyme, and pinks that have been produced by layering the stems of older plants.

Maintenance
Cut back lavender, mint, sage, tarragon, and thyme after flowering, so that the plants put on new growth before winter. Divide plants that are crowded and split clumps of mint. Remove borage flower stems as well as the flower heads of angelica to prevent abundant self-seeding. Also remove seed heads from pot marigolds to prevent them from becoming like a garden weed.

Louis Jordaan

You need to do many things now to keep the herb garden looking attractive and continuing to be productive. Plant out a supply of basil plants into containers or into the ground. Pinch out the growing shoots to make the plants bushy and to delay the onset of flowering. Cut back the spent flowering stems of lady's mantle to dry and to encourage plants to make a new flush of flowers and leaves. Prune box plants and hedges. Once you have harvested lavender flowers, cut the plants to shape.

Water plants in containers and in hanging baskets regularly as they do not retain moisture well, especially at this time of year.

Late Summer Chores

Continue to harvest flowers and leaves, especially of scented plants to use in potpourri. You will also be able to collect a variety of herbs for use in the kitchen—bear in mind you can use them to flavor vinegars and oils. Try to make use of as much plant material as possible—dry herbs and any suitable flower heads for winter use. You will also need to deadhead flowers and remove old foliage.

Dry the plant material for potpourri quickly and start to fill a large bowl with the dried produce, adding orris root and essential oils to perfume the mixture. Add trimmings from aromatic plants such as sage, thyme, and lavender to the potpourri bowl when they are dry.

INDOOR HERBS

Start thinking about your indoor herb collection for the winter. Sow annuals such as basil or biennials such as chervil and parsley so that you will have some plants to pot up for use in early winter. Take cuttings of sage and tarragon and roots of mint to force in the greenhouse for indoor use.

IN THE KITCHEN

It is worth spending some time making the most of the garden harvest. With your herb bounty, you can make herbal preserves to give as gifts or to store for your own use. Herbs can be preserved in oils, salt, sugar, and vinegars, as well as tied into small bunches to dry to make individual bouquet garnis.

VINEGARS

Use a selection of herbs to flavor a variety of vinegars, such as cider and white vinegars, which will last for some time. Suitable herbs are basil, bay, caraway, chervil, chives, cilantro, dill, fennel, lemon balm, marjoram, mint, rosemary, sage, tarragon, and thyme to flavor vinegars. For a decorative touch, you can also include the fresh flowers of many of these herbs in the vinegars.

CULINARY OILS

Suitable for savory oils, including olive, sunflower, and cornflower oil, are basil, bay, fennel, garlic, hyssop, sage, summer savory, and thyme. In sweet oils use the flowers of pinks and lavender, rose petals, lemon verbena, and scented pelargonium leaves.

SOWING SEED

Outdoors, sow seed of chervil, cilantro, lamb's lettuce, landcress, parsley, poppy, and winter purslane.

SAVING SEED

You can still harvest the foliage of herbs such as sage, rosemary, and thyme, as well as overwintered parsley and salad burnet, which should be starting into new foliage. Sorrel, too, should have new foliage. Pick flowers of sweet violet, cowslip, and primrose to crystallize. Winter purslane and American landcress leaves should also be available.

• CHECKLIST

CUTTINGS

Bay
Catmint
Cotton lavender
Curry plant
Hyssop
Lavender
Lemon verbena
Sage
Tarragon
Thyme
Winter savory
Wormwood

Wormwood

HARVEST

Anise hyssop
Cotton lavender
Hyssop
Lavender
Roses
Scented pelargonium

Cotton lavender

PRUNING

Boxwood
Lavender
Mint
Sage
Tarragon
Thyme

Box

A little heat and humidity will encourage cuttings to make roots and prevent them from drying out and wilting. An easy way of achieving this without any specialist equipment is to push stakes in around the sides of the pot and then cover the pot with plastic or clingfilm making sure it does not touch the plants. Keep the pots in a warm place out of direct sunlight. ◀

Early Fall in the Herb Garden

This is the time to take stock in the garden—to complete any remaining harvesting and to decide which herbs need special attention if they are to be kept over winter.

Clive Nichols / Chenies Manor, Bucks

A mixed herbaceous border puts on a last show of color—some of the flowers and herbs can soon be harvested for drying. As the weather cools, plants can be trimmed and the bed tidied. ▲

● PLANNER

Early fall is the time for tidying, clearing, and dividing plants, as well as a good time to plant newly bought herbs in the garden and make sowings of certain herbs. Look at your herb garden critically and see where plants are too vigorous and need to be clipped back, so that others have more space to grow.

Tidying up
Remove spent flower heads and any foliage, stems, seed heads (save attractive ones for dried flower arrangements), or dead flowers before they begin to rot. Rotting vegetation in the garden is likely to harbor pests and could encourage wilts and fungal infections. Put this waste material on the compost heap, where it can decompose and cause no harm to plants.

Pruning
It is also a good time to start pruning and shaping herb hedges of plants such as box, cotton lavender, lavender, rosemary, and thyme. If you do it now, the plants will have a chance to recover before frosts can damage new shoots.

Potting up
You can begin to make plans to pot up some culinary herbs for an indoor herb tray for fall and winter use. Chives, marjoram, mint, parsley, sage, and thyme are all suitable. Bear in mind that individual pots are easier to handle than one large one.

Apart from practical chores such as pruning, clearing, and tidying a herb garden, now is also the time to plan ahead. Mark out any changes you want to make in the garden and put up or replace trellises you may need for the next growing season. Add compost to the soil and start planting perennial and shrubby herbs. Do this on a warm day when the soil is moist. You can also start dividing clumps of perennial herbs such as artemisia, comfrey, soapwort, and tansy. If moving or potting up any plants for indoors, remove as much soil as possible, try not to damage the roots, and use clean pots to avoid spreading diseases.

Early Fall Chores

PLANTING OUT

Chives

Bay

Bay
Boxwood
Chives
Pennyroyal
Rosemary
Sage
Thyme
Welsh onion

DIVIDING

Chives
Elecampane
Fennel
Lovage
Soapwort
Tarragon
Yarrow

Tarragon

LAYERING

Honeysuckle
Sage

Sage

PRUNING

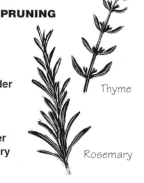

Bay
Box
Cotton
 lavender
Curry
 plant
Hyssop
Lavender
Rosemary
Thyme

Thyme

Rosemary

Boxwood, rosemary, and lavender hedges need to be clipped into shape. Any new growth will harden off before the onset of colder weather. Cut woody herbs back to at least half their year's growth. You may be able to use some of the clippings as cuttings to make new plants, or you could dry them to use in pot pourri.

Remove dead flower heads from herbs such as hyssop, lavender, and santolina. ◄

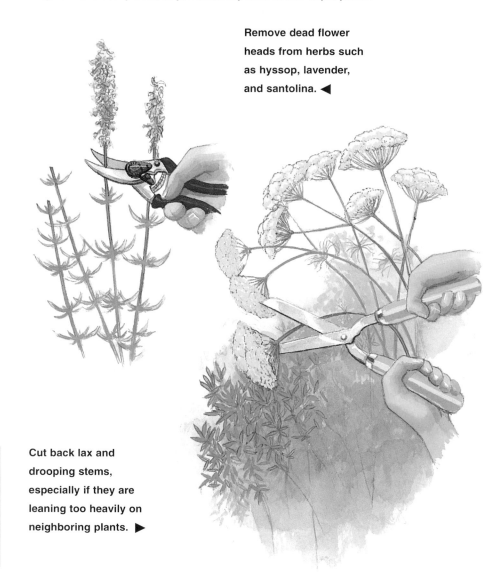

Cut back lax and drooping stems, especially if they are leaning too heavily on neighboring plants. ►

TOPIARY & STANDARDS

If you are training herbs, such as bay, lavender, and rosemary, into topiary shapes or standards, this is a good time to check their growth and remove any stems that don't fit into the overall shape you are trying to achieve.

SOWING HERBS

At this time of year, you can sow borage and chervil, as well as lamb's lettuce, sage, sweet cicely, and woodruff. Sow them directly into the ground into their growing sites, except for sage, which is best sown in rows in a nursery bed. When the plants are large enough to handle, you can plant them out into their growing sites.

HERB HARVEST

You can continue to harvest evergreen herbs such as rosemary and sage. Pick lamb's lettuce as you need it, as well as parsley and garlic chives. Dig up roots of horseradish and licorice, as well as the bulbs of garlic. Lay the garlic bulbs on wire trays or in wooden boxes to dry off before you tie them into plaits to store.

Late Fall in the Herb Garden

The colorful show of late-flowering summer flowers has faded but fall provides its own glory with tree, shrub, and plant foliage in many different colors and shades. ▼

Now is the time to complete the final cleanup of the herb garden and to bring in plants that need special protection, as well as to put in place outdoor covers for borderline hardy plants.

● PLANNER

Late fall sees an end to the cleaning, clearing, and dividing of perennial herbs. If you are starting a new herb garden, dig the ground over and fork in well-rotted garden compost or manure. Bring tender perennials such as woolly lavender and lemon verbena indoors.

Cuttings
Take cuttings from all the plants you want to increase in the garden. This is also a good policy to ensure that any plants that don't survive the winter can be replaced. Take hardwood cuttings of elder. If they have made good growth during the year, divide and replant chives, comfrey, echinacea, mint, sorrel, tarragon, and lemon-grass clumps.

Tidying up
Remove brown leaves on chive plants and cut back. Cut back comfrey plants and put foliage on the compost heap or in rows between plants to enrich the soil. Now is also the time to cut back lady's mantle plants.

Protecting plants
Tender plants that are too large to move indoors will need a winter blanket—protect their roots with a mulch of straw, leaves, or compost. You may need to peg the mulch in place, using netting to stop the material from blowing away. Cut branches from cypress and other conifer hedging and use them to make an above-ground cover for plants.

Clive Nichols / Lakemount, Cork, Eire

There is still much to clean up in the herb garden for winter. It is also time to consider and plan new planting projects. Hedging is the main activity. Mark out the site for hedges—or a knot garden if you have space—and prepare the ground. General preparation of the soil is an ongoing chore, as is the winter protection of tender plants and the taking of cuttings from these plants.

You can also plant old-fashioned roses that will provide scented blooms through the summer, as well as material for drying, use in baking, or for making scented sugars.

Hedge Planting

If you want to grow a knot garden or protect the herb garden with a low-growing hedge, now is the time to start. There are a number of herbs that respond well to clipping to make attractive hedges.

Choose strong-growing specimens of boxwood, curry plants, hyssop, lavender, and rosemary. Use two canes and a string line to keep a straight edge. Make planting holes, spacing them about two-thirds of the plants' eventual height apart. Fork in fertilizer into the base of the hole, put the plant in place, and water it and the soil in the hole.

Backfill and firm the surface. Water regularly. You may need to protect the young hedge through the winter as drying, cold winds may damage the foliage and cause wind rock to disturb the roots. Set in place a temporary windbreak. You can also protect individual plants with a light covering of conifer or cypress branches.

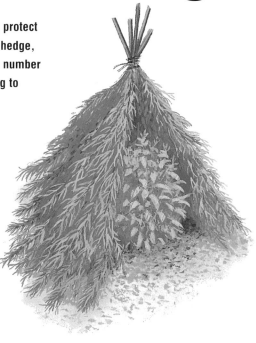

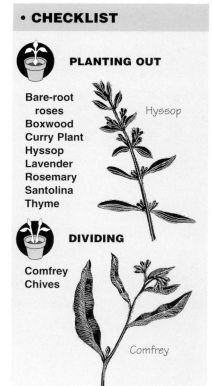

• **CHECKLIST**

PLANTING OUT

Bare-root roses
Boxwood
Curry Plant
Hyssop
Lavender
Rosemary
Santolina
Thyme

Hyssop

DIVIDING

Comfrey
Chives

Comfrey

To give young plants protection from frost until they are established, cover them lightly with offcuts of conifer or cypress. ▲

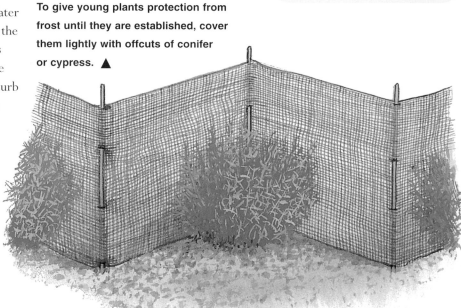

You can protect a newly planted hedge during the winter with a temporary windbreak made out of canes and burlap. ▶

PLANTING OUT

Although you can still plant out herbs if the ground is not frozen or waterlogged, it is better to wait until spring. However, it is a good time to plant out bare-root roses. Protect the roots until you are ready to plant by wrapping them in burlap and keeping them out of the wind. Make planting holes large enough to take the roots comfortably. Add compost, put the plants in place, backfill with soil, and water them in well. Firm the surface of the soil.

HERB HARVEST

You can still pick leaves of bay, parsley, rosemary, sage, and thyme—and basil, if you are growing it in a greenhouse or indoors. Freeze the herbs to use later in soups and casseroles, or dry sprigs in bundles to offer as gifts. You can also use them fresh in jams, jellies, and vinegars. Lift madder plants to dry for dyeing. Lift Welsh onions and dry them off in a sheltered sunny position before storing them indoors for use.

Early Winter in the Herb Garden

The garden takes on its winter garb and depending on whether there's been a cold snap, there may still be some fall foliage around that will need cleaning up. ▼

Planning is the keynote in the winter herb garden. You can spend some of the time choosing next year's seeds from the many specialized and general catalogs.

Photos Horticultural

● PLANNER

In early winter your indoor herb collection should start to become useful. Place the collection of potted herbs in a sunny situation in a south- or west-facing window. Keep the plants watered but don't overwater, especially plants such as rosemary, sage, and thyme, which prefer dry conditions. Never let the compost dry out completely.

Pest alert
If the herbs are attacked by whitefly, spray the plants with an insecticidal soap solution. If indoor bay plants are affected by scale insects on the back of leaves, remove them with a cotton ball dipped in the same soapy solution.

Ornamental pots
Make your indoor herb collection as ornamental as possible by grouping the herbs in a collection of attractive outer pots or cache-pots. You can also use terra-cotta window boxes.

Weather wise
Check that outdoor plants are not damaged by wind, frost or heavy snowfall. Always shake or knock snow off plants after a heavy snowfall. If the wind is strong, check roses and evergreens, especially shrubby plants, such as bay, and firm them into the ground if you think they are affected by wind rock, which disturbs the roots and weakens the plants.

In early winter, your thoughts may turn to new themes, such as a special culinary collection or a lemon-scented planting. Keep a notebook handy and jot down your ideas and make rough sketches of the plans you might put into practice in spring. If the weather is good, go out into the garden and work out the sun and shade aspects of the area you plan to plant. You might—weather and soil conditions permitting—be able to mark out the plan and begin to dig over the soil. If you are able to work the soil, incorporate some bulky organic material—garden compost, if you have your own supply—and leave it to settle over the winter. It will give you a head start in the spring.

Early Winter Chores

• CHECKLIST

PLANTING OUT

INDOORS
Parsley
Rosemary
Sage
Thyme

Parsley

ROUTINE

- apply a liquid fertilizer every few weeks
- water indoor plants sparingly
- knock snow off branches of outdoor plants
- protect with cloches, fleece, or conifer branches
- dig over soil (weather permitting)
- fork in compost

PLAN AHEAD

- order seeds
- sketch out new planting areas
- mark out (weather permitting)

Outdoor tasks depend mainly on the weather and soil conditions. Essential chores are to plan new plantings and to prepare the soil. There's also the enjoyable task of going through catalogs and ordering seeds for the next growing season. Indoors, water your herbs, keeping them on the dry side, and check for any insect problems.

Make a feature of your indoor herb garden—whether you keep it on a windowsill or a sunny porch—by using an attractive terracotta container. ◀

Pests can be a problem on indoor plants so do keep a look out for them. You may need to use an insecticidal soap solution to spray plants, or in the case of bay, wipe the leaves with a cotton ball dipped in a soapy solution. ▶

HERB HARVEST

You can still harvest foliage from evergreen herbs such as bay, rosemary, sage, and thyme, as well as from biennials, such as parsley. If you have salad burnet growing, this too will probably still have some leafy material that can be used.

You can also begin to harvest from your indoor herb collection. Wait until the plants are growing well before you cut too much material from them. Pick leaves evenly and turn the plants around in their pots so that they grow in an even shape.

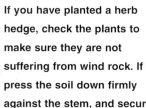

If you have planted a herb hedge, check the plants to make sure they are not suffering from wind rock. If so, press the soil down firmly against the stem, and secure with a stake if necessary. ◀

Late Winter in the Herb Garden

This is not perhaps the time of year to spend much time in the garden but, weather permitting, some input preparing the soil and removing weeds will pay dividends later.

With little color variation in the garden at this time of year—made even drabber by a light dusting of snow—interest is provided by the contrasting shapes and foliage of plants. ▶

Photos Horticultural

• PLANNER

Preparing the soil
As soon as you see any weed seedlings emerging, start to hand weed or hoe them off. Remove perennial weeds such as dock and bindweed, digging out as much of their roots as possible. Remove large stones and any bits of rubble that might be in the soil.

Once the soil is dug and weed-free, fork in some well-rotted compost. Leave it to settle, before raking the soil surface ready for planting out hardy herbs such as sage, sorrel, and chives, and for sowing more seedlings later in the spring.

Making a new herb area
If you are removing turf to make a new herb garden, wait until the ground is workable, then use a sharp-edged spade to cut small squares of turf away. The ground will be compacted so dig it over, removing debris and any weed roots, then add compost and leave it to settle.

Hard landscaping
Paths, paved areas, seats, fencing, or edging should be all be put in place before you start to plant a new garden. A network of paths that divides the area into four smaller rectangles provides a useful frame for herbs. You can use architectural herbs, such as angelica and artichoke; herbs in containers, such as bay or boxwood; or statuary to create your central or other focal points.

Place seating at the end of a path, close to where you plan to plant fragrant herbs such as lavender or lilies in pots, so that you can enjoy them in the warmer weather.

During late winter, your enthusiasm for the herb garden is often reined in by weather conditions, but you can make use of the so-called quiet time by preparing plans on paper and in your garden notebook. If the weather allows and the soil is not frosted or waterlogged, take the opportunity to do some digging. Think about the herbs you plan to sow, and make sure you have ordered seeds and plants from mail-order specialists. Always check that the seeds you are planting do not need any special treatment before you sow them—some herbs, such as angelica, need to be subjected to a cold spell before they will take.

Late Winter Chores

Now is a good time to do some general maintenance—checking, cleaning, and sharpening gardening tools, and clearing up or tidying the garden shed. To keep new plants healthy, clean any pots and trays or propagating equipment you may want to use for planting early seeds for summer.

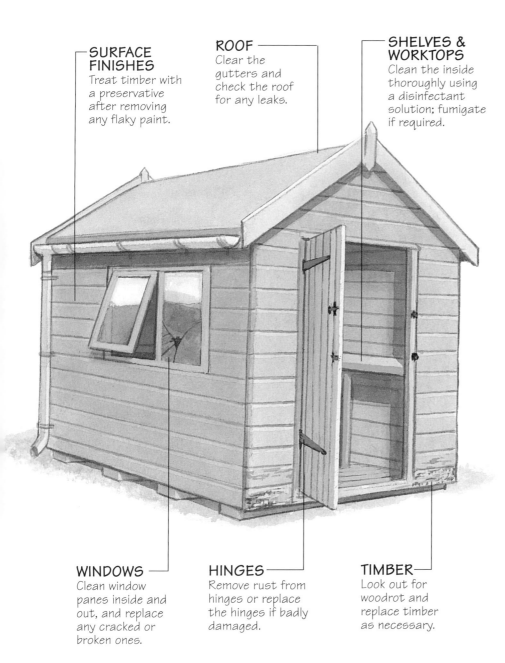

SURFACE FINISHES
Treat timber with a preservative after removing any flaky paint.

ROOF
Clear the gutters and check the roof for any leaks.

SHELVES & WORKTOPS
Clean the inside thoroughly using a disinfectant solution; fumigate if required.

WINDOWS
Clean window panes inside and out, and replace any cracked or broken ones.

HINGES
Remove rust from hinges or replace the hinges if badly damaged.

TIMBER
Look out for woodrot and replace timber as necessary.

• CHECKLIST

Start to sow seeds indoors in a heated propagator in a greenhouse or on a sunny windowsill.

Basil

SOWING

Basil
Chervil
Lemon
  eucalyptus
Parsley
Perilla
Thyme

DIVIDING

Sorrel

Chives
Costmary
Hyssop
Sorrel

PLANTING OUT

Bare root roses
Rosemary
Sage
Sorrel
Violets

Violet

MAINTENANCE

- Cutting tools: clean the blades of pruning and cutting tools by wiping them with an oily rag. You may need to use steel wool to remove plant sap from them.

- Sharpen cutting blades if necessary and adjust the tension blade on garden shears.

- Clean and oil the lawnmower and check the blades.

- Clear and clean the shed and check for rusty hinges, clean the panes of glass and check for any rotten woodwork. Scrub interior surfaces with a diluted garden disinfectant.

Planning a Rock Garden

Many herbs occur naturally in rocky places and so make ideal plants for a rock garden as they are compact and need little attention. A well-chosen selection of herbs—shrubs, perennials, and annuals—provides year-round interest in a rock garden with the added bonus of culinary supplies.

If you are creating an island bed in an expanse of lawn, for example, make the tallest part of the rockery toward the center and place the taller plants in this area. If you are including acid-loving plants such as heather, keep one area specifically for these so that you can feed them without affecting other plants. ▼

Before constructing a rock garden, it is important to consider the following:

- **position**—choose an open, sunny site that is well drained. If the rock garden is to be sited against a fence or wall, seek professional advice to avoid problems with damp.
- **size**—very small rockeries are not practical and do not make an impact. Aim for an area of about 5–6 ft. (1.5–1.8 m) wide and 9 ft. (2.7 m) long.

- **height and topography**—the highest point of an average-sized rock garden will need to be at least 2–3 ft. (60–90 cm) higher than the lowest point. Make use of natural features in your garden—a bank or slope—to create height.
- **overall plan**—a rock garden should be a natural-looking part of the overall garden design. Make sure it is linked to other items, such as a water feature, so that it does not look out of place.

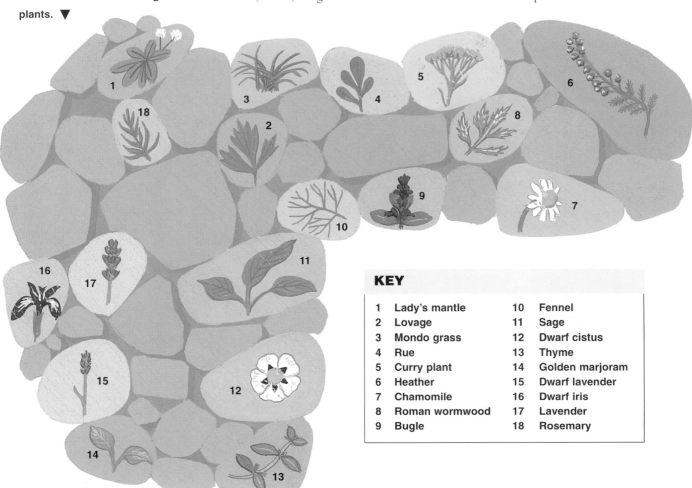

KEY			
1	Lady's mantle	10	Fennel
2	Lovage	11	Sage
3	Mondo grass	12	Dwarf cistus
4	Rue	13	Thyme
5	Curry plant	14	Golden marjoram
6	Heather	15	Dwarf lavender
7	Chamomile	16	Dwarf iris
8	Roman wormwood	17	Lavender
9	Bugle	18	Rosemary

Planning a Rock Garden

When planning a rock garden, it is important to make sure that it looks natural. Make use of a slope or bank, or create it as part of a series of "island beds" so that it blends in with the general surroundings.

- **Layout**—position the stones to look natural. To do this, the levels must be worked out carefully and the stones positioned correctly. They must then be firmly bedded or cemented in place. Keep some of the more attractive stones for the top of the rockery where they will be more visible. Pebbles around part of the area help to blend it into the surroundings and will also suppress weeds.

- **Soil**—a rock garden must be free draining and should be sited with this in mind. The soil around and between the rocks should be a rich, friable (crumbly), weed-free loam, preferably neutral to slightly alkaline. Heavier clay soils should be broken up with added compost, grit, and sand. When planting, you can add more compost for specific plants.

If the rock garden joins a patio, create the highest part where the two join. Place tall plants closest to the patio to create a hedge effect. ▲

- **Placing plants**—make sure that the eventual size of a plant will suit its position. If you have specific plants in mind before you start the rock garden, make sure you can accommodate their height and spread.

TYPES OF STONE

Although you can use whatever stones you might have lying around, a rock garden looks more effective if made with one type of stone or rock. A few large stones are particularly useful as they provide a stable base. Don't try to position large rocks yourself—have it done professionally. Garden stores and hard landscape suppliers offer a choice of quarried stone for rock gardens—these are charged according to size and weight. Generally available stones include:

Limestone—often gray; ages quickly; mosses and lichens appear readily. Lime-hating plants may not thrive in it.

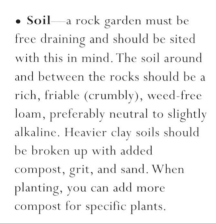

Sandstone—a popular choice as it comes in a range of attractive colors, making it possible to create a rockery that blends with the surroundings. It does not age as readily as limestone.

Granite—a tough, hard stone that looks effective but does not weather readily. It is heavy and hard to work with.

Artificial stones—made of stone and cement composites are sometimes available from garden stores and are cheaper than natural stone. They can be lighter than other types of stone.

Planting a Rock Garden

Choose the right plants for a rock garden and you will have a maintenance-free area that will also be pleasing in appearance.

A variety of drought-resistant herbs with attractive foliage fills this rocky bank. The foliage of a tall bronze fennel forms a focal point; farther down, lower growing herbs such as helichrysum, creeping thyme, ornamental toadflax, and golden marjoram provide effective contrasts of foliage, while foxglove seedlings sprout in the crevices. ▶

ACID NEEDS

Heather / Ling
Calluna vulgaris
This popular plant, available in a range of forms with different-colored flowers and foliage, makes an ideal rock garden plant with low, compact, evergreen growth and year-round interest from foliage and flowers. *Calluna* needs an acid soil that does not dry out, so these plants are best grown in a separate part of the rock garden where the soil can be kept peaty and fed with a soil conditioner.

Photos Horticultural

Shrubs and foliage plants form the mainstay of rock gardens. But in addition to the standard culinary herbs, you can add interest and color by choosing species with ornamental foliage and by planting or sowing annuals, such as marigolds, nasturtiums, and California poppies. Suitable culinary herbs for the rock garden include the following:

• **Chives** *Allium schoenoprasum* Ht.1 ft. (30 cm) Perennial, clump-forming herb; purple to pink flowers in summer

• **Fennel** *Foeniculum vulgare* Ht.6 ft. (1.8 m) Biennial or perennial with delicate foliage; umbels of yellow flowers in summer
Bronze fennel *F. vulgare* 'Purpureum' Ht.5 ft. (1.5 m) is also an attractive option; it is slightly hardier than the species

• **Golden marjoram** *Origanum vulgare* 'Aureum' Ht.8 in. (20 cm) Hardy perennial with bright foliage; makes colorful mounds with lavender flowers in summer

• **Lovage** *Levisticum officinale* Ht.6 ft. (1.8 m) Hardy perennial; needs plenty of space; attractive green foliage and seed heads

• **Rosemary** *Rosmarinus officinalis* Ht.6 ft. (1.8 m) Hardy evergreen shrub; pale blue flowers in spring

• **Sage (purple)** *Salvia officinalis* 'Purpurea' Ht.1 ft. (30 cm) Hardy, semi-evergreen shrub cultivated for its attractive purple foliage

• **Thyme** *Thymus* spp. and varieties Ht.up to 6 in. (15 cm) Evergreen herb in a choice of colors and sizes

Choosing Rock Garden Plants

CURRY PLANT ▲
The clusters of yellow flowers
can be dried for floral displays.

SUN ROSE ▲
An attractive evergreen with
white flowers in late summer.

BUGLE ▲
Provides groundcover; blue
flowers bloom in spring.

Most garden stores carry a good selection of plants suitable for rock gardens, which may be found in the herb and alpine sections. Choose a variety of plants that grow to different heights and that provide interest throughout the year.

When selecting plants, look for sturdy specimens with dense, healthy foliage:

- don't buy on impulse—go with a list or plan in mind
- do buy small plants—as long as they are healthy, these are often easier to plant in small spaces and will establish and grow more quickly
- don't choose too many plants, or varieties that will outgrow their space—check the details, especially spread, on plant labels but remember that these figures are only an approximate guide to growth over two or three years
- do choose herbs with variegated or colored leaves to provide interest during the dull winter months
- don't fill every little gap in a rock garden with perennial herbs—leave some spaces for flowering bulbs or annuals such as reticulata iris, dwarf narcissus or tulips, marigolds, and nasturtiums as well as colorful California poppies.

ORNAMENTAL PLANTS

PLANT	FEATURES
Medium	
Curry plant *Helichrysum italicum* Ht. 2 ft. (1.8 m)	Evergreen shrub, silver-gray foliage; small yellow flowers in late summer
Lady's mantle *Alchemilla mollis* Ht. 20 in. (50 cm)	Clump-forming perennial; sprays of tiny greenish-yellow flowers in mid-summer
Lavender *Lavandula angustifolia* 'Munstead' Ht. 18 in. (45 cm)	Early flowering variety with a compact habit; strongly scented and hardy
Rue *Ruta graveolens* Ht. 20 in. (50 cm)	Compact plant with blue-green foliage and bright yellow flowers in summer
Sun rose *Cistus* x *dansereaui* 'Decumbens' Ht. 30 in. (75 cm) *C.* x 'Silver Pink' Ht. 30 in. (75 cm)	Evergreen with year-round interest: these two cultivars have white and pink flowers, respectively, in midsummer
Wormwood (Roman) *Artemisia pontica* Ht. 2 ft. (60 cm)	Semi-evergreen plant grown mainly for its silvery-green filigree foliage
Low-growing	
Bearded iris (dwarf) *Iris germanica* Ht. 15 in. (37 cm)	Drought-tolerant perennial; flowers in a choice of colors from spring into summer
Bugle *Ajuga reptans* Ht. 6 in. (15 cm)	Creeping evergreen perennial; deep blue flowers in spring
Mt Atlas daisy (Pellitory) *Anacyclus pyrethrum depressus* Ht. 1 ft. (30 cm)	Hardy perennial; red-backed white flowers with yellow centers from spring to summer
Rosemary (prostrate) *Rosmarinus prostratus* Ht. 1 ft. (30 cm)	Creeping evergreen groundcover for rock garden; bright blue flowers in spring

Salad Herb Garden

The selection of green leaves and herbs planted in this ladder-style bed makes an attractive planting and provides delicious fresh produce to use in a variety of salads.

The garden is bordered with chives. This easy-to-grow herb has pretty pink pompom-shaped edible flowers and long, narrow leaves. Chives are perennial and, once established, will create an attractive edible border. Sow seed in spring into a narrow row along the edges of the bed. Chives can also be propagated by plant division.

The rungs of the ladder design are planted with salad burnet. Plant seeds or pot-grown plants in spring. This attractive plant will provide interesting leaf shapes from early spring to winter and flowers from late spring to early summer. The edible leaves are green when young and mature to a mixture of brown and green. The tiny ball-shaped flowers are green dotted with red.

Once the shape of your garden has been established, you will be able to plant a different salad leaf or herb between each rung. The mixture of leaf shape and color will give your herb garden interest.

LADDER-STYLE BEDS ▶

This type of design allows you to create interesting beds with a variety of herbs and leaves. The outline is created with chives, which provide long, narrow, grasslike leaves and pink flowers. This is contrasted with salad burnet, which has more intricately shaped leaves. The beds can be planted with lettuce and other leafy plants, and nasturtiums, which will produce colorful edible flowers.

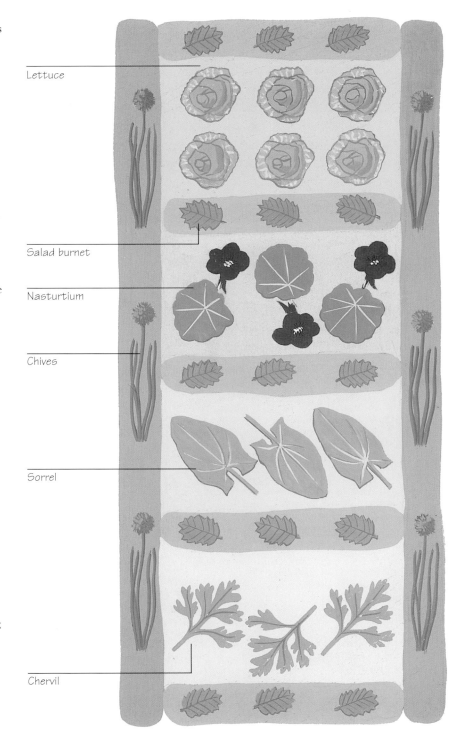

Lettuce

Salad burnet

Nasturtium

Chives

Sorrel

Chervil

Creating a Salad Garden

A salad herb garden would be ideally situated beside a patio or along a sunny fence outside the kitchen door. It should provide you with visual interest as well as many bowls of freshly picked salad herbs to tempt your palate.

Lemon balm

Arugula (rocket)

Sorrel

Mint

Leaves such as sorrel and arugula can be grown with the more traditional herbs such as lemon balm and mint. ▲

SALAD LEAVES

- **Chervil** *Anthriscus cerefolium* Ht. 10–24 in. (25–60 cm) Sow seeds on site in partial shade. Collect leaves before flowering. Good in green salads and potato salad.
- **Garlic chives** *Allium tuberosum* Ht. 20 in. (50 cm) These have flat leaves and a delicate garlic flavor, suitable for salads. The flower buds and blossoms are edible. Grow from seed in spring in a finely raked seed bed. Keep well weeded. Harvest the leaves with scissors.
- **Cilantro** *Coriandrum sativum* Ht. 6–28 in. (15–70 cm) One of the most popular leaves for flavoring; grow from seed in spring; suits partial shade; keep moist.
- **Nasturtium** *Tropaeolum majus* Ht. 3 ft. (90 cm) Sow seeds of this hardy annual in spring directly where they are to grow; the leaves and flowers are edible.

BASIL

No salad garden would be complete without a selection of basils. You need to start seeds indoors on a sunny windowsill. It is an annual and not at all hardy, so plant out only when all danger of frost is past. Watch for slug and snail damage.

- **Cinnamon basil** *Ocimum basilicum* 'Cinnamon' Ht. 2 ft. (60 cm) has purple flowers and dark green leaves with a slight cinnamon flavor and aroma.
- **Lemon basil** *Ocimum basilicum* var. *citriodorum* Ht. 1 ft. (30 cm) has light green leaves with a lovely lemon fragrance.
- **Sweet basil** *Ocimum basilicum* Ht. 18 in. (45 cm) is highly aromatic and combines particularly well with tomato salads.

Sweet basil

SALAD LEAVES

Lettuce is probably the leaf most often used in green salads. You can grow your own, although lettuces do need regular attention as they are prone to slug and snail attacks. They come in various categories:

- **Romaine** is upright with crisp, bunched leaves with good flavor. Little Gem is compact with a particularly sweet flavor.

- **Cabbage** lettuces are similar to romaine but they are round and easier to grow. Iceberg is popular for its pale, crisp leaves.

- **Loose-leaf** lettuces do not grow a heart—the leaves are harvested like sorrel. Salad Bowl and Lollo Rosso have good flavor; the latter has attractive red-tinged leaves.

Other leafy plants with good flavor for the salad bowl include:

- **Beet leaf** such as Swiss chard and spinach beet. They are easy to grow—sow seed in spring for a summer harvest. The leaves are best picked when young if they are to be used raw in salads.

- **Beetroot** leaves make a tasty and attractive addition to salads. Sow seeds on site in late spring and water during dry spells.

- **Arugula** *Eruca vesicaria sativa* Ht. 3 ft. (90 cm) Sow seeds of this hardy annual in succession from early spring. Rich, moist soil yields less bitter leaves. The leaves are best before flowering.

- **Sorrel** *Rumex acetosa* Ht. 3 ft. (90 cm) Sow seeds in spring into a finely raked soil. This spinachlike perennial will give salads an acidic flavor; use in moderation.

- **Winter purslane** *Montia perfoliata* Ht. 8–12 in. (20–30 cm) will provide a tasty winter harvest. The leaves, stalks and flowers are edible. Plant in a sunny position. Sow seeds from spring to late summer.

Hanging Baskets

Hanging baskets can be more than just a decorative item filled with flowers if you include a selection of herbs in the planting. They also extend the season as you can start them in a sheltered area in early spring and then move them outdoors in the warmer weather.

Louis Jordaan

PLANTS

Culinary herbs such as basil, chives, marjoram, oregano, parsley, and sage are all suitable for hanging baskets. If using basil, don't be in a hurry to take it outside as it is less hardy than most. A compact box, such as *Buxus sempervirens* 'Suffruticosa,' also provides a good centerpiece for a basket.

- Seedlings to crop—arugula (rocket, *Eruca vesicaria sativa*), cilantro (*Coriandrum sativum*), dill (*Anethum graveolens*), chives (*Allium schoenoprasum*).
- Creeping—lemon-scented thyme (*Thymus x citriodorus*), creeping thyme (*T. serpyllum*), catmint (*Nepeta cataria*), ivies (*Hedera*), pennyroyal (*Mentha pulegium*), creeping savory (*Satureja spicigera*), prostrate rosemary (*Rosmarinus prostatus*) and *Helichrysum*.
- Trailing—strawberries (*Fragaria vesca*), caraway-scented thyme (*Thymus herba-barone*).
- Include flowering plants such as lobelia and nasturtium to add color and interest.

WATERING

In summer, a hanging basket may need watering two or three times a day. Use either a watering can with a long neck or a hose—avoid lifting a heavy conventional can to an awkward height.

Herbs need plenty of light, so choose a sunny area to hang the basket if you are starting it indoors. If the light is directional, turn the basket regularly to prevent the plants growing unevenly.

You can start by propagating seeds in small pots or trays and then transplant them to the basket. Cuttings will quickly establish themselves in the basket to fill out the gaps between plants.

If you use a variety of different plant species, some plants may die off at different times and will need replacing. A limited number of species chosen for their foliage can look more effective.

There is a variety of products—compost, lining material, and water-retaining blocks—available specifically for hanging baskets but you can get perfectly good results without these.

Soilless compost is ideal for a hanging basket as it is very light, but it does not retain moisture well and will need to be watered regularly. Water-retentive compost with peat or coir, or compost specially formulated for a hanging basket, is preferable.

Sphagnum moss is used to line the basket—a piece of plastic inside the moss will help to retain moisture. Other lining materials include compressed paper, plastic, and sponge.

Planting a Hanging Basket

You can start the basket indoors during early spring then harden it off by hanging it outside during the day and bringing it indoors at night. Once the risk of frost is over, you can hang the basket outside permanently.

Make sure the wall bracket is strong enough to take the weight of the basket when the soil is wet. Check that the bracket is secure and not fixed to rotting wood or crumbling brickwork.

If starting the basket indoors, be sure not to overwater if you are using compost with water-retaining granules as this may make the basket too moist. You also need to check regularly for any signs of pests and diseases.

THEMED BASKETS

Hanging baskets planted with one or two varieties can look very attractive. They are also easier to maintain than baskets with a wide variety of different species.
- Culinary—include basil, chives, marjoram, curled parsley, nasturtiums, and violas
- Fragrant—green and purple basil and lemon balm combined with lobelia or nasturtiums for flowers.
- Mint—an assortment, including variegated mints and pennyroyal, makes a fragrant basket; needs copious water.
- Strawberries look good and will provide you with fruit as well.
- Thyme—an assortment, including variegated and creeping varieties, look and smell good.

Assembling a Hanging Basket

Apart from round baskets, you can also use a halfmoon-shaped basket if you want it to hang flush with a wall.

1 Balance the basket frame on a bucket or large flower pot. Line it with sphagnum moss or organic liner available from garden stores. Line this with black plastic. Make a few holes in the plastic for draining. ▶

2 Using a moisture-retentive compost, half-fill the basket. Select trailing plants to place below the rim. Make holes through the plastic and push the roots through into the basket. Rolling a piece of lightweight cardboard around the roots will make this easier. ◀

3 Add more compost to the basket and plant the top, placing upright plants in the center and surrounding them with creeping plants. Water in well and leave to drain before hanging the basket. ▶

Edging Plants

Herbs can be used to solve the problem of what to plant on the edges of borders, which provide the finishing touch to a garden.

Beds, paths, and patio edges are often dry and exposed, and require drought-tolerant plants that will provide interest from flowers or foliage over a long period. Several herbs are ideal for these spots, being relatively compact and low-growing, and requiring little regular maintenance once established.

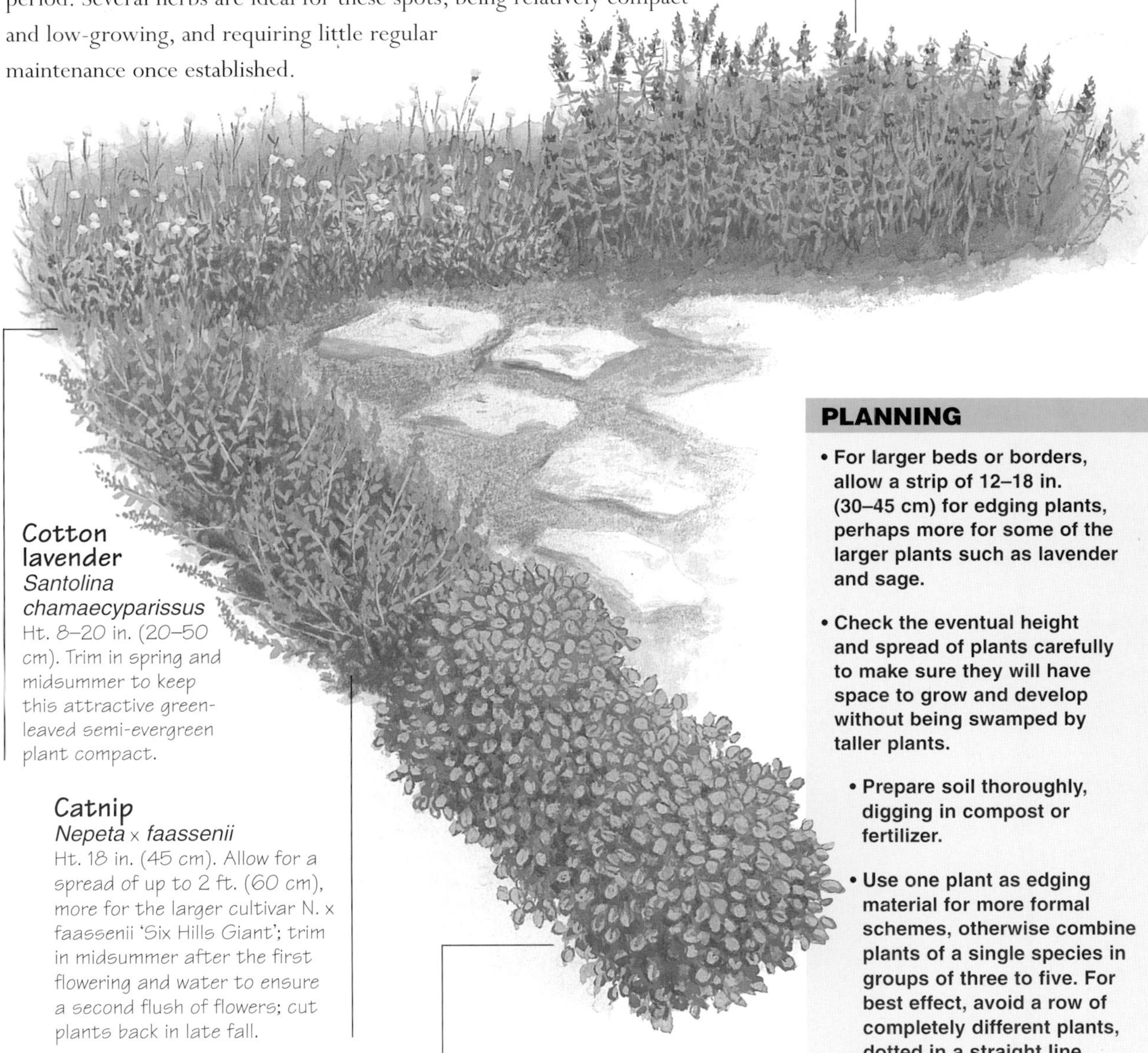

Hyssop
Hyssopus officinalis
Ht. 18–24 in. (45–60 cm). Both the purple- and white-flowered form (*H. officinalis* 'Alba') make a good dwarf hedge or edging; trim back hard in the spring.

Cotton lavender
Santolina chamaecyparissus
Ht. 8–20 in. (20–50 cm). Trim in spring and midsummer to keep this attractive green-leaved semi-evergreen plant compact.

Catnip
Nepeta x *faassenii*
Ht. 18 in. (45 cm). Allow for a spread of up to 2 ft. (60 cm), more for the larger cultivar N. x faassenii 'Six Hills Giant'; trim in midsummer after the first flowering and water to ensure a second flush of flowers; cut plants back in late fall.

PLANTING SCHEMES The plants shown here are suitable for edging beds of regular or geometric shapes, knot gardens, and bedding plots. ▲

Boxwood
Buxus sempervirens
'Suffruticosa' Ht. 7–9 in. (18–24 cm). Trim or clip to form a neat, compact, dwarf evergreen hedge.

PLANNING

- For larger beds or borders, allow a strip of 12–18 in. (30–45 cm) for edging plants, perhaps more for some of the larger plants such as lavender and sage.

- Check the eventual height and spread of plants carefully to make sure they will have space to grow and develop without being swamped by taller plants.

- Prepare soil thoroughly, digging in compost or fertilizer.

- Use one plant as edging material for more formal schemes, otherwise combine plants of a single species in groups of three to five. For best effect, avoid a row of completely different plants, dotted in a straight line.

- Use small groups of annuals or biennials to provide additional summer color.

117

Choosing Edging Plants

It is not practical to have plants flopping or spreading onto areas of lawn that require regular mowing, so opt for low-growing, compact varieties in these positions. For wide paths and paved areas, choose larger varieties which can spread and soften the effect of hard landscaping. Bear in mind too that some of the more colorful varieties of annuals and culinary herbs can make excellent edging material.

ANNUAL COLORS

Try some of these annuals and biennials for providing pockets of additional color in mixed borders from spring to autumn.

- **Curly parsley**
  Petroselinum crispum
  'Moss Curled'
  Ht. 12 in. (30 cm)

- **Chinese pink**
  Dianthus chinensis
  Ht. 6–10 in. (15–25 cm)

- **French marigold**
  Tagetes patula
  Ht. 10 in. (25 cm)

- **Heartsease** *Viola tricolor*
  Ht. 6–8 in. (15–20 cm)

Colourpacks

HEARTSEASE: The pretty and abundant blooms of the wild pansy, *Viola tricolor*, appear in spring and last through to the summer. ▲

LARGEST VARIETIES

Use these for edging broad paths or paved areas where they can spread decoratively onto brick or stonework.

- **Lamb's ears**
  Stachys byzantina
  Ht. 12–15 in. (30–38 cm).
  Silvery gray, felted leaves and spikes of mauve-pink flowers

- **Rosemary**
  Rosmarinus officinalis
  'Bendenden Blue' and
  R. officinalis 'Severn Sea'
  Ht. 3 ft. (90 cm). Brightly colored cultivars with an arching habit

- **Sage**
  Salvia officinalis 'Purpurea'
  Ht. 24–32 in. (60–80 cm).
  Attractive mauve-tinted glaucous foliage and purple-blue flowers make this one of the best plants for edgings and borders.

SHADE LOVERS

The following plants are suitable for difficult shady borders and beds where most other herbs would not thrive.

- **Ferns**
  Polypodium vulgare,
  Dryopteris filix-mas
  Ht. 16–32 in. (40–80 cm).
  Attractive foliage

- **Lily of the valley**
  Convallaria majalis
  Ht. 9–12 in. (23–30 cm).
  White flowers in early spring

- **Lungwort**
  Pulmonaria officinalis
  'Sissinghurst White'
  Ht. 12 in. (30 cm).
  Spring-flowering; mottled leaves

- **Primrose**
  Primula vulgaris
  Ht. 6–8 in. (15–20 cm).
  Soft yellow flowers in spring

COMPACT PLANTS

Use these for edging narrow beds or paths or for borders adjoining areas of lawn.

- **Chamomile** *Chamaemelum nobile* 'Flore Pleno'
  Ht. 6–8 in. (15–20 cm). Double creamy white flowers

- **Chives** *Allium schoenoprasum*
  Ht. 12 in. (30 cm). Mauve-pink flowers, neat clump

- **Lily turf** *Ophiopogon japonicus*
  Ht. 12 in. (30 cm). Lilac flowers, neat grassy clump

- **Thyme** *Thymus vulgaris,*
  T. serpyllum
  Ht. 1–10 in. (2.5–25 cm). Many forms and varieties of this popular herb make excellent edging plants

- **Thyme-leaved savory**
  Satureja thymbra
  Ht. 16 in. (40 cm). Aromatic shrub with pink flowers

- **Variegated marjoram**
  Origanum vulgare 'White Anniversary'
  Ht. 6–10 in. (15–25 cm).
  White variegated leaves

- **Wall germander**
  Teucrium chamaedrys
  Ht. 4–8 in. (10–20 cm).
  Spreading, shrubby perennial, purple-pink flowers

- **Wormwood**
  Artemisia caucasica
  Ht. 6–12 in. (15–30 cm) Dwarf shrub, silvery green leaves.

FEVERFEW: Another compact choice is *Tanacetum parthenium*, which has creamy white flowers. ▼

Planting for Potpourri

Sweet-smelling leaves and blossoms—roses, lavender, violas, pinks, marjoram, mint, and lemon balm, and many more—can be planted to create a colorful and fragrant potpourri garden.

In this octagonal garden, the entrance is marked with two pots containing lemon verbena complemented with violas round the bases of the pots. A bay tree surrounded by roses and lavender marks the center. ▼

PLANTING LIST

FRAGRANCE:
- **Artemisia**
  Artemisia abrotanum 1
- **Bay**
  Laurus nobilis 2
- **Honeysuckle**
  Lonicera japonica 3
- **Jasmine**
  Jasminum officinale 4
- **Lavender**
  Lavandula 5
- **Lemon balm**
  Melissa officinalis 6
- **Lemon bergamot**
  Monarda citriodora 7
- **Lemon thyme**
  Thymus x *citriodorus* 8
- **Lemon verbena**
  Aloysia triphylla 9
- **Marjoram**
  Origanum majorana 10
- **Mints**
  Mentha spp. 11
- **Pinks**
  Dianthus spp. 12
- **Roses**
  Rosa spp. 13
- **Sage**
  Salvia officinalis 'Tricolor' 14, *S. sclarea* 15
- **Violas**
  Viola odorata 16
- **Yarrow**
  Achillea millefolium 'Cerise Queen' 17

COLOR:
- **Annual cornflowers**
  Centaurea cyanus 18
- **Larkspur**
  Consolida ambigua 19
- **Love in a mist**
  Nigella damascena 20
- **Pot marigold**
  Calendula officinalis 21

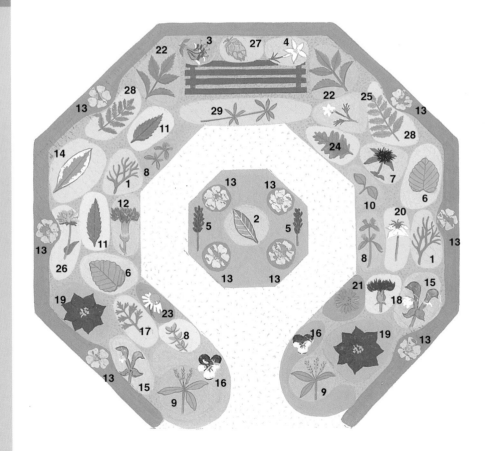

PLANTS TO USE AS FIXATIVES

- **Angelica roots and seeds**
  Angelica archangelica 22
- **Chamomile flowers**
  Chamaemelum nobile 23
- **Cilantro seeds**
  Coriandrum sativum 24
- **Cumin seeds**
  Cuminum cyminum 25
- **Elecampane root**
  Inula magnifica 26
- **Hops seed heads**
  Humulus lupulus 27
- **Sweet cicely roots and seeds**
  Myrrhis odorata 28
- **Sweet woodruff leaves**
  Galium odoratum 29

Planting a Potpourri Garden

Rose petals and leaves, and dill seed heads. ▼

The fragrant mix of herbs and flowers found in potpourri can be grown in a corner of the garden. The planting will also create a haven for butterflies and bees.

Although a wide variety of plants is suitable for potpourri, some are a must. Include the apothecary's rose (*Rosa gallica* var. *officinalis*) alongside lavender (*Lavandula angustifolia* 'Hidcote' has rich, scented, purple flowers). Dried lavender and rose petals keep their scent for quite some time without needing a fixative. A standard bay tree makes a good focal point and will provide plenty of leaves for potpourri and for culinary use in the kitchen.

Include climbers such as fragrant honeysuckle, jasmine, and golden hops, the latter for sleep-inducing flowers. Grow these over a trellis near a small bench. Place sweet woodruff under the bench. When dried, the leaves will have the fragrance of newly mown hay.

If you have room, an hydrangea, with its pink or blue flowers, will make a colorful addition to potpourri mixes.

Lavender, lemon verbena, mint, and rose petals. ▲

Rose petals, rosebuds, and bay leaves. ▲

Lemon verbena and lavender. ▲

HARVESTING

- Harvest flowers, petals, and leaves in the morning when the dew has dried. Pick foliage just before the plants flower—this is when the fragrance is strongest. Spread in a shady, airy spot in large, flat baskets or on muslin-covered frames to dry. Alternatively, dry leaves and flowers in small bunches hung from a rail in an airy spot. If possible, also harvest rosebuds and hips, and dry them to add interest and an opulent look to your potpourris.

- Dig up roots in summer, wash them and leave to dry in a shady well-ventilated spot. When thoroughly dry, grate and then pound to a powder ready for use.

- Harvest seeds when ripe and store in small envelopes.

- When your plant material is quite dry, store in boxes lined with tissue paper and covered, away from the light in a dry spot. Add labels to the boxes.

PLANNING A POTPOURRI GARDEN

A cottage-garden-style layout is a good shape for planting fragrant flowers and foliage and seed-pod-producing plants. When gathered and dried, the produce can be used to make potpourris.

Sketch out a planting plan and mark the placing of plants, taking into consideration height and color, and putting sun-loving plants on the sunniest side of the garden. Include a trellis for climbing roses to provide petals and buds, often the base ingredient of potpourri.

PLANT SPECIES

Choose species that will provide good color and fragrance. Plant the border with a mixture of scented herbs and flowers. Lemon-scented bergamot can be grown from seed. Place low-growing thymes, chamomile, mints, and marjoram in the front of the border. *Salvia viridis* 'Claryssa' has colorful bracts that dry well.

A large clump of pinks, including *Dianthus*, should be planted to provide a spicy fragrance to potpourri. Pinks grow easily from cuttings taken in summer. Pineapple-scented chamomile, sweet marjoram, costmary, rosemary, and lemon balm (bear in mind it is invasive) can be planted in the second row of the border. Plant modern rose cultivars as well as old-fashioned ones—*Rosa* 'Albertine' and *R.* 'New Dawn' are both fragrant with blooms in shades of pink.

Organic Gardening

Herbs and organic gardening are natural allies. Grouped together naturally in a border or vegetable patch, herbs are an essential part of the organic garden.

Comfrey (bottom left) is planted here in a self-contained area to control its spread. Other plants include lungwort, marguerite, and sweet woodruff. ▼

Louis Jordaan

Herbs are invaluable not just for their culinary and medicinal uses, but also as a means of weed control. Some herbs also make good liquid fertilizers, or composts, while others have insecticidal properties or else provide food for insects that are generally beneficial to the garden.

USEFUL HERBS

- **Comfrey** *Symphytum officinale*
  Ht. 2–4 ft. (60 cm–1.2 m).
  Strong-growing, hairy-leaved perennial high in potash, a vital element for promoting vigorous plant growth.
- **French marigold** *Tagetes patula*
  Ht. 8–12 in. (20–30 cm).
  An aromatic, bushy annual with bright yellow or orange flowers, popular for summer bedding or containers. Contains substances that help control eelworms and limit weeds.
- **Pyrethrum daisy** *Tanacetum cinerariifolium*
  Ht. 12–30 in. (30–75 cm).
  Fine-leaved perennial with single white daisy flowers in summer. Contains pyrethrin, a highly effective insecticide.
- **Wormwood** *Artemisia absinthium*
  Ht. 3 ft. (90 cm).
  Subshrub with ferny gray-green foliage, easily grown in a sunny, well-drained spot. It contains thujone, an insecticide.

DO	DON'T
• control weeds by hoeing, handweeding, or mulching	• use weedkiller or sprays
• use organic insect traps, natural products, or biological controls for insect pests	• use chemical insecticides or fungicide sprays
• use compost, animal waste, or plant liquids as fertilizers	• use artificial fertilizers
• rotate crops and different species of plants.	• discard leaves, grass clippings, or vegetable waste that could be used for compost
	• grow the same plants in the same places for too long.

Organic Gardening

Comfrey is no longer recommended as a culinary herb. However, it can be cultivated to make a natural liquid fertilizer. To use the fertilizer, dilute the liquid with about 10–15 parts of water and use it to feed plants every two to three weeks during the summer.

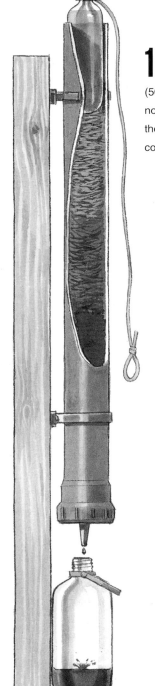

1 Fix a 4 ft. (1.2 m) length of wide-bore drainpipe to a fence, with the bottom end about 20 in. (50 cm) above the ground. Attach a cap with a nozzle or short length of tubing on to the bottom of the drainpipe, placing a bucket or large plastic container underneath. ◄

2 Wearing gardening gloves, push several handfuls of comfrey leaves down the top of the pipe. ▼

3 Compress the leaves with a plastic bottle filled with water and attached to a length of strong string to allow easy removal. The process can be accelerated by adding a small amount of water to the leaves—about 2 cups (500 ml). The leaves can be topped up as they rot down. A concentrated brown liquid will begin dripping out of the pipe in about 10–12 days. ▲

GROWING COMFREY

Remember that comfrey can be invasive and difficult to eradicate when established in moisture-retentive soil, so plant it in an out-of-the-way corner where it can be controlled.

• grow comfrey in sun or part-shade

• the soil should be deeply dug and moisture-retentive

• space two or three plants 18–24 in. (45–60 cm) apart

• keep plants watered in prolonged dry spells

• pick flower heads before seeds develop and scatter.

Medicinal Herb Gardens

Medicinal herb gardens have a long tradition, dating back to ancient times. Some of these traditional gardens are so well recorded that it is possible to recreate them, albeit on a smaller scale.

HERBAL MEDICINES

Plant remedies were once the domain of physicians, apothecaries, monks, and herbalists. Today it is qualified professionals who are skilled in the exact properties of plants and the doses required to be effective at healing specific ailments.

The earliest evidence of herb gardens dates back some 4,000 years to Ancient Egypt. The Chinese, Aztecs, and Romans also cultivated herbs specifically associated with healing. In fact, herbs were grown primarily for their medicinal rather than culinary values and gave rise to many folk remedies.

Some plants were associated with traditional rituals and worship, and so became established in religious gardens, such as those near temples, monasteries, and burial sites. These gardens included plants such as bay, chamomile, fig, frankincense, lotus, myrrh, poppy, and rosemary. In Islam, paradise is regarded as an enclosed garden with fragrant flowers such as roses and fruit such as almonds and pomegranates. Islamic gardens were designed with this vision of paradise in mind.

Monasteries, in an attempt to be self-sufficient, created gardens that incorporated areas specifically set aside for vegetables, fruit, herbs, and flowers. Special attention was given to plants used in the infirmaries. Over the years, these monastic gardens were developed to look as attractive as they were functional. Today, these ancient designs can be used as inspiration in planning a modern garden.

Lyndon Parker

Traditionally, medicinal beds were laid out in straight rows, with plants grouped according to their families for identification purposes. Many of the older physic or botanic gardens used this design, which gave them a formal appearance. The design also provided easy access for planting and harvesting. ▲

Planting a Medicine Garden

Themed gardens have become popular, and although the medicinal garden is limited in its use, it can provide attractive plantings. Traditionally, this type of planting would have had a fairly formal appearance.

The four-square garden, where a rectangle is divided into four sections, surrounded by paths and with a central plant for a focal point, is a popular design for a themed garden. So long as the four sections are not too large the paths will provide access to the beds.

A more modern variation is in a checkerboard design. Here the plants are set in blocks, making a good display and separated from each other by paving stones. You can either have a rigid pattern of paving and plants, or group the paving into larger sections, so that you can include a seat.

Make sure that you know just what you are planting, and that you know how to use it safely.

Draw a detailed sketch to scale and indicate the plant placings. ▲

KEY: Symbols indicate the plants used above.

 white echinacea
 evening primrose
 lavender
 marigold
 celandine
 dill

 borage
 periwinkle
 purple echinacea
 meadowsweet
 chamomile
 angelica
alecost

- **Angelica** *Angelica archangelica* Ht. 6 ft. (1.8 m). Hardy biennial or short-lived perennial; infusions stimulate the digestive system

- **Borage** *Borago officinalis* Ht. 1–3 ft. (30–90 cm). Hardy annual, edible blue flowers; use in poultice to soothe bruises

- **Chamomile** *Chamaemelum nobile* Ht. 1–6 in (2.5–15 cm). Hardy, evergreen perennial; nonflowering form has a wonderful fragrance. A flowering form, valued for its oils, can be used to make a soothing tea and a safe and gentle hair wash

- **Dill** *Anethum graveolens* Ht. 2–5 ft. (60 cm–1.5 m). Hardy annual; yellow flowers in summer; rich in mineral salt; infusion good for digestion and flatulence

- **Lavender** *Lavandula angustifolia* Ht. 2–3 ft. (60–90 cm). Hardy evergreen; flowers in summer; use a weak infusion for headaches

- **Lesser celandine** *Ranunculus ficaria* Ht. 6 in (15 cm). Perennial; flowers from spring onward; used externally to treat piles

- **Madagascar periwinkle** *Catharanthus roseus* Ht. 1–2 ft. (30–60 cm). Tender perennial; flowers through summer; poultices staunch bleeding and ease insect stings

- **Meadowsweet** *Filipendula ulmaria* Ht. 2–5 ft. (60 cm–1.5 m). Hardy perennial; flowers in summer; weak infusions used for acid stomach and heartburn

- **Nasturtium** *Tropaeolum majus* Ht. up to 10 ft. (3 m) Hardy annual; flowers in summer; used externally to combat skin problems and heal small wounds

Other herbs to consider: fennel, fenugreek, hyssop, lemon balm, mint, rosemary, and verbena.

A Fragrant Herbal Bower

The climbing roses will cover the hard outline of the archway and the surrounding plants will add to the overall effect. Place a seat in position once the chamomile is established. ▼

An archway smothered with fragrant roses underplanted with chamomile, soapwort, scented sweet peas, and pinks, with a chamomile carpet, creates a bower fit for a princess.

Choose a quiet sunny corner in the garden for your fragrant bower, siting it where it can be seen at its best. Remove any weeds from the site and improve the soil by digging in plenty of well-rotted manure or good garden compost. The archway can be ready-made in metal or wood available from garden centers. Dig holes for the posts and place in position. Make sure they are secure in the ground. Rake the soil to a fine tilth before planting.

PLANTING THE BOWER

Start by planting two types of climbing rose to grow up and cover the bower. Once mature, the rose branches and foliage will create a "wall" between the posts.

A chamomile lawn is planted under the archway. *Chamaemelum nobile* can be grown from seed. The apple-scented nonflowering cultivar *C. n.* 'Treneague' must be propagated by division.

Include a selection of other fragrant plants and herbs in the scheme. Consider the colors and when the plants will be in flower to balance the overall planting.

SWEET PEAS
Lathyrus odoratus
Ht. 10 ft. (3 m)
Fast-growing climber, flowers in shades of pink, white, purple, and blue.

ROSES
Climbing roses such as *Rosa* 'Zephirine Drouhin,' carmine pink, and 'Kathleen Harrop' pink are suitable for covering the archway.

PINKS
Dianthus caryophyllus
Ht. 8–20 in. (20–50 cm). Deep pink to purple flowers.

LEMON-SCENTED THYME
Thymus × citriodorus
Ht. 10–12 in. (25–30 cm). Lemon-scented leaves with lilac flowers.

CHAMOMILE LAWN
Chamaemelum nobile
Ht. 6 in. (15 cm). Provides a fragrant groundcover.

SOAPWORT
Saponaria officinalis
Ht. 1–3 ft. (30–90 cm). Clusters of pale pink flowers.

Creating an Herbal Bower

Remove all weeds from the area around the roses and fork it over well. Improve the quality of the soil by adding compost or well-rotted farmyard manure. Stamp the earth down well and start planting.

- **Chamomile** can be propagated by seed sown in spring or fall or by root division in spring. Root division is by far the quicker method. Plant rooted chamomile cuttings 4 in. (10 cm) apart. Water in well. Chamomile lawns need regular weeding until they are established.

- **Lemon-scented thyme** is planted beside the pinks. This hardy evergreen dwarf perennial is low-growing and enjoys the same conditions as pinks. Lemon thyme is best propagated from cuttings—take a heel cutting in early summer, plant in a cutting bed, and water well. Plant out once the cutting has taken and roots are established.

- **Pinks**—a hardy perennial that enjoys a well-drained site in full sun. A popular plant, especially in cottage-type gardens, pinks flower in midsummer, filling the air with an aromatic spicy scent. To propagate pinks take 6 in. (15 cm) cuttings in late spring, remove any flower heads, and set in sandy soil. Water well and wait. Once cuttings have rooted plant in 4 in. (10 cm) pots to grow on or directly into the growing site. Old-fashioned cultivars have a single flowering period in midsummer but some modern cultivars are repeat flowering. Try *Dianthus* 'Alice' or *Dianthus* 'Denis,' which has double, magenta clove-scented blossoms.

- **Soapwort** has frothy pink ice-cream-fragranced flowers from summer to fall. It can be invasive but the abundance of blossom and leaf will lend an opulence to the area surrounding the bower. Propagate from root cuttings.

LAVENDERS

To the overall scheme you could add some lavender for its colour as well as its fragrance. *Lavandula angustifolia* 'Folgate' is compact with violet flowers, while *L. a.* 'Rosea' has pink flowers. *L. stoechas leucantha* has white flowers.

Lavender complements the roses and adds to the overall scent. ▲

Choose an archway that will fit comfortably in the chosen site, allowing space for the plants so that they will not end up being cramped. Check that the seat or bench fits inside the structure. ▶

Two rambling roses in different colors have been used very effectively here to cover an archway. ▲

Plant cuttings into clean, well-composted soil in spring, about 4 in. (10 cm) apart.

- **Sweet peas**—choose a fragrant old-fashioned variety. Grow from seed sown in early spring. Plants will need a little assistance at first, but once established, the tendrils will cling to the rose branches and will eventually give a wonderful display of fragrant flowers.

Kitchen Herb Tub

Growing a selection of herbs in a tub provides a convenient source of fresh flavorings for use in cooking, while the tub itself gives a decorative focus. You need to ensure that the plants get enough light and water and are not exposed to strong sun or severe frost.

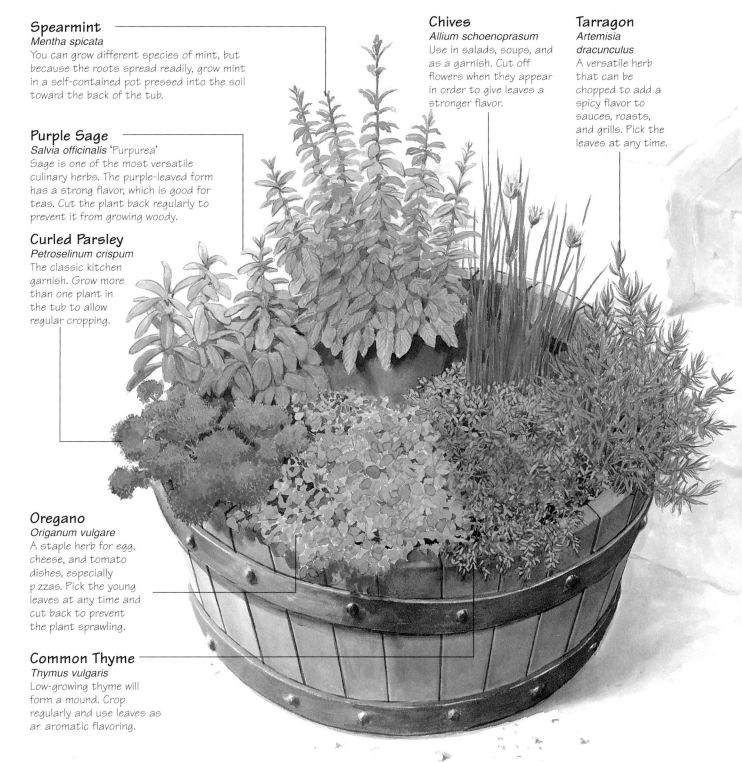

Spearmint
Mentha spicata
You can grow different species of mint, but because the roots spread readily, grow mint in a self-contained pot pressed into the soil toward the back of the tub.

Purple Sage
Salvia officinalis 'Purpurea'
Sage is one of the most versatile culinary herbs. The purple-leaved form has a strong flavor, which is good for teas. Cut the plant back regularly to prevent it from growing woody.

Curled Parsley
Petroselinum crispum
The classic kitchen garnish. Grow more than one plant in the tub to allow regular cropping.

Chives
Allium schoenoprasum
Use in salads, soups, and as a garnish. Cut off flowers when they appear in order to give leaves a stronger flavor.

Tarragon
Artemisia dracunculus
A versatile herb that can be chopped to add a spicy flavor to sauces, roasts, and grills. Pick the leaves at any time.

Oregano
Origanum vulgare
A staple herb for egg, cheese, and tomato dishes, especially pizzas. Pick the young leaves at any time and cut back to prevent the plant sprawling.

Common Thyme
Thymus vulgaris
Low-growing thyme will form a mound. Crop regularly and use leaves as an aromatic flavoring.

127

Although a half-barrel is an ideal size and shape, other containers will suffice as long as you arrange suitable drainage. Choose your herbs carefully, with their decorative appearance as well as their practical use in mind. For convenience, you can buy mature plants in pots and transfer them to the tub.

Planting Herbs in a Container

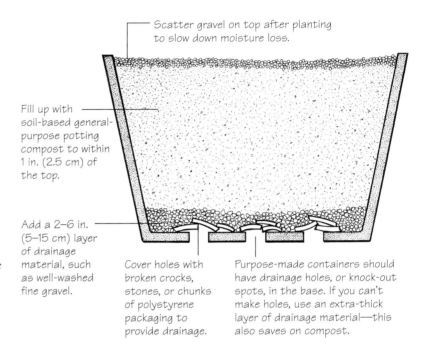

Scatter gravel on top after planting to slow down moisture loss.

Fill up with soil-based general-purpose potting compost to within 1 in. (2.5 cm) of the top.

Add a 2–6 in. (5–15 cm) layer of drainage material, such as well-washed fine gravel.

Cover holes with broken crocks, stones, or chunks of polystyrene packaging to provide drainage.

Purpose-made containers should have drainage holes, or knock-out spots, in the base. If you can't make holes, use an extra-thick layer of drainage material—this also saves on compost.

Plan the tub according to the size of the herbs. For the best effect, put the largest plants in the center and step down to the smallest herbs. Popular choices include:

Large: borage, dill, fennel, lemon balm, tarragon.

Medium: chervil, cilantro, mint, pot marjoram, oregano, sage, sweet marjoram.

Small: basil, parsley, arugula (rocket), summer savory, thyme.

Rosemary and bay eventually become large shrubs but grow slowly, so a small plant can be kept for a few years. Fast-growing herbs such as mint must be restrained by constant cropping. Although a decorative species of mint makes a good central plant, you must confine it in a separate pot or the roots will smother the other plants.

Surround the central plant with the herbs you use most, spacing them to allow for growth. Plant more than one of those you use most often to allow for regular cutting.

PLANTING AND AFTERCARE

Place the container in a sheltered, sunny spot. Put in a drainage layer followed by a layer of compost. Water the potted herbs and gently ease them out of their pots. Plant firmly, starting in the center, and top up with compost.

Water in well and keep the compost moist, but do not soak—most herbs like fairly dry conditions. You don't need to feed the plants, as regular cutting for the kitchen will stimulate the plants to grow vigorously. Trim back if they get too large. Most herbs are annuals or biennials grown as annuals and discarded at the end of summer. Perennials such as mint, sage, and rosemary can be reused until they get too big. Take cuttings for new plants and plant out the old ones.

TYPES OF CONTAINERS

KITCHEN SINK
Scrap items like old stoneware sinks, tin baths, or even a stack of old car tires can all be pressed into service.

STRAWBERRY OR PARSLEY POT
If you want a lot of one particular herb, say parsley or cilantro, put them into parsley pots—tall containers with holes all over for planting in.

TRADITIONAL TERRA-COTTA FLOWERPOT
Attractive but heavy; choose one that is wide enough to plant a good range of herbs and ensure it is frost-proof.

WOODEN PLANTING BOXES
Choose a readymade box or make one yourself. Make sure that the wood is well treated with nontoxic timber preservative to prevent rot.

Growing Edible Flowers

Apart from the thistlelike globe artichoke, the plants listed here are not usually associated with food. Being colorful and decorative, they are seen essentially as garden plants. Grow them in mixed borders or to add color to a vegetable or herb garden, and then use some of the flowers for culinary purposes. Bear in mind that the plants may not all flower at the same time—in fact, it's a good idea to plan the garden so that you have blooms from spring, through summer into the fall.

Make more out of your garden by growing plants for food as well as for their ornamental value. Flowers are a source of vitamins and trace elements, making them nutritious as well as decorative. They can make an attractive addition to salads, and can be used to garnish soups and vegetable dishes.

Being fairly permanent, these plants need to be sited where they will not shade or overcrowd smaller plants, particularly in a herb garden. Plant them at the back of beds, or in their own patch if you have a large vegetable garden. ▼

Artichoke
Cynara scolymus
Takes a couple of years to reach harvesting size, and is best replaced every few years with a new plant. ▲

Rose
Rosa gallica 'Cardinal de Richelieu'
This makes a lovely plant for a mixed border, combining well with purple, blue, or mauve flowers and with silver-foliaged plants. ▶

Elder
Sambucus racemosa
Some varieties have attractive gold or purplish foliage, and all have heads of large, creamy white flowers. ▼

Rosemary
Rosmarinus officinalis
This well-known shrubby herb needs a sunny, well-drained spot and makes a good container plant. ▼

Chrysanthemum
Chrysanthemum coronarium
Long-lasting flowers that provide a good show of color.
◀

Harry Smith Collection

Harry Smith Collection

Harry Smith Collection

Deni Bown/Oxford Scientific Films

Growing Edible Flowers

Shrubs and tall perennials may require positions different from smaller perennials and annuals. When you're planning your planting, think about where the plants will look best and place them where they won't shade or block access to smaller plants. With plants that grow in the wild, such as elder, it's unwise to eat anything that you are not sure is correctly indentified. With garden flowers, such as chrysanthemums and roses, the old-fashioned species used by herbalists, for example *Chrysanthemum coronarium*, an annual, and *Rosa gallica officinalis*, are the best ones to use for culinary purposes.

The "globe," which is edible, will form a flower if left on the plant. The choke inside the globe is not edible. ▼

PLANT	WHEN TO PICK	HOW TO USE
Artichoke *Cynara scolymus* Ht. 60–80 in. (1.5–2 m). The unopened flower bud of this highly ornamental thistle forms the familiar vegetable. Several varieties are available.	Early to late summer, while buds are still tight and firm (open flowers are not edible)	Trim and steam, boil or braise; use with mayonnaise or in vegetable dishes and salads
Chrysanthemum *Chrysanthemum* species Ht. 32–54 in. (80 cm–1.35 m) These popular border plants that provide fall color need a sunny position and well-fed, well-watered soil to produce the best flowers.	Late summer to late fall, when flowers have just opened	Use petals lightly blanched in fruit and vegetable salads, soups, sauces, and cakes
Elder *Sambucus racemosa* Ht. 80–110 in. (2–3 m). A large, woody shrub that favors moisture-retentive soil. Useful for filling gaps in a hedge or back of a border.	June, just before flower heads are fully open	Dip in batter to make fritters, or use in soups, jams, and drinks
Rose *Rosa gallica* Ht. 60–100 in. (1.5–2.5 m) Deeply scented, crimson-flowered cultivars 'Emperor of Morocco,' 'William Lobb,' 'Belle de Crecy,' and 'Cardinal Richelieu'.	Usually May–July, though some cultivars have later flowers; use when flowers have just opened	Use petals to make jam and tea or in salads
Rosemary *Rosmarinus officinalis* Ht. 40–80 in. (1–2 m) This well-known shrubby herb needs a sunny, well-drained spot and makes a good container plant. Choose one of the bright blue cultivars, such as 'Sissinghurst,' 'Benenden Blue,' or 'Severn Sea.'	Early to late summer while buds are still tight	Use in salads and sauces or to flavor marinades and drinks or fruit dishes

Plant Diseases

To help reduce the risk of common diseases, it is important to provide good growing conditions and to know the general requirements of particular plants.

Since most plant diseases are encouraged by particular environmental or climatic conditions, they can sometimes be avoided or reduced by, for example, making sure plants are well ventilated and not subject to extremes of drought or wet. We have no control over weather conditions, of course, so inspect plants regularly for symptoms—then you need to act promptly to avoid the disease spreading.

Some of the most common diseases are caused by minute fungi that thrive in particular conditions. Most of these plant diseases can be identified by the symptoms on leaves, flowers, or stems, so check them carefully.

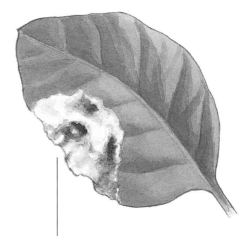

Gray mold
Furry gray fungal patches on flowers, leaves, and shoots; attack a variety of plants, particularly those with soft leaves, and seedlings.

Downy mildew
Whitish mealy patches on lower surface of leaves; upper surface becomes blotched and brown; common on alliums, asters, borage, brassicas, and evening primrose.

Leafspot
Blackish spots that enlarge and spread on leaves, found on ivy, holly, lavender, parsley, roses, and other plants.

Rust
Orange-brown spots appearing first on undersides of leaves; common on tarragon, mint, periwinkles, roses, and other plants.

Scab
Dark blistery patches on leaves, branches, and fruit, particularly on loquat, ornamental fruit trees, and pyracantha.

IDENTIFICATION: Diseased leaves have particular characteristics— use them to decide what the problem is and then use the appropriate treatment.

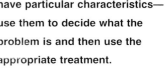

Powdery mildew
Whitish, powdery patches with discoloration on upper surface of leaves appearing later.

Treating Diseases

Spraying with fungicide is sometimes the only effective way to control a fungal disease, but many established plants will survive attacks without severe damage if they are growing healthily. Remember that providing good ventilation for plants and avoiding excessive wet will help to reduce disease, especially for indoor or container-grown plants.

DISEASED PLANTS

Although a healthy plant may survive an attack from a disease, young plants are more vulnerable and may die if left untreated. ▲

CAUSE AND EFFECT

Bacteria and fungi that cause diseases in plants are too small to see and identify. But recognizing the damage they cause gives an indication of the type of treatment necessary to eradicate the problem.

- **Leafspot**
  Minute bacteria spread by insects, wind, or rain-splash; more common in damp conditions. Leaves turn yellow and fall.

- **Downy mildew**
  Fungi thriving in humid conditions. Leaves fall, plant growth is stunted; patches of dieback may occur on plants.

- **Gray mold**
  Fungi especially common in cool, damp, still conditions. Spreads rapidly, spoiling flowers and fruit; can cause plant to collapse.

- **Powdery mildew**
  A variety of minute fungi thriving in hot, dry conditions; some have restricted host ranges while others attack a much wider range of plants. Leaves fall; flowers and fruit are spoiled.

- **Rust**
  Minute fungi that thrive and spread especially in damp, humid conditions. Leaves fall; flowers and fruit are spoiled.

- **Scab**
  Fungi thriving in damp weather. Disfigures leaves and branches; early leaf fall; branches may die.

Pest	Control	Eco-friendly alternative
Downy mildew	fungicide with mancozeb	improve ventilation; reduce watering and damp conditions
Gray mold	as for leafspot	improve ventilation and air circulation; avoid excessive damp and remove dead material
Leafspot	fungicide containing benomyl or carbendazim	keep foliage dry if possible, remove fallen leaves
Powdery mildew	fungicide containing benomyl or sulfur	water or mulch affected plants; cut off affected plants
Rust	spray with fungicide containing mancozeb or propiconazole	improve air circulation around plants; avoid excessive feeding and watering
Scab	as for leafspot	remove diseased parts and all fallen leaves; prune bushes/trees to keep plants open in their overall shape

Cooking with Herbs

One of the joys of growing herbs is having a year-round supply to use in the kitchen. This section on cooking with herbs contains more than 30 mouth-watering, yet simple-to-follow recipes that make the best use of the herb garden, combining flavors in both traditional and creative ways.

Most recipes call for herbs that are readily available, whether fresh or dried, and there is something here for all occasions—soups, starters, and snacks; meat, poultry, and fish meals; pasta and vegetable dishes; herb breads, butters, and cheeses; and delicious drinks and desserts.

The "Cooking with Herbs" chapter will show you how to add flavor and interest to all your meals, whether a traditional pasta dish with homemade pesto sauce, chicken with tarragon sauce, or a delectable dessert to delight the family such as lavender ice cream.

Fennel & Bean Soup

Fennel and spinach are combined to make this flavorful soup, enhanced with mixed beans. It makes a hearty lunch eaten with country-style bread and cheese. Make it vegetarian or add chunks of Serrano ham for a meatier version.

Making the Soup

Use Serrano ham, available from Spanish delicatessens, to flavor the soup. Ask for an end piece so there will be more rind. If you prefer vegetarian soup, leave out the ham.

Ingredients: *Serves 8 1 cup (100 g) mixed dried beans • One small onion • One bay leaf • Nutmeg • Black pepper • 5 oz. (125 g) chunk of cured ham rind • 2 cups (500 ml) vegetable stock • Small head of fennel • Pinch of saffron • 5 oz. (125 g) fresh spinach*

Saffron threads

1 Soak the beans overnight in cold water. Drain and put in a pan with 2 cups (500 ml) of fresh water. Bring to a boil and skim off any foam with a spoon. ▶

2 Peel, halve, and slice the onion. Add to the pan, along with the bay leaf, a good pinch of freshly grated nutmeg, and some black pepper. ▶

3 Add the ham, cut into large chunks, and add the stock. Simmer over a low heat for 40 minutes. ▼

4 Cut the top and base off the fennel and slice thinly. Add to the pan and cook for another 10 minutes, stirring well. ▶

Whole fennel bulb

5 Test to see if the beans are soft, then stir in a good pinch of saffron and the spinach. Heat through, remove the chunks of ham, and check the seasoning. Serve the soup hot. ▶

135

Basil & Zucchini Soup

A substantial soup, thick and with a hint of sweetness to counteract any slight bitterness from the zucchini. It makes a lunch on its own, served with a herb salad or sun-dried tomato bread.

Making the Soup

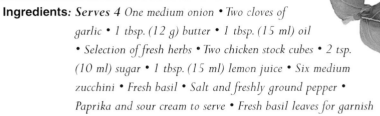
Basil

You can also use squash or pumpkin instead of zucchini in the soup, as long as you remove the seeds and any fibrous pieces.

Ingredients: *Serves 4 One medium onion • Two cloves of garlic • 1 tbsp. (12 g) butter • 1 tbsp. (15 ml) oil • Selection of fresh herbs • Two chicken stock cubes • 2 tsp. (10 ml) sugar • 1 tbsp. (15 ml) lemon juice • Six medium zucchini • Fresh basil • Salt and freshly ground pepper • Paprika and sour cream to serve • Fresh basil leaves for garnish*

Equipment: *Large heavy-based saucepan • Food processor*

Paprika

1 Peel and finely chop the onion and garlic. Melt the butter in a saucepan and add the oil, onion, garlic, and herbs and cook gently, stirring, for two minutes. ▶

2 Add 2½ cups (625 ml) of water to the pan, crumble in the stock cubes and add the sugar and lemon juice. Chop and dice the zucchini and add to the pan. ▼

3 Bring to a boil, then reduce the heat and simmer, uncovered, for 20 minutes, or until the zucchini are tender. Chop a large handful of basil and stir into the mixture. ▼

4 Process the soup in batches in a food processor until smooth. Return to the pan and reheat, seasoning to taste. Serve topped with soured cream and paprika, and garnish with fresh basil leaves. ▶

Zucchini slices

Kashmiri Lamb Chops & Cilantro Chutney

These delicious lamb chops are cooked twice—first boiled in milk for tenderness, then coated in a spicy yogurt mixture and fried. Serve with rice and a piquant cilantro chutney.

Making the Kashmiri Lamb Chops

Cooking the chops in milk tenderizes the meat, while the spicy yogurt keeps them moist during frying. The end result is exceptional tenderness. Serve the chops with boiled rice and a herb salad.

Ingredients: *12 lamb chops or cutlets • 2 cups (500 ml) milk • One cinnamon stick • One bay leaf • ¹/₂ tsp. (2.5 ml) fennel seeds • ¹/₂ tsp. (2.5 ml) black peppercorns • Three whole green cardamom pods • 1 tsp. (5 ml) salt • ¹/₂ cup (125 ml) evaporated milk • ³/₄ cup (150 g) plain yogurt • 2 tbsp. (30 ml) flour • 1 tsp. (5 ml) chili powder • 1 tsp. (5 ml) of finely grated fresh ginger • ¹/₂ tsp. (2.5 ml) garam masala • ¹/₂ tsp. (2.5 ml) crushed garlic • Pinch of salt • Vegetable oil • Mint sprigs and lime quarters*

1 Trim away excess fat from the lamb chops and place in a large saucepan. ▶

2 Add the milk, cinnamon stick, bay leaf, fennel seeds, peppercorns, cardamom pods, and salt. Bring to a boil over a high heat. ▼

3 Simmer over a low heat for 10–15 minutes or until the milk has reduced by about half. Add the evaporated milk and lower the heat. Simmer, stirring occasionally, until the chops are cooked through and the milk has evaporated. ▼

139

4 Meanwhile, blend the yogurt and flour with the chili powder, grated ginger, garam masala, crushed garlic, and a pinch of salt. ◀

◀ **Cinnamon sticks, bay leaves, cardamom pods, black peppercorns, and fennel seeds provide the flavoring, and salt, the seasoning for the Kashmiri lamb chops.**

5 Remove the the chops from the pan and discard any whole spices stuck to them. Add the chops to the yogurt mixture, turning them to coat them all over. ▲

6 Pour oil into a deep, heavy-based frying pan to a depth of 1 in. (2.5 cm). Heat the oil then turn down the heat and add the chops a few at a time. Fry until golden brown, turning them once or twice as they cook. Serve garnished with sprigs of mint and lime quarters. ▼

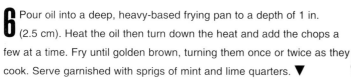

Cilantro Chutney

A fresh-tasting, slightly sweet chutney with the wonderful taste of cilantro, perfect for serving as an accompaniment to the Kashmiri lamb chops. For a more authentically sweet-sour Indian flavor, use tamarind pulp instead of plain yogurt. Extract the pulp from 2 oz. (50 g) of tamarind pods by soaking them in hot water.

Cilantro

Ingredients: *12–15 sprigs of fresh cilantro • One small onion • One or two cloves of garlic • 1 oz. (25 g) fresh root ginger • One or two green chilies • ¹/₂ cup (125 ml) plain yogurt • 2 tsp. (10 ml) cumin seeds • 2 tbsp. (30 ml) sugar • ¹/₂ tsp. (2.5 ml) salt • Five sprigs of fresh mint*

Equipment: *Food processor*

1 Wash the cilantro and remove the stalks. You can use more or less cilantro, according to preference. Place in a food processor. ▲

2 Peel and slice the onion, garlic, and ginger. Cut open the chilis and remove and discard the seeds. ▶

3 Add the onions, garlic, ginger, and chilis to the food processor. Add the yogurt and cumin seeds. ▼

4 Add half the sugar, all the salt, and the mint leaves, and blend until smooth. Check taste, and add more sugar, if necessary. ▲

Beef with Red Wine, Cumin, & Thyme

A wonderfully rich stew, with a surprising heat from the chilies and a partnership of unusual flavors—olives, red wine, cumin, thyme, bay leaves, and parsley—this dish is perfect served with country bread or baked potatoes.

Cooking the Beef

Choose a full-bodied red wine for this recipe, otherwise its flavor will be lost among the herbs and spices. Cook's perk—you get to drink the leftovers if you choose. Preheat the oven to 350°F/180°C/gas mark 4.

Ingredients: *Serves 6–8 2¹/₂ cups (275 g) flour • 1 tbsp. (15 ml) dried thyme • 1 tsp. (5 ml) salt • ¹/₂ tsp. (2.5 ml) black pepper • 3 lb. (1.35 kg) lean braising beef, cubed • 6 tbsp. (90 ml) olive oil • 1 cup + 2 tbsp. (270 ml) red wine • 1¹/₂ cup (375 ml) beef stock • 14 oz. (350 g) canned tomatoes • Two small red onions, chopped • 2 tbsp. (30 ml) cumin seeds, crushed • 1 tsp. (5 ml) ground chilies • Two bay leaves • Six cloves of garlic, chopped • Handful of parsley, chopped • 8 oz. (200 g) pitted black olives • Sour cream to serve*

1 Sift the flour, thyme, salt, and pepper into a large bowl and toss the cubes of meat in the mixture, making sure they are well coated.▼

2 Heat the oil in a casserole dish and brown the cubes of beef, a few at a time, over a high heat, turning constantly. Transfer to a plate and keep warm. ►

3 When all the meat is browned, discard the oil, and add the wine, stock, and canned tomatoes to the casserole. Bring to a boil, scraping in the brown bits from the bottom and sides of the casserole dish. ►

4 Return the beef to the pan and add the chopped onion, cumin seeds, chiles, and bay leaves. Put the lid on the casserole and cook in the oven for 1¹/₂ hours, stirring occasionally. ▼

5 Add the garlic, parsley, and olives to the casserole and return to the oven until the stew is thick— about another hour. Serve with a swirl of sour cream. ►

Handy Hint

Put the casserole dish on a baking tray in the oven to catch any spills that may occur during the long cooking time.

Black olives

143

Chicken with Tarragon Sauce

Chicken with tarragon is a classic combination of culinary flavors. Here orange and ginger are added as a variation to give zest to an old favorite.

Making the Salad

Use king shrimp where possible—buy peeled if you can't get unpeeled, or buy fresh shrimp and cook them. You can substitute ordinary shrimp if you prefer. Reserve a few unpeeled shrimp to use as a garnish when serving.

Ingredients: *2 lb. (1 kg) king shrimp, cooked • Two ripe mangoes • Fresh cilantro • Fresh mint • One small Spanish onion • 2 tbsp. (30 ml) Thai sweet chili sauce • 3 tbsp. (45 ml) orange juice • Arugula (rocket) leaves • Romaine lettuce*

1 Wash the shrimp and peel away the shells including the heads and the tails. Place the shrimp in a colander. ▲

2 Chop the stalk end off the mango, stand upright on the flat base, and slice through either side of the center to remove the stone. Cut vertically and horizontally through the flesh of the two remaining pieces and turn through to remove the cubes. ▶

Fresh cilantro

Mint leaves

3 Wash the cilantro and chop finely to produce 3 tbsp. (45 ml). Wash the mint and chop finely to produce 2 tbsp. (30 ml). Put the mango and shrimp into a large bowl and add the chopped herbs. ◀

4 Peel the onion, chop finely, and add to salad. Mix the sweet chili sauce with the orange juice and pour over the shrimp and mango mixture. ▼

5 Toss the salad. Shred the arugula and lettuce, and line a serving plate. Pile the salad on top and garnish with fresh shrimp to serve. ▶

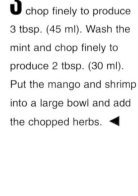

151

Cajun-style Sea Bass

This is a delicious way to serve fine fillets of this fish, quickly fried in a spicy herb seasoning and accompanied by a well-flavored mayonnaise. Serve with a green salad or mixed bean salad and rice, or new potatoes for a perfect light lunch.

Making the Cajun-style Sea Bass

Catfish is an even more traditional option. Buy the fish as fresh as possible on the day that you intend to use it.

Dill

Ingredients: *Serves 4 For the mayonnaise:* One egg yolk • One clove garlic • ¹/₂ cup (120 ml) olive oil • 1 tsp. (5 ml) grainy mustard • Sea salt • Black pepper • Anise liqueur • 1 tbsp. (15 ml) chopped dill

For the cajun fish: ¹/₂ tbsp. (7.5 ml) garlic powder or garlic salt • ¹/₂ tsp. (2.5 ml) cayenne pepper • 1 tsp. (5 ml) black pepper • 1 tsp. (5 ml) dried thyme • ¹/₂ tsp. (2.5 ml) dried oregano • Pinch dried basil • Pinch cumin • Four sea bass fillets • 1 tbsp. (15 ml) olive oil • Butter

Equipment: *Pestle and mortar • Heavy-based saucepan*

1 To make the mayonnaise, grind the egg yolk with a pestle and mortar. Chop the peeled garlic clove and grind in the mortar. Slowly drizzle in the olive oil while grinding until the mixture thickens. ▶

2 Add the mustard, salt and pepper, a dash of anise, and the chopped dill and mix well in. Cover and chill until required. ▼

3 Make the cajun seasoning in a large flat dish by combining the garlic powder, cayenne, and black pepper then adding the thyme, oregano, basil, and cumin. ▶

4 Lay the fish fillets on a board and pinch the flesh together along the center. Use a sharp knife to score through the flesh at even intervals so that the thicker parts will cook through at the same time as the thinner edges. Lay face down in the seasoning. ▶

5 Heat the oil and a knob of butter in a pan until almost smoking. Fry the fillets quickly, the seasoned side first, until black on each side. Serve at once with the flavored mayonnaise. ▲

Cayenne pepper

153

Smoked Trout and Spinach Tart

A very effective dish for a lunch party—a soufflé wrapped in filo. It has a healthy filling full of flavor—smoked trout, horseradish, dill, and spinach, combined with the low-fat elements of ricotta cheese and lightweight filo pastry.

Making the Tart

If you have trouble obtaining smoked trout, you can use smoked mackerel instead. Remove the bones and skin from the fillets and break the flesh into 1/4 in. (6 mm) pieces. Preheat the oven to 350°F/180°C/gas mark 4.

Arugula

Ingredients: *Serves 4 14 oz. (350 g) spinach leaves • 1/2 stick (60 g) butter • 1/4 cup (50 g) flour • 1 cup (250 ml) milk • Nutmeg • Salt and pepper • Fresh horseradish • Six eggs • 4 1/2 oz. (110 g) ricotta cheese • Fresh dill • Two fillets of smoked trout • 8 1/2 oz. (210 g) filo pastry*

Equipment: *9 in. (23 cm) pie tin*

1 Remove any large stalks from the spinach leaves. Wash thoroughly and blanch in a pan of rapidly boiling salted water. Drain, rinse in cold water, drain, and squeeze out as much water as possible. Chop finely. ▼

3 Grate sufficient horseradish to provide 1 tbsp. (15 ml) and separate the eggs. Add the yolks to the mixture with the horseradish, ricotta, 1 tbsp. (15 ml) chopped dill, chopped spinach, and the smoked trout. ◄

2 Melt 1/4 stick (25 g) of butter in a saucepan. Stir in the flour and then gradually whisk in the milk. Bring to a boil, reduce heat to simmer, and add a pinch of nutmeg and salt and pepper to taste. Whisk occasionally for 10 minutes until thick. ▲

5 Beat the egg whites to stiff peaks. Fold into the mixture in two batches, then pour into the pie tin and fold the filo pastry over the top. Brush with more melted butter and cook until golden brown and firm—about 15 minutes. ◄

4 Lay the filo pastry on a work surface, covered with a damp tea towel. Brush one sheet of filo at a time with melted butter and line the tart tin in overlapping layers, protruding above the edges of the tin. ▲

155

Roasted Fennel

The aniseed flavor of fennel needs no other enhancement apart from the addition of olive oil and a little salt. Roast it in the oven to serve with roast meat, or chop with other roasted or grilled vegetables into a fresh tomato sauce to serve with pasta.

Roasting the Fennel

Use fresh, young fennel bulbs where possible, as the older, larger bulbs tend to be tough. If using large ones, cut them into wedges through the stem to keep them intact and parboil the wedges for 10 minutes. Leave to drain and then roast them. Preheat the oven to 450°F/220°C/gas mark 7.

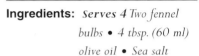

Ingredients: *Serves 4 Two fennel bulbs • 4 tbsp. (60 ml) olive oil • Sea salt*

Fennel bulb

1 Trim the fennel bulbs, removing the feathery leaves and tips and tough base of the bulb. ▲

2 Chop each bulb in half vertically then, depending on size, chop each in half again to form wedges. ▶

3 Put the wedges in a nonstick baking tray and pour over the olive oil. ▲

Handy Hint
If serving the fennel hot, grind some black pepper over it. You can also add a sprinkling of finely grated Parmesan cheese.

4 Sprinkle sea salt over the wedges and bake for 15–20 minutes, depending on the size of the wedges. ▲

Stuffed Eggplant

An unusual twist on a traditional Greek recipe, halves of eggplant are stuffed with a herby lamb mixture, along with diced fried eggplant, then baked in the oven. Serve as a starter or a light lunch with a tomato salad.

Stuffing the Eggplant

It is important to use ground lamb—it's used in the traditional Greek dish and it produces less fat in what is already a rich dish. Preheat the oven 300°F/150°C/gas mark 2.

Ingredients: *Serves 6 Four eggplants • Salt and pepper • Olive oil • Two cloves of garlic • One onion • 18 oz. (450 g) ground lamb • Four ripe tomatoes • 1 tbsp. (15 ml) parsley • Two eggs • ¹/₄ cup (60 ml) milk • 2 tsp. (10 ml) dried mixed herbs*

1 Dice one eggplant and season with salt and pepper. Heat the olive oil in a frying pan and fry the eggplant lightly. ▶

2 Slice the remaining eggplants in half lengthways, remove the pulp, and discard. Sprinkle salt over the insides and leave for 40 minutes. Rinse well, sprinkle with olive oil, place in a baking tray, and bake for 15 minutes. ▼

3 Peel and finely chop the garlic and onion and brown in olive oil. Add the lamb and fry until browned. Add the peeled and deseeded tomatoes, the chopped parsley, and half the eggplant pulp. Season. Cover and simmer for 20 minutes. ▶

4 Put the cooked eggplant halves in a serving dish, cut side up, and stuff each one with layers of ground lamb and fried eggplant. ▲

Handy Hint

You can top the eggplants with a little grated cheese 10 minutes before the end of cooking time.

5 Beat the egg with the milk and season with salt and pepper. Add the dried herbs. Pour over the stuffing. Place the dish in a roasting tin. In the oven, pour boiling water into the tin to come halfway up the sides of the serving dish. Bake for 40–60 minutes. ▲

Tapenade-stuffed Cherry Tomatoes

Tapenade, an olive paste flavored with garlic, is used to stuff scooped-out cherry tomatoes. This flavorful dish makes the ideal canapé or finger-food for a buffet or party.

Stuffing the Tomatoes

The quantities given here make enough to serve as one of a selection of canapés for a buffet or party. If you require less—for an appetizer, for example—simply reduce the ingredients in proportion.

Ingredients: *30 cherry tomatoes, about 18 oz. (450 g) • 8 oz. (225 g) black olives, stoned • 2 oz. (50 g) green olives, stoned • Two small cloves of garlic • Three small canned anchovy fillets • 1 tbsp. (15 ml) virgin olive oil • 5 tbsp. (75 ml) mayonnaise • Small sprigs of fresh thyme • 1 tbsp. (15 ml) dry sherry • Fresh parsley or cilantro*

Equipment: *Kitchen paper • Food processor*

1 Wash and dry the cherry tomatoes and take a small slice off the top of each one. Using a small spoon, scoop out the inside and discard the flesh and seeds. Place the tomatoes on kitchen paper, cut side down, to drain. ▶

2 Put the olives, garlic, anchovy fillets, olive oil, and mayonnaise in a food processor. Strip the leaves from the thyme stems and add to the processor. ▶

3 Process for one minute, scraping the mixture down the sides as necessary. Add the sherry and process briefly. Taste the mixture, and if it is too strong, add a little more mayonnaise. ▼

Cilantro

Black olives

Handy Hint

Any leftover tapenade can be used as a spread on crackers or Italian-style breads such as ciabatta.

4 Using a small spoon, fill each tomato with some of the mixture, then garnish with parsley or cilantro. ◀

Roasted Peppers with Herbs in Oil

This is a truly delicious way of making the most of peppers—flavored with herbs and roasted. Serve the peppers with bread and cheese for a light lunch or snack.

Roasting the Peppers

After all the peppers have been eaten, strain the oil and use it to add a delicious herbal flavor to your cooking and salad dressings. Preheat the oven to 400°F/200°C/gas mark 6.

Ingredients: *Red, yellow, and green peppers • Olive oil • Spring onions • Salt and pepper • A selection of fresh herbs such as chives, lavender, thyme, lemon thyme, curry plant leaves, sage, and parsley*

White lavender

Equipment: *Preserving jar*

1 Wash the peppers and cut off the tops and bases. Slice large portions out of each pepper either side of the ribs. ▶

Lemon thyme

2 Oil a baking tray with olive oil then place one layer of peppers on the tray. ▼

3 Pile the mixed fresh herbs on the peppers, season with salt and pepper, and drizzle with olive oil. ▼

Curry plant   *Garden thyme*

4 Cook in the oven for 45 minutes or until slightly blackened. Leave to cool. Transfer to a preserving jar and cover with oil. ▶

163

Roast Root Vegetables with Fresh Herbs

A trouble-free way of cooking a wonderful selection of vegetables to serve with a Sunday lunch—roast the vegetables in the oven with a mouthwatering mix of fresh herbs. Once the preparation is done, the dish requires very little attention.

Roasting the Vegetables

Use herbs such rosemary, thyme, oregano, and chives. Prepare the vegetables by scrubbing them, peeling only those where the skin is too tough to eat, and chopping them into roughly equal chunks. Preheat the oven to 400°F/200°C/gas mark 6.

Ingredients: *Serves 4–6 2 lb. (1.8 kg) mixed vegetables such as new potatoes, carrots, celery root, rutabaga, and sweet potato •Vegetable or olive oil • Selection of fresh herbs, such as chives, rosemary, thyme, and oregano • 2 tbsp (30 ml) balsamic vinegar • Salt and pepper*

Chives

Oregano

1 Scrub the potatoes and carrots. Top and tail the carrots and chop them roughly into 3 in. (7.5 cm) lengths. Peel the celery root and cut into wedges.◄

2 Peel the rutabaga and chop into chunks. Peel the sweet potatoes and chop into chunks. ▼

3 Pour ¹/₂ in. (1 cm) of oil into the roasting tin. Add the prepared vegetables to the tin and turn them in the oil until they are well covered. ◄

4 Chop or cut the herbs into sprigs about 4 in. (10 cm) long so that they are easy to remove once the vegetables are cooked. Spread the herbs over the vegetables and stir them in. Roast for about an hour, stirring the vegetables two or three times during cooking. ▶

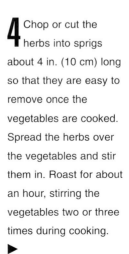

5 Test the vegetables with a knife to make sure they are cooked. Pour the balsamic vinegar over the vegetables, season with salt and pepper, and remove the large herb sprigs before serving. ▲

165

Dill Potatoes

Serve this potato dish with fresh fish, such as salmon or tuna steaks, or with pork or chicken. It's very quick and easy to make and it can be put in the oven to cook while you prepare your main course. It is also suitable to be served as part of a vegetarian meal.

Making the Dill Potatoes

Fresh dill

Dried dill

It's better to use dried dill rather than fresh in this dish, as fresh dill can develop a rather unpleasant texture during the lengthy cooking. However, you can garnish the finished dish with the fresh herb. Preheat the oven to 350°F/175°C/gas mark 4 before you start to prepare the potatoes.

Ingredients: *1 lb. (450 g) of potatoes • Dried dill • Garlic salt • 1 cup (250 ml) milk • 1 oz. (25 g) butter • Fresh dill to garnish*

1 Wash the potatoes and cut into slices about 1/4 in. (6 mm) thick, using a sharp knife. Start to layer the potatoes in a dish. ▲

2 Sprinkle each layer of potatoes with about 1/2 tsp. (25 ml) each of dried dill and garlic salt, building up the layers until the dish is full. ▶

3 Sprinkle the top layer with dill and garlic salt, and carefully pour the milk over so it spreads evenly throughout the dish. ◀

4 Chop the butter into small pieces and dot all over the top of the potatoes. Cook in the oven for 45 minutes to 1 hour, until golden brown. Serve hot. ▶

Pasta with Basil, Parsley, & Lime

This is a simple light lunch or supper dish, which relies on the flavor of the herbs and lime to provide a wonderful fresh taste, spiced up with the addition of the cayenne pepper.

Cooking the Pasta

Cook the pasta first until *al dente*, then drain and keep warm. Be careful not to overcook the garlic—it will catch and burn easily, which will spoil the taste of the finished dish.

Lime

Ingredients: *Serves 4* 12 oz. (300 g) of medium-sized pasta shapes, such as fusilli • Four cloves of garlic • Handful of fresh parsley • One lime • 4 tbsp. (60 ml) olive oil • Handful of basil, chopped • ¹/₄ tsp. (1.5 ml) cayenne pepper, or to taste • Salt and pepper

1 Peel the garlic cloves, chop the ends off, and slice them as finely as possible. ▲

2 Wash and chop the parsley. Grate the lime rind or use a zester, and then squeeze the juice. ▶

3 Heat the oil in a pan, add the garlic and cook until golden. Remove from the heat and add the lightly chopped basil, which will turn bright green and glossy. ◀

4 Add the cooked, drained pasta to the pan and toss the mixture well. ▶

Fresh parsley

5 Add the grated lime, lime juice, chopped parsley, cayenne pepper, and salt and pepper. Toss well and serve at once. ▲

Sage & Spinach Gnocchi

These spinach and sage gnocchi, or dumplings, are quick and easy to make and impressive as a starter. Fresh sage and Parmesan add a wonderful flavor—serve on a bed of mixed and unusual leaves for a final touch.

Nutmeg

Making the Gnocchi

Ingredients: *Serves 4 as a starter 11 oz. (275 g) fresh spinach • 4¹/₂ oz. (110 g) ricotta cheese • One egg • Nutmeg • Sea salt • Black pepper • ³/₄ cup (100 g) freshly grated Parmesan • Fresh sage • ¹/₂ cup (50 g) flour • ¹/₄ cup (25 g) seasoned flour • ³/₄ stick (60 g) butter • Mixed leaves in season to serve—sorrel, spinach, red swiss chard, or mixed herb salad*

You will need an ovenproof dish and a deep frying pan capable of holding all the gnocchi in a single layer. Preheat the oven to 230°F/ 110°C/gas mark low.

1 Wash the spinach and remove the stalks. Cook in a pan of boiling water for one minute. Drain and refresh in cold water. Squeeze all the water out, then chop roughly. Put in a bowl and refrigerate. ▶

2 Add the ricotta, beaten egg, nutmeg, seasoning, and ¹/₂ cup (75 g) of grated Parmesan to the spinach. Finely chop the sage leaves and add 1 tbsp. (15 ml) to the bowl. Stir in the flour and refrigerate for one hour. ▲

3 Dust a tray with seasoned flour. Form the mixture into golf-ball-sized pieces— it should make about 12—and roll in generous amounts of flour. Warm the ovenproof dish in the oven. ◀

4 Half-fill the frying pan with salted water and bring to a boil. When the water is bubbling, carefully lower the gnocchi into it and let them simmer for 10 minutes or until they float. ▲

5 Remove the gnocchi with a draining spoon and place in the warmed ovenproof dish. Pour over the melted butter and place in the preheated oven for 10 minutes. Serve on a bed of leaves sprinkled with the remaining Parmesan and a little black pepper. ◀

Red chard

171

Carrot, Date, & Pecan Salad

A variation on the popular carrot and nut salad, this version contains pecan nuts rather than peanuts, and dates for added sweetness. A dressing of fresh cilantro, basil, and orange juice adds piquancy.

Making the Salad

Serve the salad well chilled as an accompaniment to barbecued meats and fish. Because of its sweetness, a little goes a long way, and the salad is packed with goodness from the carrots, nuts, and dates.

Pecans

Ingredients: *Serves 6–8 1 1/8 lb. (450 g) carrots • 12 oz. (300 g) fresh dates • Small handful of fresh cilantro and basil leaves • 1/2 cup (125 ml) freshly squeezed orange juice • 1 1/2 cup (150 g) pecan nut halves • Salt and freshly ground black pepper*

1 Peel the carrots, top and tail, chop in half, then cut into matchstick strips. ▶

2 Cut one end off the dates, cut in half vertically, separate the two halves, and remove the stone. Chop the dates into quarters. ▼

3 Finely chop the cilantro and basil, and combine with the orange juice to make a salad dressing. ▼

4 Put the chopped carrots and dates into a large bowl along with the pecan-nut halves. Pour the dressing over and mix well. Season to taste and chill for a couple of hours before serving. ◀

Dates

173

Chickpea & Pine Nut Salad

A quick-to-make standby, perfect for unexpected guests. The salad can be made more substantial by serving it warm with sausages and potatoes.

Making the Salad

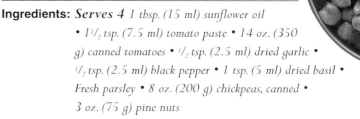

If you can't get canned chickpeas, you can use dried ones for this recipe, although it requires advance planning. Soak them overnight, drain, refresh, and boil according to the instructions on the packet.

Ingredients: *Serves 4* *1 tbsp. (15 ml) sunflower oil • 1¹/₂ tsp. (7.5 ml) tomato paste • 14 oz. (350 g) canned tomatoes • ¹/₂ tsp. (2.5 ml) dried garlic • ¹/₂ tsp. (2.5 ml) black pepper • 1 tsp. (5 ml) dried basil • Fresh parsley • 8 oz. (200 g) chickpeas, canned • 3 oz. (75 g) pine nuts*

Chickpeas

2 Add the canned tomatoes to the pan and mash slightly with a fork. Add the dried garlic, black pepper, and dried basil and stir in. ▼

1 Heat the oil in a saucepan, add the tomato paste, and stir well over a low heat. ▶

3 Simmer the mixture for 10 minutes, then wash and chop a large handful of fresh parsley and add to the sauce, stirring in well. ▲

4 Drain the canned chickpeas, rinse well, and put in a bowl. Pour the sauce over the chickpeas, add the pine nuts, and mix well together. Serve warm or cold. ◀

Parsley

175

Herb Bread

This alternative to herb or garlic butter with bread uses olive oil as the base. You can use any fresh culinary herbs with soft leaves, such as mint, sage, basil, parsley, chives, and tarragon. Choose herbs that complement the food accompanying the warm herb bread.

Making the Salsa

The salsa is best eaten fresh, so make up only as much as you need. You can chop the ingredients by hand or use a food processor—in which case, the texture will be smoother and the salsa more runny. Use less chili if you prefer. Garlic is optional.

Ingredients: *Serves 6* • *Four tomatoes* • *One bunch of spring onions* • *Two limes* •
Two green chilies • *2 tbsp. (30 ml) fresh cilantro leaves* • *Salt and black pepper*

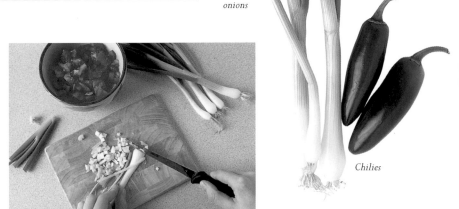

Spring onions

Chilies

1 Wash the tomatoes and cut each one into eighths. Then chop them finely. ▲

2 Wash and trim the spring onions at both ends. Chop finely and add to the chopped tomatoes. ▲

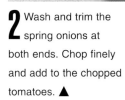

3 Squeeze the juice from the limes and add the juice to the vegetable mixture. Add salt and freshly ground black pepper. ▶

4 Wash the cilantro leaves and chop finely, removing the excess stems. Add to the mixture in the bowl. ▼

5 Cut the chilies in half and deseed using a knife. Chop finely and mix into the salsa. (Wash your hands after handling chilies. Don't touch your eyes as the chilies will burn.) ◀

Traditional Pesto

Although pesto is is now widely available commercially, once you have experienced the true Mediterranean flavors of the homemade variety, you will be loathe to eat anything else. Serve in the traditional way, tossed with fresh pasta, or use as a base on pizza instead of tomatoes or stir into cooked rice.

Making Pesto with Basil

Pesto is usually made with basil, nuts, and strong cheese (usually pine nuts and Parmesan), blended with garlic and olive oil. The finished product has a wonderful sharp aroma and a fresh, green color. It keeps well in the fridge for up to two weeks stored in an airtight container. The oil will separate a little from the mixture quite naturally, and you can add a little more oil to help preserve the pesto.

Basil

Ingredients: *3 cups of basil leaves • $^1/_3$ cup of pine nuts • $^1/_2$ cup of Parmesan cheese, coarsely grated • 3 cloves garlic, chopped coarsely • $^1/_2$ cup (120 ml) olive oil • Salt and black pepper*
Equipment: *Grater • Sharp knife • Cup measures • Food processor*

1 Measure out the pine nuts using the small $^1/_3$ cup measure. Use the full cup to measure out the fresh basil leaves. ▲

2 Peel the garlic and chop coarsely—it's going in a food processor so there's no need to crush it. ▶

3 Place the basil, pine nuts, Parmesan cheese, and garlic in the food processor. Add the salt and pepper. ◀

4 Process until everything is well chopped, then slowly add the oil in a thin stream to form a fairly smooth paste. Put into airtight glass jars to store in the fridge. ▶

181

Pesto with Tarragon

Tarragon and parsley—curly or flat-leaf—are used here. Serve with pasta or chicken, and include some black olives.

Ingredients: *1 cup of loosely packed parsley leaves • $^1/_2$ cup of loosely packed tarragon leaves • $^1/_4$ cup of spring onions • $^1/_3$ cup of pine nuts • $^1/_2$ cup of Parmesan cheese • $1^1/_2$ tsp. (7.5 ml) of fresh lemon juice • 4 tbsp. (60 ml) of vegetable or olive oil • Salt and pepper*

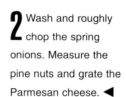

Pasta

1 Remove any stems from the parsley and tarragon and measure them. ▶

2 Wash and roughly chop the spring onions. Measure the pine nuts and grate the Parmesan cheese. ◀

3 Place the parsley, tarragon, spring onions, pine nuts, Parmesan cheese, lemon juice, and salt and pepper in a food processor and blend until well chopped. Then drizzle in the oil to form a smooth paste. Check seasoning. ▼

FACT FILE...

CUP MEASURES

These are quick and accurate ways of measuring all sorts of things—solids and liquids—in the same measure. Measures of fresh herbs must always be somewhat approximate: a handful of this, a loosely packed cup of that. However, when using dried herbs, exact weight measures are easy since dried herbs are sold by weight, usually in ounces.

Pesto with Dill

This recipe works particularly well with fish and fish soups—stir a spoonful into the soup when serving. Mature Cheddar, which is strongly flavored, is used here so that the cheese won't be overpowered by the herbs.

Ingredients: *1 cup of loosely packed dill • ¹/₂ cup of chopped fresh chives • ¹/₂ cup of mature Cheddar cheese • ¹/₂ cup of walnut pieces • 4 tbsp. (60 ml) of vegetable or light olive oil • Salt and pepper*

1 Remove any tough stems or stalks from the dill. ▼

2 Wash and chop the chives into short lengths. ▼

3 Grate the Cheddar cheese—it doesn't have to be too fine. ▼

4 Place the dill, chives, cheese, walnuts, and salt and pepper in a food processor. Blend until well chopped. Then slowly drizzle in the oil in a thin stream and blend to form a paste. ▼

Pesto with tarragon

Pesto with basil

Pesto with dill

183

Herb Butters and Cheeses

Herb butters can be used in a variety of ways. Apart from using them to add flavor to sandwiches, you can also serve them with meat, fish, poultry, and vegetables. They are particularly suited to barbecues—with any grilled food. You can use the herb cheeses to make canapés or serve them on a cheeseboard.

Making the Chive Butter

The herb butters keep as well as ordinary butter, so you can make them in bulk and store them in the refrigerator until required. Flavors can be changed according to the herbs you have available.

Ingredients: *4 tbsp. (60 ml) chives • 1 stick (100 g) butter, softened • 1 tbsp. (15 ml) lemon juice • Salt and pepper*

Equipment: *Food processor or blender*

1 Wash and roughly chop the chives. Place them in a food processor. ▲

2 Chop the butter roughly with a knife and add it to the food processor. ▶

3 Add the lemon juice to the butter and chives. Process and check seasoning, adding salt and pepper to taste. This butter is good with baked potatoes and grilled fish. ◀

Chives

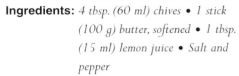

Handy Hint

For special occasions, roll the butter in waxed paper to form a cigar shape and chill in the fridge. Slice or cut to shape using cutters.

Garlic & Cilantro

Garlic and cilantro produce an excellent combination of flavors. Use the butter with grilled meats and vegetables.

Ingredients: *1 stick (100 g) butter • 1 tbsp. (15 ml) cilantro seeds • 6–8 cloves of garlic, peeled • 1 tbsp. (15 ml) lemon juice • Salt and pepper*

Garlic　　*Cilantro*

Place butter in food processor. Add peeled garlic cloves and cilantro. Blend, then season to taste with salt, pepper, and lemon juice. ▶

Top to bottom: *Garlic and cilantro butter, chili butter, and chive butter.*

Chili butter

The piquancy of this butter goes well with rich, spicy foods. You need to handle the chilies with care—avoid touching sensitive areas, such as your eyes.

Ingredients: *• 1 stick (100 g) butter • 1 tbsp. (15 ml) paprika • 3–6 chilies, deseeded • 1 tbsp. (15 ml) lemon juice • Salt and pepper*

Chilies

Place the butter in a food processor. Add the paprika and deseeded chilies. Blend, then season to taste with salt, pepper, and lemon juice. ▲

Soft Cheeses with Herbs

The creaminess of soft cheese and the fresh taste of green herbs make a perfect combination of flavors. A selection of cheeses can be decorated to provide a mouthwatering centerpiece for a lunch party or a fitting finale to a more formal dinner.

Ingredients: *8 oz. (250 g) soft cheese, such as cream cheese, goat's cheese, or ricotta • 1–2 cloves of garlic • Fresh herbs, such as parsley, chives, dill, and cilantro*

1 Peel and finely chop 1 or 2 cloves of garlic (according to taste) using a sharp knife. ▼

2 Finely chop the herbs using a sharp knife. The quantity will vary according to taste—you can always add more to the cheese mixture as you go. ▼

3 Put the cream cheese in a bowl and blend with a fork. Gradually add the chopped herbs and garlic in equal quantities, forking them well into the mixture. ▼

4 Fork a little of the cheese into the palm of your hand, then roll it once or twice between your palms to form a cylindrical shape. ▼

Handy Hint

If you find the taste of garlic too strong, use chives or garlic chives for a milder flavor. Chop the chives, add to the cheese, and shape into cubes. Tie with lengths of chives to form packages.

5 Chop more herbs, as necessary, and roll the cylinders of cheese in the herbs, leaving the ends clear. ▼

Lavender Ice Cream

Fresh lavender flowers can be used to make an unusual and fragrant ice cream. Honey is also used to complement the flavor of the lavender. Serve this distinctive ice cream with brandy snaps to make a perfect summer treat.

Making the Ice Cream

Lavender flowers

The type of honey you use will affect the flavor of the ice cream—choose lavender honey if you can find it. An ice-cream machine makes it easier to produce a smooth, creamy dessert, but you can also make it in the freezer.

Ingredients: *Serves 4 • $^{1}/_{2}$ cup (150 g) honey • 1 tbsp. (15 ml) lavender flowers • $1^{1}/_{2}$ cup (375 ml) double cream • Brandy snaps to serve, optional*

Equipment: *Small saucepan • Mixing spoons • Ice-cream machine (optional—see Handy Hint below for an alternative method using a freezer)*

1 Spoon the honey into a small saucepan and heat it gently over a low heat. If the honey has crystallized, heat it until it is clear. ▲

2 Crush the lavender flowers and add them to the honey. ▶

Handy Hint

If you don't have an ice-cream machine, whisk the double cream until thick and make the ice cream in the freezer of your fridge. Beat the ice cream every 30 minutes or so to break down the crystals that form while freezing.

Brandy snaps

3 Stir in the cream and mix lightly. Transfer to an ice-cream machine, and use it according to the manufacturer's instructions to stir the ingredients until frozen. Serve with brandy snaps or dessert cookies. ▶

Raspberry & Tarragon Torte

Amaretti cookies soaked in liqueur add an unusual and delicate flavor to this striking raspberry torte, perfect as a rich finale for a special occasion such as a summer wedding or a summer lunch or dinner party.

Making the Torte

Before you start to prepare the torte, line the base of the tart tin with greaseproof paper and melt the gelatine in the anise in a pan over gentle heat. Set aside to cool. If using frozen raspberries, ensure that they are fully thawed.

Amaretti cookies

Ingredients: *Serves 8 1 cup and 1 tbsp. (150 ml) anise • 1 tbsp. (15 ml) gelatine • 5 oz. (125 g) amaretti cookies • 7 oz. (175 g) mascarpone cheese •14 oz. (350 g) sugar • 2 tbsp. (30 ml) fresh tarragon, chopped • 11 oz. (275 g) raspberries, fresh or frozen • 1 cup (250 ml) whipping cream*

Equipment: *Loose-based 9 in. (23 cm) tart tin with fluted edge • Greaseproof paper*

Tarragon

1 Put the amaretti cookies in a large bowl and crush them with the back of a spoon. Pour into the lined tin to cover the base evenly. ▶

2 Whisk the mascarpone cheese and sugar together and pour the cooled gelatine mixture over it. Stir in well. ▼

3 Add the chopped tarragon to the mixture, along with the raspberries and any juice, stirring in gently. ▲

4 Whip the cream and fold into the mixture, then pile this on to the crushed amaretti cookies in the tart tin. Leave to set in the fridge for at least two hours, then invert on to a serving dish so that the cookie layer is on top. ▶

Mint Julep

This is a great cocktail, with the warmth of bourbon and spiked with the refreshing taste of mint. Mint julep is the perfect way of translating a warming winter nightcap into a special drink for a hot summer's day.

Making the Mint Julep

Mint julep, which originated in the Deep South, is perfect for anyone with a taste for bourbon. A touch of bitters is complemented by a little sugar and fresh mint adds the final touch.

Sprig of mint

Ingredients: *Serves 2 1–2 tsp (5–10 ml) powdered sugar •*
Eight medium-sized mint leaves • $^1/_4$ *tsp. (1.5 ml)*
Angostura bitters • 3 tbsp. (45 ml) bourbon • Ice
• Sprig of mint
Equipment: *Electric blender*

1 Put the sugar in the blender. Strip the mint leaves from the stems and add to the blender. ▼

2 Put the Angostura bitters in the blender and add the bourbon. Blend for 20–30 seconds until the leaves are finely processed. ▼

Handy Hint

To serve the drink icy cold, make the cocktail and chill it along with the glasses before serving on ice.

3 Strain into a glass full of ice and serve at once, garnished with a sprig of fresh mint. ◀

Herbal Beauty and Health

Herbs have been used for thousands of years for their cosmetic and medicinal properties, and many people today prefer to use the natural ingredients of herbs in cosmetics and homemade medicinal remedies. The more than twenty-five cosmetic and medicinal preparations in the "Herbal Beauty and Health" chapter draw on both centuries-old folklore and modern scientific evidence of herbal properties.

Using all natural ingredients, there are recipes here to pamper and treat the body from top to toe, from soothing eye cream and fennel-and-honey toner, to juniper massage oil and rosemary-mint foot cream.

Recognizing the powerful healing and soothing properties of herbs, many modern medicines contain herbal extracts. The medicinal remedies in this chapter can be used to treat some common ailments, but always consult a physician if symptoms persist.

Lavender Leg Gel

With its lavender scent, this gel is ideal for soothing legs after hair removal. Keeping it in the refrigerator adds to its cooling properties. It is also suitable for skin that has been exposed to the sun. Apply in small quantities, smoothing the gel into the skin.

Preparing the Leg Gel

The leg gel is perfect for soothing skin after hair removal. It has a lovely cooling effect—enhanced by keeping it in the fridge. Although creamy in appearance, it has a gel-like texture, making it easy to apply. Lavender has an antibacterial effect.

Ingredients: *1 tbsp. (15 ml) glycerine • 1 tbsp. (15 ml) powdered arrowroot • $^1/_2$ cup (120 ml) water • Lavender essential oil*

Handy Hint

It's important to stir the mixture over boiling water after the arrowroot has been added, otherwise it will not thicken.

1 Measure the glycerine into a small bowl and place it over a pan of warm water over a low heat. As the glycerine thins, add the powdered arrowroot. ▲

2 Pour the measured amount of water into the mixture. Allow the water in the pan to bubble rapidly, and stir the mixture well until it starts to thicken. ▶

3 Remove the bowl from the heat and add four drops of lavender essential oil. ▼

4 Stir the mixture well until it cools to prevent lumps forming, then spoon into a small container and keep in the fridge. ▼

Herbal Body Scrub

The wonderful scent of this invigorating body scrub is provided by the orange peel and roses. Although the peel and the rose petals are dried in the microwave to produce the right texture, they will retain their scent. Thyme adds to the overall fragrance of the scrub.

Making the Body Scrub

The astringent effect of thyme combined with the grittiness of oatmeal makes a perfect exfoliating body scrub when applied after a bath. To use the scrub, rub it gently into damp skin, avoiding the facial area, then shower or rinse off with cool water.

Ingredients: *2 oranges • 4 large scented red roses • arrowroot • 1 cup dried thyme • 3 cups of oats or coarse oatmeal*

Equipment: *Vegetable peeler • Microwave • Kitchen paper • Food processor*

1 Peel the orange with a vegetable peeler, producing fine strips of peel. Place it on kitchen paper to absorb moisture during the drying process. ▼

2 Transfer the orange peel on its paper to a plate in the microwave and microwave on medium power for two minutes. Check to see if the peel is brittle to the touch—microwave for another minute if necessary. ▶

3 Remove the petals from the roses and spread out on kitchen paper. Microwave the petals on medium power, as for the orange peel, checking after one minute and repeating as necessary, until dry. ▶

4 If using oats, process to coarse oatmeal by whizzing in the food processor for a few seconds. Alternatively, put the oatmeal in the processor. Add the dried orange and dried rose petals and process for five seconds. Store in an airtight container. ◀

Handy Hint

Microwave times will vary depending on the power of your microwave—if it's high wattage, reduce the length of the drying and checking times.

Rose

Soothing Eye Cream

Keep a little pot of the cream in the fridge—the coldness adds to the soothing effect—and apply it in the evening. The very simple ingredients mean there is little likelihood of any allergic reaction to the cream, a bonus for eyes that may already be inflamed.

Making the Eye Cream

When making the cream, stir constantly and keep an eye on the heat—the cream starts to thicken very quickly, and if it "catches," you will have to start again. Add the rosewater in small amounts once you've heated the mixture—it's easy to overdilute it.

Ingredients: *3 tbsp. (45 ml) of cornstarch • About 5 tbsp. (75 ml) rosewater*
Equipment: *Small pan • Pots with lids*

1 Put the cornstarch into a small pan—level the spoons when measuring the cornstarch. ▼

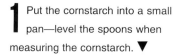

2 Add 3 tbsp. (45 ml) rosewater to the cornstarch. ◄

3 Blend the ingredients to the consistency of single cream. Heat very gently over a low heat, stirring, until it starts to thicken. ▼

4 Remove the pan from the heat at once and keep on stirring well to prevent lumps forming. ▼

5 Add rosewater to the mixture, a teaspoon at a time, to thin it down—you'll probably need to add about five teaspoons altogether. ▼

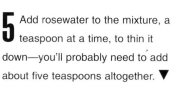

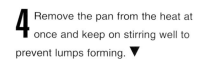

6 Transfer the mixture to pots using a small spoon. Do this at once before the mixture sets. ►

Handy Hint

If you add too much rosewater, return the pan to a very low heat and heat gently to thicken the mixture again.

Rosemary & Mint Cologne

Herbal eau de cologne is easy to make from a blend of your favorite aromatic oils with alcohol and water. You can vary the essential oils to produce a unique scent—your own individual signature. These light fragrances also make perfect gifts for friends, male or female.

Preparing the Cologne

The recipe is a traditional one, using vodka as an alcohol base. The cologne is valued purely for its scent—it has no medicinal properties—and can be used as a refreshing splash or added to the bath. It will keep in a cool place or in the fridge for up to two weeks.

Mint

Rosemary

Ingredients: *1 tbsp. (15 ml) of any fresh mint leaves— Eau de cologne (lemon) mint (Mentha x piperata f. citrata) is best • 1 tbsp. (15 ml) fresh rosemary leaves• ¹/₄ cup (60 ml) vodka• 1 orange • 1 lemon • ¹/₄ cup (120 ml) rosewater*

Equipment: *Bowl • Small saucepan • Grater*

1 Wash the mint and rosemary leaves. Shake dry and place in a bowl. Warm the vodka in a small pan and pour over the herbs. ▲

2 Wash the orange and lemon, then finely grate the peel from each one. Add the peel to the herbs. ▶

3 Warm the rosewater gently in a small saucepan, then tip into the mixture and stir well. ▼

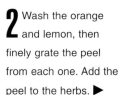

4 Cover the mixture and keep it in the fridge for a week. Stir every day. Strain the mixture through a plastic sieve into a jug, then pour the liquid into a bottle and seal with a stopper. ▼

Strawberry & Mint Face Mask

This face mask has a cleansing, refreshing effect, thanks to the action of the strawberries and the mint. It's a perfect mask to make in the summer when you have plenty of strawberries and mint in the garden.

Making the Face Mask

If the strawberries are very ripe, you may need to thicken the mixture with a little powdered milk. Store, covered, in the fridge, and use the mask within 24 hours. Apply the mask, avoiding the eye area, leave for up to 20 minutes, then rinse off.

Ingredients: $^1/_2$ cup (100 g) of fresh strawberries • 4 sprigs of fresh mint • 1 tbsp. (15 ml) of freshly squeezed lemon juice • Powdered milk

Equipment: Food processor

1 Wash the strawberries and remove the leaves, and the hulls if they come away easily. ▲

3 Put the strawberries, mint leaves, and lemon juice in a food processor. Add 2 tbsp. (30 ml) of powdered milk. ▼

2 Wash and dry the mint, and separate the leaves from the stem. Discard the stems. ▲

4 Blend everything together for 10–15 seconds, then spoon out into a bowl ready for use. ▼

Parsley Skin Pack

This skin pack is ideal for greasy skins—particularly teenage skin—because the parsley combats oiliness while the natural yogurt regulates the bacteria level on the skin and helps to clear up any blemishes.

Making the Skin Pack

The consistency of the pack will vary depending on how thick the yogurt is. Use a set yogurt if you prefer. Apply the pack to your skin and leave it in place for 10–15 minutes. Splash off with cold water. Keep covered in the fridge for up to 24 hours.

Ingredients: *6 tbsp. (90 ml) fresh parsley • 2 tsp. (10 ml) cider vinegar • 3 tbsp. (45 ml) natural yogurt*
Equipment: *Chopping board • Sharp knife • Food processor*

1 Remove the large stalks from the parsley and chop the leaves roughly. ▼

2 Place the parsley in the food processor and blend it briefly. Add the vinegar to the parsley and process. ▶

3 Add the yogurt to the mixture in the food processor and blend again. ▲

Handy Hint

If you drain the yogurt in cheesecloth first, the pack will be thicker and adhere to the skin more readily.

4 Transfer the parsley skin pack to a small container, cover, and chill until required. ▲

Juniper Massage Oil

Juniper essential oil, blended with sweet almond oil, is recommended for revitalizing the body and for giving the spirits a lift. A massage, in which you are sure of receiving total one-to-one attention, is a wonderful way of enjoying this oil's reviving benefits.

Preparing the Oil

When you're feeling low and your body is tired, add a few drops of a suitable essential oil to a base oil for a revitalizing massage. Juniper essential oil has a warm, woody scent and is used to treat aching limbs. It reinforces the immune system and has a cleansing and healing effect on both mind and body.

Ingredients: *¹/₂ cup (120 ml) of sweet almond oil • A few drops essential juniper oil*

Handy Hint

You and a friend or partner can learn a few simple massage techniques from the many books available on the subject.

1 Carefully pour the sweet almond oil into a glass bottle, making sure you decant it all—it's an expensive oil so don't waste it. ▲

2 Carefully add 10 drops of juniper essential oil to the sweet almond oil. If you want a stronger scent, you can add up to 25 drops of essential oil per ¹/₂ cup (120 ml) of base oil. ▲

3 Cork the bottle well, then invert a few times to mix the ingredients. ◄

CAUTION
Don't use this massage oil on the face or temples— some aromatherapy oils are too strong to use close to the eyes or nose.

Fennel & Honey Toner

Use this toner on your face after cleansing. The alcohol preserves the ingredients and adds a refreshing tingle, as does the fennel, which has an aniseed scent and an astringent action. Honey softens the skin and helps smooth out fine lines.

Making the Toner

This toner is quick and simple to make, and much less harsh than many of the commercially made preparations. Apply the toner with cottonballs.

Ingredients: *1¹/₂ tbsp. (22 ml) honey • 1 tbsp. (15 ml) fennel seeds • 2 tbsp. (30 ml) vodka*

Equipment: *Small container • Sieve • Small glass bottle with stopper*

Handy Hint

The toner can be diluted—add 2 tbsp. (30 ml) of water before using.

1 Measure the honey into a small container and sprinkle the fennel seeds over it. ▲

3 Stir the mixture well to spread the fennel seeds evenly throughout. Allow to stand for three days in a cool place to infuse. ▲

2 Add the vodka to the honey and fennel-seed mixture in the container. ▲

4 To remove the fennel seeds from the infusion, strain the mixture into a bottle. ▲

Honey

Fennel seeds

Sage & Rosemary Hair Rinse

Rosemary has antibacterial properties, helps clear dandruff, and promotes a healthy scalp. Sage adds shine to hair. The combination of the two herbs in this rinse gives hair a healthy sheen, which is particularly noticeable on dark hair.

Making the Hair Rinse

It's best to make the rinse the day before you use it, but it will keep for up to a week in bottles in the fridge. Decant the rinse into a jug to use it, or pour it from the bottle over your hair after shampooing. Leave for 30 minutes, then rinse again and dry as normal.

Ingredients: *2 oz (50 g) fresh rosemary sprigs • 2 oz (50 g) fresh or dried sage leaves • 2 cups (500 ml) boiling water*

Eqiupment: *Kitchen scissors • Heatproof glass bowl • Sieve • Bottles with well-fitting stoppers to store the hair rinse*

1 Snip the fresh rosemary into a heatproof glass bowl using a pair of kitchen scissors. ▲

2 Add the sage leaves, then carefully pour in the boiling water. Leave the herbs to infuse for at least two hours. ▲

3 Strain the infusion through a sieve into a jug. Transfer to storage bottles and keep in the fridge until required. ▲

Dried sage

Handy Hint

To prevent dandruff, mix a little borax into the rinse and use regularly after shampooing your hair.

Herbal Shampoo

This shampoo is ideal for normal hair, but you can tailor it to suit other hair types—such as dry or damaged hair—by varying the essential oils. As a finishing touch, add some fresh herbs to the container.

Making the Shampoo

Use a mild, unscented shampoo as a base for your own herbal mixture—choose the essential oil from the table below and add an appropriate sprig of the fresh herb.

Ingredients: *Lavender essential oil • Orange essential oil • Rosemary essential oil • ¹/₂ cup (120 ml) clear, unscented shampoo in a screwtop container • Fresh rosemary*

1 Add s x drops of lavender essential oil, four drops of orange, and two drops of rosemary to the unscented shampoo. ▼

2 Replace the top of the container securely and shake well to disperse the oils. ▼

3 Wash a couple of sprigs of rosemary and add these to the bottle for additional scent and as a decoration. ◄

Essential oils

PERSONALIZING YOUR SHAMPOO

Try adjusting the recipe to suit your hair type:

HAIR	DROPS OF OIL PER 4 FL OZ (120 ML)	DECORATION
Gray hair	6 geranium, 4 grapefruit, 2 juniper	add grapefruit peel
Dandruff	6 rosemary, 4 sage, 2 tea tree	sprig of rosemary
Dry hair	6 lavender, 4 geranium, 2 yarrow	sprig of lavender
Damaged	6 chamomile, 4 lavender, 2 thyme	sprig of lavender

Parsley Juice Preconditioner

This treatment stimulates hair growth, conditions the hair, and helps balance the sebaceous glands, as well as heal scalp problems. The parsley stimulates the circulation and therefore the flow of blood to the scalp.

Making the Preconditioner

Massage the preconditioner well into dry hair, especially the scalp. Leave on the hair for one hour, wearing a shower cap to catch the drips. Rinse thoroughly, then wash hair as usual.

Ingredients: *Parsley • Boiling water*
Equipment: *• Heatproof jug • Food processor*

1 Take a large handful of parsley, wash it thoroughly, and chop roughly. ▲

2 Put the parsley in a jug and pour $1/2$ cup (120 ml) of boiling water over it and leave to infuse for 30 minutes. ▲

3 Put the whole infusion, leaves and liquid, into a food processor, along with two more large handfuls of parsley, and blend to a runny paste. ▲

4 Check the consistency and, if necessary, add either more boiling water or more parsley, until it is the right consistency to stay on the hair. ▲

Oregano Hair Detangler

A detangler to add the wonderful scent of oregano and vanilla to your hair, and great for helping to comb out knots and tangles painlessly—especially good for children.

Making the Detangler

Use this detangler regularly after shampooing and conditioning. Spray on to the ends of your hair to saturate it and comb through, but do not rinse off.

Ingredients: *Fresh oregano leaves • Water • 1 tsp. (5 ml) pure vanilla extract*

Equipment: *Sieve • Funnel • Spray bottle*

1 Remove the leaves from a couple of handfuls of fresh oregano and put in a pan. ◄

2 Add 1 cup (240 ml) of water to the pan and then the vanilla extract. ►

Oregano

3 Bring to a boil, then remove from heat and leave to infuse for 30 minutes. Strain through a sieve into a jar. ▲

4 Pour the leaves into the sieve and press with the back of a spoon to extract as much of the oregano as possible. ◄

5 Use a funnel to pour the liquid into a spray bottle and store in the fridge for up to three days. ►

Chamomile & Rosemary Cleanser

Chamomile soothes as well as cleanses, making this cleanser ideal for sensitive skins. Rosemary has a slightly astringent action and a wonderful scent.

Making the Cleanser

Dried chamomile flowers

Keep the cleanser in the fridge and use night and morning, applying it to the face with a soft cloth or cottonwool. Repeat several times within five minutes, before splashing off with water.

Ingredients: •*Dried chamomile flowers* • *Dried rosemary*
Equipment: • *Heatproof bowl* • *Sieve* • *Small plastic funnel*

1 Put a handful of dried chamomile flowers into a bowl and add a handful of dried rosemary. ▼

2 Pour 2 cups (500 ml) of boiling water over the herbs, stir well, and leave until cold. ▼

3 Strain the herbal infusion through a sieve, collecting the liquid in a jug. ▼

4 Use a spoon to press down on the herbs remaining in the sieve to extract all the liquid from them. Pour the liquid through a funnel into a bottle, seal, and store in the fridge. ▼

Chamomile & Cucumber Moisturizing Lotion

Use the lotion liberally after a bath while the skin is still warm. Cucumber is soothing and chamomile has restorative properties—together they make an excellent moisturizer for dry and chapped skin

Making the Lotion

As with all cosmetic products made from fresh ingredients, the finished mixture should be kept in the fridge to preserve it. If you have a juice extractor, the lotion can be made in minutes. Use within 10 days.

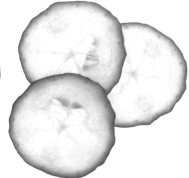

Ingredients: *One cucumber • $^1/_2$ cup (25 g) dried chamomile flowers • 2 tbsp. (30 ml) glycerine*
Equipment: *Sharp knife • Sieve • Jugs • Bowl • Glass bottle • Funnel*

Cucumber

1 Peel the cucumber, using a sharp knife or vegetable peeler. Chop in half and then into small chunks. Press the cucumber through the sieve to extract the juice. Use a juicer if you have one. ▲

2 Put the dried chamomile into a heatproof cup and pour in boiling water up to the 2 cups (500 ml) mark to make a strong infusion. ◄

3 Leave the chamomile to infuse for 20 minutes and then strain through a sieve into a bowl. Leave to cool. ►

4 Spoon the glycerine into the cooled, but not cold, chamomile infusion. Stir in well. Pour the cucumber juice into the glycerine and chamomile mixture and stir. ▼

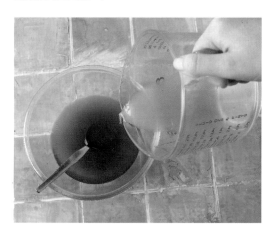

5 Use a funnel to pour the mixture into a glass bottle that can be made airtight. Keep in the fridge and use as required. ►

Lavender & Rose Bath Oil

Bath oils are easy to make using varied combinations of herbs and essential oils. Lavender and rose make a particularly delightful partnership, ideal for a relaxing bath at bedtime thanks to the soothing properties of lavender.

Making the Bath Oil

Use good-quality essential oils when making preparations to be used on your skin. Pop sprigs of lavender and rose petals in the bottles of your bath oils as a reminder of what they contain. Dried herbs work best—fresh herbs retain moisture, which can cause mold to form.

Ingredients: *Dried lavender • Cord, raffia, or ribbon • 1 scant cup (210 ml) of almond oil • Five drops of rose essential oil • Five drops of lavender essential oil*

Equipment: *Sharp scissors*

Handy Hint

If you are giving the bath oil as a gift, tie a decorative ribbon and a sprig of lavender around the bottle neck.

1 Cut a few sprigs of lavender slightly shorter than the bottle and tie with a length of cord, raffia, or ribbon. ▲

2 Put the lavender sprig into the bottle and add a few rose petals taken from a dried rose flower head. ▶

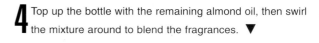

3 Pour half of the almond oil into the bottle. Add the rose essential oil drop by drop and then the lavender essential oil. ▼

4 Top up the bottle with the remaining almond oil, then swirl the mixture around to blend the fragrances. ▼

Herbal Bath Bouquets

Enjoy the delicate fragrance of fresh herbs in the bathroom by suspending this posy from the hot water tap when you run the bath. Use different herbs, depending on whether the effect you want to achieve is relaxing or stimulating.

Lemon balm

Lavender

Making the Bath Bouquet

Fresh herbs add a lovely scent to the bathroom and bath water if they are hung from the taps and allowed to infuse in the warm water before you get in the bath. Choose whichever herbs you have in season in the garden.

Ingredients: : *White and purple lavender* • *Lemon balm* • *Winter savory*
Equipment: *Floristry wire* • *Narrow satin ribbon*
To relax: *Chamomile* • *Hops* • *Jasmine* • *Lime flowers* • *Valerian*
To stimulate: *Bay* • *Eucalyptus* • *Fennel* • *Mint* • *Pine* • *Rosemary* • *Thyme*

1 Cut 12 in, (30 cm) lengths of white and purple lavender. Wire seven or eight stems together in separate bunches. ▲

2 Wire four or five long stems each of lemon balm and winter savory, and add to the bunches of lavender. ▲

3 Mix into one large bunch and tie two 24 in. (60 cm) lengths of ribbon around the stems. Add extra lengths of ribbon to help tie the bunch to the tap. ▲

Handy Hint

Before assembling the bouquet, give the herbs a good shake, or rinse them and allow to dry, to remove any insects.

Aphrodisiac Bath

A sweetly scented mixture to add to your bath water to encourage a romantic mood. Pour under the running water, open the champagne, light the candles, put out the fluffy towels—and let the lovely sweet scent of this herbal combination work its magic.

Making the Mixture

Materials: *Rosemary • Bay leaves • Nasturtium leaves • Arugula (rocket) leaves • Rose petals • 1 tbsp. (15 ml) dried ginseng root • Neroli essential oil*

Use fresh herbs from the garden in summer when possible, and pick fresh, unsprayed roses that are free from greenfly. Choose dark pink roses to add a delicate pink hue to the mixture, so the mixture will add a hint of color to the bath water.

Rose

Rosemary

1 Put a large handful of fresh rosemary, bay leaves, nasturtium leaves, and arugula into a large pan containing 6 cups (1.5 l) of water. ▶

2 Tear the petals off a rose or two until you have a large handful. Add these to the pan along with the dried ginseng root. Bring the water to a boil, cover the pan, and simmer for 15 minutes. ▲

3 Allow to cool a little and strain the mixture through a sieve into a jug or bowl. Press down on the herbs with the back of a spoon to extract all the scent. ▲

4 Add four drops of neroli essential oil to the mixture and stir well. Pour into a suitable jug or bowl to take into the bathroom, and add to the hot running water. ▶

Nasturtium leaves

Dill Aftershave

This aftershave, or facial splash, has the distinctive aroma of dill. It has a slightly astringent action thanks to the witch hazel, and keeping it in the fridge adds to the bracing effect.

Making the Aftershave

Clear honey

This aftershave will keep for several weeks in the fridge. Keeping it at a low temperature also makes it invigorating to splash on first thing in the morning.

Dill seeds

Ingredients: *1 tbsp. (15 ml) honey • 1³/₄ cup (420 ml) still mineral water • 4 tbsp. (60 ml) dill seeds • 1 tbsp. (15 ml) witch hazel*

1 Measure the honey into a small saucepan, add the mineral water and the dill seeds. Bring to a boil, then simmer for about 20 minutes. ◀

2 Allow the mixture to cool in the saucepan. Add the witch hazel to the liquid and stir it to blend the ingredients. ▲

3 Strain the mixture through a fine sieve into an airtight bottle and store in the fridge. ▲

Sage & Mint Tooth Powder

This is an unusual and totally natural tooth powder, made according to an old-fashioned recipe. Sage has antibacterial and antiseptic properties, while mint has a refreshing aroma and flavor. Salt is a traditional tooth cleanser thanks to its abrasive qualities.

Making the tooth powder

Preheat the oven to 350°F/150°C/gas mark 2. Don't use fine table salt—even though you are going to crush the coarse salt finely—because the coarser grains help crush the herbs.

Ingredients: • *¹/₂ oz. (12 g) fresh sage leaves* • *¹/₂ oz. (12 g) fresh mint leaves* • *1 oz. (25 g) coarse sea salt*
Equipment: *Pestle and mortar*

1 Wash and dry the sage and mint leaves and then chop roughly. ◄

2 Spread the chopped herbs in an even layer on a baking sheet, then sprinkle the salt over the top. Put in the preheated oven for about 20 minutes, or until the sage is crisp and dry. ▼

Sage leaves

3 In a pestle and mortar, pound the herb mixture in batches until finely crushed, paying particular attention to the salt. ▲

Mint leaves

4 Rub the mixture through a sieve with fine mesh, using the back of a spoon. You may need to return what is left in the sieve to the pestle and mortar and repeat Steps 3 and 4. Store the resulting powder in a small container with an airtight lid. ◄

Fresh Mouthwash

Caraway and anise are both strong flavors that can be used to scent the breath. Here they are combined to make a mouthwash mixture—perfect to freshen the breath after a rich meal heavy on pungent flavorings.

Making the Mouthwash

Fennel seeds

Use the mouthwash frequently to fight halitosis, but do not drink the liquid. If bad breath persists, consult a doctor or dentist.

1 Put 4 cups (1 l) of water in an enamel or glass pan and add the caraway, anise, fennel seeds, and orris root. Leave to stand for 10 minutes. ▼

Ingredients: $1/2$ oz. (12 g) caraway seeds • $1/2$ oz. (12 g) anise seeds • $1/2$ oz. (12 g) fennel seeds • $1/2$ oz. (12 g) orris root

Equipment: *Teapot or heat-resistant glass • Strainer*

2 Bring to a boil, cover, and simmer for 10 minutes. Remove from the heat and leave to stand, covered, for a further 10 minutes. ▶

3 Strain through a sieve lined with muslin to remove any pieces that rise to the surface. Leave to cool and keep in the fridge. Use as required. ◀

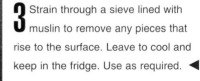

Caraway seeds

234

Rosemary & Mint Foot Refresher

This lotion is the perfect way to revitalize tired feet, particularly in hot summer weather, when the herbs used will be growing in profusion in the garden. The wonderful scent of rosemary combined with mint will also uplift the senses when you use the lotion.

Making the Foot Refresher

You can double the quantities of the ingredients to make a footbath rather than a lotion if you prefer. Refrigerating the lotion before use will add to its refreshing qualities.

Materials: *1 cup (240 ml) milk • Fresh mint • Fresh rosemary • Peppermint extract*
Equipment: *Heatproof bowl*

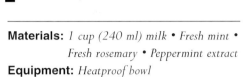

1 Put the milk in a pan and add a large handful of whole mint leaves and six 6 in. (15 cm) sprigs of fresh rosemary. Simmer over a low heat for 15 minutes. ◄

Mint leaves

2 Turn off the heat and let the mixture cool a little, then strain through a sieve into a bowl. Discard the herbs. ►

3 Add 2 tsp. (10 ml) of peppermint extract to the bowl and stir in gently. Soak some cottonwool or a soft cloth in the mixture and dab all over the feet. Then splash gently with cool water. ▲

HEALING PROPERTIES
Rosemary has antibacterial and antifungal properties—perfect for hot, sweaty feet. Mint has invigorating and cooling properties. Milk contains lactic acid, which is soothing.

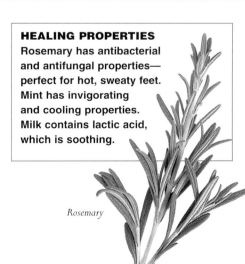

Rosemary

Steam Inhalation

Herb-scented steam offers effective natural relief for a stuffy nose or breathing problems. The steam helps to open the nasal passages, while inhaled microdroplets of the herbal oils also aid clear breathing.

Herbs and essential oils for inhalation are used in the same way. The difference between the two is that the essential oils are more concentrated. You must seek professional medical advice if symptoms persist after using an inhalant.

Essential oils

General method:

Fresh herbs

Crush 1–2 oz. (25–50 g) fresh herbs and add 2 cups (500 ml) of boiling water. Cover your head and the bowl with a towel and inhale the steam. Use for up to five minutes, once or twice a day.

Essential oils

Use three or four drops of oil with 2 cups (500 ml) of boiling water. Inhale as for fresh herbs, but for no more than one or two minutes at a time.

Ingredients: *Herbs or essential oils, according to complaint (see chart for details)*

Equipment: *Large, heatproof bowl • Boiling water • Towel*

Making a Citrus Decongestant

1 Slice two lemons thinly, discarding both ends of each lemon, and put the slices in a large, wide-mouthed heatproof bowl. ▲

2 Bring 4 cups (1 l) of water to a boil and pour it over the lemon slices in the bowl. ▲

3 Add five drops of eucalyptus oil to the boiling water, being careful not to get the oil on your fingers—the scent of the undiluted essential oil is very difficult to remove. ▲

HERBS AND OILS FOR EASING RESPIRATORY PROBLEMS
* Widely available as fresh herbs

	BRONCHITIS	CATARRH	COLDS	COUGHS	HAY FEVER	INFLUENZA	LARYNGITIS	SINUSITIS	SORE THROAT	TONSILITIS	WHOOPING COUGH
BENZOIN OIL	■		■	■					■		
* BERGAMOT									■		
* CHAMOMILE		■						■			
CINNAMON			■			■					
* EUCALYPTUS	■	■	■	■	■	■		■			
FRANKINCENSE	■	■		■			■				
* LAVENDER	■		■			■	■		■	■	
LEMON			■						■		
* MARJORAM			■	■	■						
* MELISSA					■						
MYRRH		■							■	■	
* PEPPERMINT			■			■		■			
* PINE	■	■	■				■	■			
SANDALWOOD				■					■		
TEA TREE	■	■	■			■			■		■
* THYME	■			■			■				■

Sage Infusion for a Sore Throat

Gargling can be very effective for treating a sore throat caused by a cold or lingering cough. For the gargle, use an infusion made from dried sage—its astringent, antiseptic qualities are very soothing.

Making the Sage Infusion

Dried sage

Gargle holding your head back and keep the sage tea in contact with your sore throat for as long as possible. You can drink the rest of the infusion if you like. Do not take more than a couple of cups a day, half a cup at a time.

Ingredients: *Dried sage leaves • Cider vinegar*
Equipment: *Teapot or heat-resistant jug • Strainer*

Handy Hint

For a compress, use 2 tsp. (10 ml) of sage per cup. Make as above, then dip a cotton scarf in the hot tea, wring it out, and wrap around the throat. Secure with another scarf and leave for 20 minutes.

1 Crumble the sage leaves into a jug or teapot, allowing about 1 tsp. (5 ml) of sage leaves per cup. ▲

2 Pour boiling water over the sage leaves, cover, and leave to infuse for 10 minutes. ▲

3 Add about 1 tsp. (5 ml) of cider vinegar, or less if you are making only one cup. Stir gently to mix it in. ▲

4 Strain the infusion into a cup or glass and use as a gargle, checking the temperature first. ▲

240

Comfrey Ointment

The healing properties of comfrey are ideal as a base for the ointment, which can be used to treat bumps, grazes, and damaged skin. The addition of a little borax to the mixture helps preserve it.

Making the Comfrey Ointment

Beeswax sets quickly when cooled, so you may find it helps to use a warmed spoon and keep the beeswax over a pan of hot water until required. The cocoa butter is solid but melts at body temperature. As the ointment contains borax, it will keep for a while—use within three months.

1 Make an infusion by putting the comfrey leaves into a jug and adding 2 cups (500 ml) of boiling water. Leave to cool, then strain. ▲

Materials: *1 oz. (25 g) comfrey leaves • 2 tbsp. (30 ml) of melted beeswax • ¹/₂ cup (125 ml) of almond or olive oil • 2 tbsp. (30 ml) cocoa butter • 2 tsp. (10 ml) of honey • 1 tsp. (5 ml) borax*

2 If using solid beeswax (rather than granules), melt in a bowl over hot water. Spoon 2 tbsp. (30 ml) of beeswax into the almond oil in another bowl set over a pan of hot water. ◄

3 Add the cocoa butter to the oil and beeswax mixture and stir well. ◄

4 Add ¹/₂ cup (125 ml) of the comfrey infusion to another pan. Spoon in the honey and borax. Warm gently while stirring the mixture. Pour it into the bowl of oil, beeswax, and cocoa butter (off the heat). ▼

Handy Hint

If the cocoa butter has set hard and is difficult to measure out, stand the jar in warm water to make it a little less solid.

5 Beat steadily— the mixture will gradually thicken as it cools. (You could use an electric whisk instead.) While still a little runny, pour into a little jar and label the ointment. ▶

Sleep-Easy Tea

There's nothing like the overindulgence of a rich meal to give you a restless night. This herbal tea aids digestion and soothes an upset stomach—drink it after dinner to promote uninterrupted sleep.

Making the Tea

The herbs used here all aid digestion and together they make a soothing tea that will settle an upset stomach to promote a good night's sleep.

Fennel seeds

Dill seeds

Ingredients: *Two handfuls of fresh mint leaves*
- *¹/₂ oz. (12 g) of fennel seeds*
- *¹/₂ oz. (12 g) of dill seeds*

1 Strip the mint leaves from the stems and chop finely. Add to an enamel or glass saucepan. ▲

2 Add the fennel and dill seeds to the pan. Add 3 cups (750 ml) of water and leave to stand for 10 minutes. ▶

3 Put the pan on the heat, bring to a boil, cover, and simmer for 10 minutes. Remove from the heat and leave to stand for a further 10 minutes, still covered. ▼

4 Strain the mixture through a sieve into a jar and leave to cool. Reheat as necessary and drink as required. ▼

Athlete's Foot Remedy

Tackle stubborn athlete's foot the natural way with this soothing oil, which combines the healing properties of marigold, safflower, and tea tree.

Making the Remedy

The marigold helps to heal damaged skin, while the tea-tree oil has a strong antibacterial effect to tackle the fungal infection. Smooth the oil on to clean, dry feet twice a day.

Materials: *2 oz. (50 g) dried marigolds • 3 cups (750 ml) safflower oil • ¹/₂ tsp. (2.5 ml) tea-tree oil*
Equipment: *Muslin • Sieve • Sterilized preserving jar*

Dried marigold

1 Put the marigolds in a preserving jar. Pour safflower oil over to cover the marigolds. Seal the jar and put it on a sunny windowsill, turning occasionally, for three weeks. ▶

2 Set a piece of muslin in a sieve and pour the marigold infusion through the muslin. ▶

3 To get the full benefit of the dried marigold, gather up the muslin and squeeze to extract the last drops of oil. ▲

Handy Hint

If you have fresh marigolds on hand, use these instead of dried. You will need to repeat Steps 1 and 2 using a fresh batch of marigolds.

4 Add the tea-tree oil to the infusion and stir well. Transfer to the preserving jar, seal, and use as required. ▲

Herbal Health Tonics

Tonics can be made to act as pick-me-ups for a specific time of year, or to have a calming, restorative effect on the system. They are medicinal, so not always very palatable—you may need to add honey to sweeten them.

Making the Health Tonics

The winter tonic contains sage for its antiseptic properties, rosehips for Vitamin C, and hibiscus for sweetness. Dandelion leaf in the summer tonic has diuretic properties, chicory root is anti-inflammatory, a laxative, and has a tonic effect on the gall bladder and liver. Hop flowers and valerian root in the calming tonic are potent sedatives and the lavender is an antidepressant.

CALMING TONIC

Dried hop flowers

Ingredients: ¹/₂ oz. (12 g) dried lavender • ¹/₂ oz. (12 g) dried orange flowers • ¹/₂ oz. (12 g) dried lemon-balm leaves • ¹/₂ oz. (12 g) dried hop flowers • ¹/₂ oz. (12 g) dried valerian root

1 Measure out all the dried ingredients into a jar, ensuring you have equal quantities of each. Break the hop flowers from the stems when adding them to the jug. ▼

2 Add 4 cups (1 l) of boiling water to the jug and leave to infuse for 5–10 minutes. ▲

3 Strain the infusion through a sieve into another jug and keep it in the fridge. Take two cups of the gently warmed tonic per day. ▼

WINTER TONIC

Ingredients: ¹/₂ oz. (12 g) dried sage leaf • ¹/₂ oz. (12 g) dried hibiscus flowers • ¹/₂ oz. (12 g) dried rosehips

1 Put the dried sage leaf into a jug and add the hibiscus flowers and the rosehips. Pour over 2 cups (500 ml) boiling water and leave to infuse for 5–10 minutes, then strain. Take four to five cups per day, warmed. ▶

Hibiscus flowers

SUMMER TONIC

Ingredients: ¹/₄ oz. (6 g) dried dandelion leaves • ¹/₄ oz. (6 g) dried mint leaves • ¹/₄ oz. (6 g) dried chicory root • ¹/₂ oz. (12 g) dried rosehips

1 Put the dried dandelion and mint leaves into the jug and add the chicory root and rosehips. Pour over 2 cups (500 ml) boiling water and leave to infuse for 5–10 minutes, before straining. Take three cups per day, hot or cold. ▶

Dried rosehips

Backache Remedy

This backrub is made by crushing fresh and dried herbs in heated oil, in the same way that you might make an infusion with water. Scented with essential oils such as eucalyptus and wintergreen, which have a head-clearing and warming effect, this rub is ideal to ease backache and relax aching muscles caused by overexertion or exercise.

Making the Backache Remedy

Massage the oil into the affected areas by applying a small amount to the palm of your hands, rubbing your hands briskly together to warm the oil and your hands, then applying the oil with smooth massaging movements. Alternatively, you can use a wooden massaging aid.

Ingredients: *Dried valerian root • Dried sage leaf • Chamomile • Fresh ginger root • Sunflower oil • Essential oils: camphor, chamomile, clary sage, eucalyptus, ginger, and wintergreen*
Equipment: *Bottles with stoppers*

1 Put the valerian root, sage leaf, and chamomile into a heavy-based pan. Peel and slice the ginger root into the pan. ▲

2 Cover the herbs with sunflower oil and heat for several hours by heating the mixture up, but not to boiling, then turning the heat off and allowing the mixture to cool. Reheat in the same way several times. ▲

3 Strain the herbs through a sieve, pressing down on the herbs to extract all the goodness. Strain the oil again through a double layer of muslin to remove traces of dried chamomile flowers. ▲

4 Add five drops each of camphor, eucalyptus, and wintergreen oils, and one drop each of chamomile, clary sage, and ginger oil. Stir well and bottle. ▲

Dried sage leaf

Root ginger

Herbs in the Home

There are few things more satisfying than making objects to perfume and beautify the home or to give as gifts. The herbal crafts in this "Herbs in the Home" chapter include instructions for making such items as decorative candles, potpourris, and herbal baskets, as well as drawer fresheners, herbal displays, and wreaths. Whether you grow herbs mostly to use in the kitchen or more specifically for herbal crafts, you will gain great enjoyment from the creative expression that herbal craftmaking will give you.

Share your enthusiasm with friends and family by making gifts of your homemade herbal displays or traditional flower posies. Alternatively, you can use herbs in household items such as a herbal flea powder to treat the family dog, or an all-purpose cleaner to use around the home instead of the chemically based commercial preparations.

Fresh Herbal Basket

A fresh arrangement of herbs makes a striking and unusual centerpiece for a table, as well as adding a wonderful scent to the room. Herb flowers are complemented by pansies to add color.

Arranging the Basket

Keep the arrangement out of direct sunlight as the herbs with fleshy stems (those that are wired) are prone to wilting if they get too warm. Revitalize the arrangement with a misting of water from a plant sprayer as required.

Materials: *Fresh herbs: rosemary and chives in flower, flat (Italian) parsley, poppy buds, 'Dark Opal' (purple) basil, arugula, and eucalyptus • Pansies • Sheet of plastic • 22 gauge floristry wire • Block of florist's foam • Florist's frog • Flat basket with handle*

Equipment: *Hot glue gun or floristry tape*

Chives in flower

1 Soak the florist's foam in water for 15 minutes. Attach the florist's frog to the base of the basket using a glue gun or floristry tape. Cover the base with a piece of plastic to prevent leakage. Add the foam to the basket, cutting off the corners, as necessary, to fit. ▲

2 Cut lengths of eucalyptus up to 12 in. (30 cm) long. Remove some of the leaves at the base and push the stems into the florist's foam, around the outer edge, to fan out over the basket. Add rosemary to the central part of the foam. ▲

3 Add the poppy buds and foliage randomly, aiming for a loose, unstructured feel, which the poppies will provide as the buds have a natural tendency to droop. ▶

4 Use precut lengths of floristry wire to wrap around the base of the bunches of herbs. This allows you to insert them easily into the arrangement—their stems are too fleshy to use individually. Add the bunches randomly. ▼

5 Wire three or four chive flowers into bunches and add to the arrangement. Add wired bunches of pansies for a pleasing color effect. Make sure all the wired stems are pushed into the florist's foam. Spray with water. ◀

Decorated Pots

Terra-cotta pots can be given an original touch by sponging them with paint and then adding pressed ivy leaves as a decoration. Sponging is very quick and the paint dries within minutes—all you have to do then is to add the ivy. Use the pots to grow herbs.

Decorating the Pots

To create the paint finish, you need to use clean, dry terra-cotta pots. Apply two colors of acrylic or emulsion paint to give a mottled finish. When sponging, load the sponge lightly with paint. Don't worry if it looks uneven to start—you can easily spread the paint along with the sponge. You could match the pressed leaves to the contents of the pot for an effective touch.

Materials: *Paint: acrylic in yellow and pearl luster was used here • Terra-cotta pots • Varnish, matt silk or gloss • Pressed ivy or other leaves*

Equipment: *Natural sponges • Varnish brush*

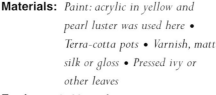

Ivy leaves

1 Dab a sponge in the paint (yellow acrylic in this case), and apply it to the terra-cotta pot, dabbing it lightly all over the pot to provide a base coat. ▲

2 Using a clean sponge, apply a second color (pearl luster). Do this lightly, allowing some of the base color to show through. Leave to dry. ▲

3 Dab varnish on to the pot in the first area you want to decorate with pressed leaves (the varnish is used as glue). ▶

4 Add the pressed leaves (ivy was used here) in a random fashion, pressing them down gently with your fingers. Repeat as required, adding more leaves around the pot. ▲

Handy Hint

Don't cover the whole pot with paint—it works well if some of the pot or the base coat shows through.

5 Allow the varnish to dry, then varnish the whole pot, working over the leaves, using a dabbing action. Leave to dry, then varnish again. ◀

255

Sage and Lavender Mirror

Lavender

Sage

A simple ready-made frame can be transformed by dressing it up with small bunches of dried herb foliage in a given colorscheme— misty blues and greens of dried sage and lavender are used here. Bay leaves and ribbons soften the overall effect.

Decorating the Mirror

Prepare the frame by painting it with blue emulsion paint diluted with a little water and leave it to dry. Keep the overall color scheme simple and avoid adding too much foliage around the mirror as the end result will appear cluttered.

Materials: *Unfinished pine-framed mirror • Blue emulsion • Dried sage • Dried lavender • Dried bay leaves • Floristry wires*

Equipment: *Ribbon • Scissors • Hot glue gun*

1 Choose small sprigs of sage, about 3-4 in. (7.5–10 cm) long, and wire them together to make two bunches. ▼

2 Cut stems of lavender about 5 in. (12 cm) long and wire two bunches together as before. ▼

3 Cut two lengths of ribbon about 12 in. (30 cm) long and form each into a bow—tie it as though tying shoelaces. ▼

4 Position a bunch of sage leaves at each bottom corner of the mirror, leaves pointing outwards, and glue in place using a glue gun. ▼

Handy Hint

To add scent, you can rub lavender essential oil on to the back of the mirror frame—choose a part that doesn't touch the wall or it will stain.

5 Use the glue gun to attach a bunch of lavender on top of the sage at each corner. ▼

6 Glue the bows in place to hide the wires on the dried bunches. ▼

7 Tuck dried bay leaves under the bows and over the stem bunches to hide the wires and cut ends. ▶

Herb Flower Greeting Cards

Press herb flowers and foliage in spring and summer when they are in their prime to provide a colorful selection to make your own greetings cards.

Making the Greetings Cards

To press flowers, choose small specimens of everything—flower heads such as wild pansies and daisies, and foliage such as thyme, bay, and ivy leaves. You will need round-ended tweezers to position the pressed items as they are very fragile and break easily. Apply glue using a toothpick for the same reason.

1 Lay sprigs of thyme out on the card until you have a pleasing design. Use tweezers to lift and move the herbs, and handle them gently. ▲

Materials: *Selection of pressed herbs and flowers, such as thyme, lavender, heather, wild pansy, daisy, and alchemilla • Card blanks (from craft shops) • ¹/₈ in. (3 mm) wide ribbon • Latex glue •*

Equipment: *Round-ended tweezers • Toothpicks or small skewers*

2 To secure the thyme, use a little glue on the end of a toothpick and smear it along the stem. Add lavender and heather in the same way. Glue stalks to the base of the flowers. ▶

3 Glue the centers of wild pansy and daisy flower heads in place, using tweezers to position them. Lightly press the heads in place with your fingertips. ▼

4 Add tiny heads of alchemilla to fill in the background of the design, then glue on small ivy leaves, sliding them in behind the flower heads. Tie a length of ribbon into a neat bow and glue to the base of the design. ▼

Handy Hint

Use any pressed flowers you have on hand, keeping to a single species or color for best effect. Depending on your artistic abilities, you could also add a pen and ink border, or write in the Latin name of the flower, or even add a short message for the recipient.

Air Freshener

This liquid mixture freshens the house, deters insects, and keeps lingering smells at bay. The fragrance is provided by eucalyptus, peppermint, and lavender essential oils.

Making the Air Freshener

Use the air freshener sparingly as the essential oils can be strongly scented. Avoid using it in the kitchen or around food-preparation areas.

Materials: *1 tbsp. (5 ml) each of eucalyptus, peppermint, and lavender essential oils*
Equipment: *Measuring jug • Glass jar with lid • Spray container • Funnel*

1 Measure out 2 cups (500 ml) of boiling water and leave to cool. Add 1 tbsp. (15 ml) of eucalyptus oil to the water. ▼

2 Carefully measure out 1 tbsp. (15 ml) of peppermint essential oil and add to the water. ▼

Eucalyptus

Peppermint

Lavender

3 Measure out 1 tbsp. (15 ml) of lavender essential oil and add to the water. ▼

4 Secure the lid on the jar and shake well to mix the ingredients. ▼

5 Using a funnel, decant the mixture into the spray container. ▲

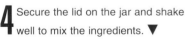

Handy Hint

Substitute 1 tsp. (5 ml) of pennyroyal oil for the lavender to act as an effective insect deterrent. It is particularly good against animal fleas.

Sweet-Smelling Box of Herbs

A fragrant box of herbs is the perfect way of adding a sweet scent to a room that may not be used frequently. The blue-grays of the dried lavender and sage combine well together in a simple cardboard box.

Making the Herb Box

Fill the box with bunches of herbs cut to stand with their flowering or foliage stems protruding above the top of the box. Tie the individual bunches so that they stand well.

Materials: *Dried lavender • Dried sage • Raffia • Paper string • Box about 8 in. (20 cm) square • Lavender and sage essential oils • Florist's scissors*

1 Tie a large bunch of lavender using raffia. Tie a large bunch of sage together in the same way. Make several generous bunches of each herb. ▼

3 Wrap string or paper string tightly around the box several times. Tie a knot at the back, trim the ends, and tuck them away behind the string. ▼

2 Use florist's scissors to trim the stems to the right height, so the herbs protrude from the box. The stems are thick, so only trim away a few at a time. ▲

4 Arrange the bunches of sage and lavender alternately into the box. You should be able to fit at least three rows consisting of three bunches into the box. ▼

Handy Hint

To maintain the scent of the herbs, sprinkle one or two drops of the appropriate essential oil onto each bunch in the completed box.

Dried sage

263

Decorative Candles

Combine dried herbs with glycerined foliage and preserved flowers to decorate pillar candles for special and festive occasions. Tie on the sprigs with a length of festive ribbon to add a finishing touch.

Decorating the Candles

You can decorate a single candle for a centerpiece or, for a more spectacular effect, use three or more candles of varying lengths and thicknesses.

Materials: *Glycerined ivy • Dried golden rod*
• Dried roses • Dried sage leaves
• Lengths of ribbon, ¹/₂ in. (12 mm) wide
• Sharp scissors • Medium-gauge floristry wire
• Pillar candles in varying heights and diameters

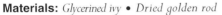

1 Snip small bunches of leaves from the ivy, leaving stems of about 3 in. (7.5 cm) and including preserved berries where possible. ▼

2 Snip small sprigs of golden rod flowers – you will need three or four sprigs per bunch, depending on the size of the candle. ▼

> **CAUTION...**
> For safety, never leave burning candles unattended. Either use the candles solely as decoration, or blow them out as soon as the flame nears the foliage.

3 Snip a single rose head and a sprig of sage to about 2 in. (5 cm) long, depending on the size of the candle. ▶

4 Combine the sprigs, with the ivy at the back, and bind the stems together with a length of floristry wire. ▼

5 Place the sprig close to the base of the candle. Trim the floristry wire and stems. Wrap a length of ribbon around the decoration to secure it. Tie the ribbon into a neat bow, leaving the ends to trail down. ▶

Lavender & Tansy Drawer Fresheners

Make these simple sachets to add a scent to linens and sweaters stored in drawers and cupboards, with the added bonus that the contents will repel insects such as moths.

Making the Drawer Fresheners

Make the sachets out of offcuts of calico—they are small enough to sew by hand. Add small bows to the completed sachets for a decorative finishing touch.

Materials: *Dried southernwood • Dried mint • Dried lavender flowers • Dried tansy, leaves and flowers • Offcuts of calico for the sachets • Ribbon bows*

1 Put 5 tbsp. (75 ml) of dried southernwood into a bowl. Add 5 tbsp. (75 ml) of dried mint. ▲

2 Add 10 tbsp. (150 ml) of dried lavender flowers to the bowl. ▲

Dried southernwood

Dried lavender

3 Add 5 tbsp. (60 ml) of dried tansy to the bowl. Mix everything together. ▲

4 Sew two plain calico rectangles 5 x 3½ in. (12 x 9 cm) together on three sides. Turn right sides out and spoon in some of the mixture. ◀

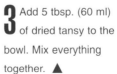

5 To secure the sachet, oversew the open end with small stitches. Decorate with a small readymade ribbon. ▲

Spicy Marigold Potpourri

The herbs and spices used in this potpourri combine well to provide a distinctive scent. You can choose to add other favorite herbs and essential oils to give it an individual touch.

Making the Potpourri

To make the most of the finished potpourri, set it in a pretty bowl. Decorate the top with sprigs of hops, dried lime, and fresh or dried marigolds. Fresh marigolds are particularly pretty, so use them if they are in season.

Dried marigolds

Materials: *2 oz. (50 g) dried marigold • Equal amounts of mixed dried herbs such as oregano, sage, mint, and thyme to make 4¹/₂ cups (1 l) • 1 oz. (25 g) dried lavender • 2 cinnamon sticks • 1 oz. (25 g) orris root powder • 5 drops cinnamon essential oil • 3 drops orange essential oil • 1 drop clove essential oil • ¹/₂ tsp. (2.5 ml) each of allspice and caraway seeds • Hops, dried lime, and fresh or dried marigold for decoration • Bowl • Kitchen scissors • Plastic bag*

Handy Hint

When the scent fades, put the potpourri back in a plastic bag, add more drops of essential oils, shake, and reseal the bag. Leave for a few days.

1 Place the dried marigold in a bowl. Snip the oregano and add to the marigold. ▶

2 Snip the sage and other dried herbs into the bowl, and mix well. Add the lavender. Crush the cinnamon sticks and add to the bowl. ▼

3 Add the drops of essential oils. Mix in the allspice, caraway seeds, and orris root powder. Place the mixture in a polythene bag, seal, and leave for a week. Turn into a bowl and add the decorations. ▶

269

Fresh Bay-Leaf Wreath

The wreath has the classic appearance of a laurel crown, and its sheer simplicity makes it very attractive and effective. It can be used as a wall decoration in the kitchen.

Making the Wreath

The wreath consists solely of overlapping fresh bay leaves, glued in a herringbone pattern to an unpeeled willow wreath.

Materials: *Fresh bay leaves • 12 in. (30 cm) unpeeled willow wreath*

Equipment: *Glue gun*

Handy Hint

If you have a bay hedge, simply use the clippings to make the wreath.

1 Sort the perfect whole leaves from the branches, discarding any that are discolored or damaged. ▲

2 Apply the leaves alternately to the wreath to form a herringbone pattern, using a glue gun to secure them in place. ▲

3 Continue the design, applying glue to the base of each leaf and then sticking it down. ▼

4 Fill in any gaps with smaller leaves to avoid a sparse appearance. As the wreath becomes fuller, snip off the stems of the leaves to make it easier to secure them. ▲

Pressed Herb Picture

The simplest arrangement of pressed flowers makes a strikingly effective picture, set on roughly torn handmade paper and corrugated cardboard for a modern feel.

Making the Picture

Press your flowers at the height of summer when they look their best. Pick them mid-morning, when early dew has had a chance to dry and before the full sun hits them. Press for several weeks before use.

Materials: *Picture frame 10 x 10 in. (25 x 25 cm) • Corrugated cardboard • Handmade paper • Pressed rosemary, thyme, heather, and lavender*

Equipment: *Glue • Toothpicks • Tweezers*

1 Cut a piece of corrugated cardboard to the same size as the glass in your picture frame. Tear a piece of handmade paper to a slightly smaller size than the card. ▲

Heather

2 Glue the paper lightly to the card at each corner, then start to lay out your design using tweezers to handle the delicate stems, and putting pressed rosemary in the bottom righthand corner. ◄

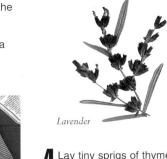

Lavender

4 Lay tiny sprigs of thyme in the adjacent top corner, pointing upward rather than in toward the center. Glue in place. ►

3 Using a toothpick, apply glue in a line down the back of the rosemary stems once you are happy with their position. Set out pressed heather flowers in an adjacent corner and glue in place in the same way. ▲

Rosemary

Thyme

5 Lay tiny sprigs of lavender in place in the remaining corner of the picture and glue in place. Carefully replace the glass in the picture and secure the frame. ◄

Rose & Daisy Basket

A small arrangement like this makes a perfect welcoming decoration in a guest bedroom, on a sideboard or hall table, or as the centerpiece at a special lunch party.

Making the Rose & Daisy Baskets

A fresh arrangement made in a small container works best, using small flowers and a simple color scheme.

Materials: *Florist's foam • Small basket 8 x 3 in. (20 x 7.5 cm) • Fresh ivy leaves • Fresh peony leaves • Cream roses • Orange chrysanthemums • Orange rosebuds • Daisies*

Chrysanthemum

1 Soak the florist's foam in water and put into the basket. Cut short lengths of ivy and peony foliage, and insert all around the block to hide it. ▶

2 Cut 10 or 12 cream rosebuds in varying stages of openness and add to the middle of the arrangement, putting the fuller roses in the center and the buds at each end. ▲

3 Cut short stems, about 4 in. (10 cm), of orange chrysanthemums and dot in among the roses, using the vivid color as a highlight. ◀

Rosebuds

4 Cut several orange rosebuds and add to the arrangement in between the chrysanthemums and among the roses. ▶

5 Cut short stems of daisies and set them in groups of two or three randomly through the arrangement. ▲

275

Gift Display for Drying

A clever idea for bringing lasting enjoyment to a friend—an arrangement put together from your herb garden, designed to be easily separated into bunches for hanging and drying.

Making the Display

Choose from whatever herbs you have available in your garden, depending on the season. Look for a mixture of flowers and different types of foliage, and select plants of varying heights.

Materials: *A selection of fresh herbs, some in flower. The following were used here: White lavender • Lady's mantle • Marjoram •Wormwood • Hellebore foetidus • Lemon balm • Flowering mint •Weeping pear foliage*

Equipment: *Rubber band • Raffia*

Flowering mint

1 Make two or three bunches of each species you have picked, depending on availability. Don't be tempted to pack too much into each bunch or they will not dry well. ▼

2 Start to assemble the arrangement, putting the tallest plants to the back and adding the bunches to balance color, flowers, foliage, and height. ◄

Marjoram

3 Assemble all the bound bunches together, making a final check for color balance and graduation of height. Secure with a rubber band. ▲

Handy Hint

The arrangement can be displayed for two to three days before hanging, but if you don't want to dry it, the bunches are easily arranged in a vase.

4 Tie the raffia loosely around the finished arrangement to hide the rubber band, wrapping it around at least twice and tying a double knot or a loose bow. ▲

Lady's mantle

Herbal Laundry Rinse

The scent of this rinse and spray adds a special outdoor-dried freshness to your sheets, pillowcases, and general linens and cottons.

Making the Laundry Rinse

Add this to the final rinse of your laundry or put into a spray container and mist your laundry lightly before use.

Materials: *One large handful of mint • Three large handfuls of lavender • Borax*

1 Put the mint in a large mixing bowl. Add the lavender, chopping it into short lengths and including leaves, flowers, and stems ▲

2 Pour 2 cups (500 ml) of boiling water over the herbs until they are well covered, adding more water as necessary.

3 Allow to cool, strain into a jar, and add a pinch of borax. Stir well. ▲

4 Pour the liquid into a bottle, allowing any sediment or stray herb leaves to remain in the jar. Store the bottle in a cool, dark place and decant into a spray as required. ▲

Handyman's Skin Protector

Use this skin-softening lotion to apply to hands after work that may have left them roughened or chapped—for example, after sanding, painting, or gardening.

Making the Hand Protector

You need to know the capacity of the container you are using—check it by filling with water and measuring the water quantity. Apply the salve to clean hands and rub in.

Ingredients: *Glycerine • Rosemary essential oil • Orange essential oil • Bergamot essential oil*

Equipment: *Measuring jug • Funnel • Storage container with stopper*

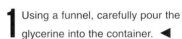

Essential oils

1 Using a funnel, carefully pour the glycerine into the container. ◀

2 Add the essential oil to the container, in the ratio of three drops each of rosemary and orange essential oils, and two drops of bergamot essential oil to $\frac{1}{4}$ cup + 1 tbsp. (75 ml) of glycerine. ▲

Handy Hint

You can use the salve in winter to treat chapped hands.

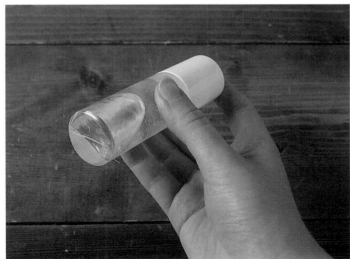

3 Shake the bottle well, inverting it a few times to mix the oils well into the glycerine, which is quite a thick mixture. ▲

Gardener's Face and Hand Screen

This soothing, moisturizing cream helps protect the face and hands against overexposure to the wind and other elements when outside in the garden. Apply before going outdoors and again when you come in.

Making the Face Cream

Cocoa butter sets hard and is difficult to remove from the pot. If you have a full pot, you can melt it all then pour half off and save the rest. Alternatively you will have to scrape it out of the jar.

Materials: *2 oz. (50 g) cocoa butter*
- *2 tbsp. (30 ml) almond oil*
- *Lime essential oil*
- *Lavender essential oil*

1 Put the cocoa butter jar container in a bowl of very hot water. As it starts to melt, use a metal teaspoon to scrape it down and stir it around until evenly blended. ◄

Lime essential oil

Lavender essential oil

2 Add the almond oil to the melted cocoa butter and stir well in. ►

3 Add six drops of lime essential oil and six drops of lavender essential oil to the mixture. Stir well to blend, allow to cool, and seal. Use as required. ◄

Almond oil

CAUTION

If you have sensitive skin, do a patch test first as essential oils may irritate the skin.

Dried Herb Topiary Trees

Topiary trees make striking dried flower decorations, enhanced by their simple shape. Used singly or in pairs, they make original presents.

Making the Topiary Trees

Dried sage leaves work well as the foliage for the pot because of their color contrast.

Dried oregano flowers & eucalyptus

Materials: *Small 3 in. (7.5 cm) diameter terra-cotta pot • Block of florist's foam • Cinnamon sticks • 2³/₄ in. (7 cm) florist's foam ball • Bunch of dried carthamus • Dried sage leaves*

Purple marjoram & carthamus leaves

1 Press the top of the pot into the foam block, then use a sharp knife to carve the foam into shape to fit in the pot, tapering it toward the base. ▼

2 Press the foam into the pot. Hold together three 6 in. (15 cm) long cinnamon sticks and push them into the center of the foam, down to the base. ▼

3 Carefully push the florist's foam ball on to the sticks so that it is secure, but avoiding pushing the sticks through to the top. ▶

4 Cut several carthamus heads with ³/₄ in. (2 cm) stems. Starting at the base of the ball, push the stems into the foam, working round and upward to cover the ball. ▲

5 Cut individual leaves of dried sage with ³/₄ in. (2 cm) stems and push these into the foam in the pot so that the leaves stand upright. ◀

Carthamus heads & sage leaves

285

Quick Lavender Bags

These bags are super quick to make and require no stitching. They can be tucked into drawers or the linen cupboard, or hung in wardrobes or in rooms to delicately scent the air. Very inexpensive, but striking to look at, they make delightful, affordable gifts.

Making the Lavender Bags

Use a slightly transparent fabric—squares in different toning colors look particularly attractive—so that the dried flowers are visible inside. Cut 12 in. (30 cm) squares of the chosen fabrics. They can also be used as Christmas tree decorations.

Materials: *Dried lavender flowers • Rubber bands • Crystal organza*

1 Put about ¹/₂ oz. (12 g) of dried lavender flowers into the center of a square of fabric. ▼

Dried lavender flowers

2 Gather the fabric up around the lavender into a bag shape and secure close to the lavender with a rubber band, wound around the top two or three times. ▼

Handy Hint

You can use pinking shears when cutting out the fabric to give a pretty finish to the bags.

3 Wrap a 12 in. (30 cm) length of narrow ¹/₈ in. (3 mm) ribbon around the elastic band to hide it, then tie the ribbon into a bow and leave the ends trailing. ▲

Fall Fruit & Flower Arrangement

Pumpkins do not just make jack-o'-lanterns at Halloween, or pumpkin pies, they also make good containers for seasonal fruit and flower displays, like this stunning arrangement of fall leaves and berries.

St. John's wort

Globe amaranths

Creating the Display

Saw the top off the pumpkin using a very sharp knife, then hollow out the inside, removing the seeds and fibrous strands, using a spoon or scissors.

Materials: *Florist's foam • Large pumpkin, about 10 in. (25 cm) in diameter • A selection of fall foliage and berries—the following were used here: smoke tree (Cotinus), fruiting ivy (Hedera), red berries (Cotoneaster), astilbe, stems of orange chilies, St. John's wort (Hypericum), dahlias, globe amaranths (Gomphrena globosa)*

1 Put a large block of well-soaked florist's foam into the pumpkin. Cut 8–10 in. (20–25 cm) lengths of foliage (smoke tree). ▶

3 Tuck the ivy berries in separately, then cut a stem of cotoneaster berries into three lengths and add to the display so that the berries protrude at pleasing angles. ▶

2 Build up the base with the foliage, adding height at the back. Use single leaves to help cover the foam. Separate berry stems of ivy from the leaves, keeping the stems as long as possible. Add the leaves to the pumpkin. ▲

4 Build up the display, inserting 5 in. (12 cm) lengths of astilbe and 8 in. (20 cm) lengths of chilies. Snip 6 in. (15 cm) lengths of St. John's wort berries, stripping away the leaves, and insert in display. ▶

5 Cut four or five dahlia flower heads and spread them through the display. Strip the leaves from the stems of the globe amaranths and add to the display in groups as a final touch. ▲

Dahlia

289

Flowers in a Tank

A glass tank makes the perfect vessel for this colorful spring flower arrangement. Add interest to the container itself using pebbles and glass nuggets, which serve the dual purpose of being decorative and anchoring the flower stems.

Making the Arrangement

If you don't have any of the suggested flowers, use others, but don't mix large flower heads such as peonies with smaller varieties. In season, the spring blossom can be almond or cherry, or whatever is available.

Eucalyptus

Freesia

Materials: *Glass tank • Assorted pebbles • Glass nuggets • Fresh rosemary • Eucalyptus • Hyacinths • Spring blossom • Paper white narcissi • Pink freesias*

1 Put several medium to small pebbles in the base of a glass tank, and scatter glass nuggets in two or three colors among them. ▶

2 Cut stems of rosemary about 12 in. (30 cm) long and strip away the leaves two-thirds of the way up the stem. Push the stems in among the pebbles, wedging the base of the stems with more pebbles and nuggets as necessary. ▼

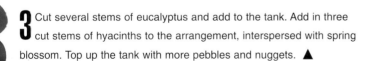

3 Cut several stems of eucalyptus and add to the tank. Add in three cut stems of hyacinths to the arrangement, interspersed with spring blossom. Top up the tank with more pebbles and nuggets. ▲

4 Use pink freesias and white narcissi to finish the arrangement, cutting the stems to varying lengths so that the flowers will radiate through the arrangement. Use remaining nuggets to secure the stems firmly, and top up with water. ▶

Herbal Hot Towels

For a wonderful treat for your guests after a meal involving messy finger foods—such as shellfish or meat on the bone—serve up these deliciously scented lemon and rosemary hot towels as a hand refresher.

Lemon essential oil

Making the Hot Towels

If it is the right time of year, use fresh lemon balm from the garden or lemon mint. Rosemary is a good option because it is available throughout the year.

Materials: *Six thin, cream-colored handtowels • Lemon essential oil • Fresh rosemary*

Equipment: *Atomizer • Bamboo steamer*

1 Put ¹/₂ cup (125 ml) water into an atomizer and add five drops of lemon essential oil. Replace the lid and shake the atomizer well. ▶

Handy Hint

In hot weather, you may prefer chilled towels as a refresher. After spraying with scented water, place in the fridge until cold.

2 Spread each towel out on the work surface and spray well all over with the atomizer of scented water until it is thoroughly damp. ▶

3 Fold each damp towel in half and lay a sprig of rosemary over it. Roll up, enclosing the rosemary, and set on a plate to protect your work surface from the moisture. ▲

5 Give the towels a final misting of scented water, then put the lid on the steamer and put over the heat for 3–5 minutes, until hot. Use tongs to distribute them to your guests, and warn them that the towels will be hot. ◀

4 Lay a couple of sprigs of rosemary in the base of the bamboo steamer and pile the towels on top. Bring a pan of hot water to a boil, so that steam is rising. ▲

Rosemary

293

Spiced Scented Coasters

These coasters contain crushed spices that release their aroma when a warm tea or coffee mug is placed on them. The layers of padding within the coasters help protect polished wood surfaces from the heat.

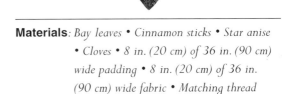

Making the Coasters

Use warm, woody spices to create the filling for the coasters. Crush them in a pestle and mortar rather than using powdered spices, which will filter through the fabric. Cut the fabric and padding into 12 x 6 in. (15 cm) squares to make six coasters.

1 Crush six bay leaves, a couple of cinnamon sticks, some cloves, and star anise with the pestle and mortar— you can vary the spice quantities according to preference. ▶

Cloves

Materials: *Bay leaves • Cinnamon sticks • Star anise • Cloves • 8 in. (20 cm) of 36 in. (90 cm) wide padding • 8 in. (20 cm) of 36 in. (90 cm) wide fabric • Matching thread*

Equipment: *Pestle and mortar • Pins • Scissors • Needle*

2 Lay the squares of wadding on the wrong side of the fabric squares. Place the squares of fabric right sides together, pin, and backstitch or machine stitch around all sides, leaving a 2 in. (5 cm) gap on one side and taking 1/2 in. (12 mm) seams. ▼

3 Turn the coasters through and press. Add a teaspoon or so of the crushed spices to the coaster and shake to disperse evenly through the coaster. ▲

Cinnamon

4 Close the gap in the coaster with close overstitches to prevent any spices escaping. If using a sewing machine, overstitch all around the outside, close to the edge. ▶

Traditional Flower Bouquet

This is a beautifully scented bouquet, with roses in a delicate shade of pink and foliage in several shades of green, from blue-green to bright green. The flowers have been chosen for their 19th-century associations when formal posies were far more widely used than they are today.

Making the Bouquet

The bouquet is designed to be presented as a gift, so you can tie the stems with a length of lace to emphasize the period feel, or wrap them in colored tissue paper. Set the posy in a vase on a low table to display the arrangement at its best.

Materials: *Pink roses*
- *Lavender*
- *Heather*
- *Rosemary*
- *Bay leaves*
- *Ivy • Rubber band*
- *Length of lace*

1 Take alternate stems of roses and lavender, cutting the stems of lavender short to avoid the woody lower stems. Put the stems together to form the center of the bouquet, using five roses. ▼

Heather

2 Add in alternate stems of heather and rosemary, revolving the posy in your hand as you work so that it builds evenly from the center. Tuck two or three stems of heather into the center among the roses. ▼

3 Work around the posy, adding in stems of fresh bay leaves and cut stems of trailing ivy in various lengths to encircle the flowers with foliage. When you are happy with the finished effect, trim the stems to an even length. ▼

Lavender

4 Use a rubber band to hold the stems firmly together. Take a long length of broad lace edging and tie around the posy into a bow, with long trailing ends to hide the rubber band. ▲

297

Herbal Flea Powder

Dried lavender

This flea powder for dogs is made using herbal rather than chemical ingredients, with strong-smelling dried herbs that insects dislike, but which will have the dual effect of keeping the fleas away and making your dog smell nicer.

Making the Flea Powder

Rub this flea powder into your dog's coat, paying particular attention to the spine and back of the neck—the areas that are hard for your dog to reach and therefore where the fleas tend to congregate. Brush out with a stiff brush.

Materials: *1 oz. (25 g) dried lavender • 1 oz. (25 g) dried pennyroyal • 1 oz. (25 g) dried rosemary • 8 oz. (200 g) baking soda • 1 lb. (450 g) cornstarch • Citronella, lemon, pennyroyal, and rosemary essential oils*

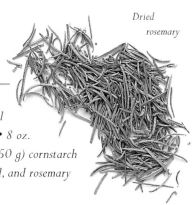

Dried rosemary

1 Put the dried lavender, pennyroyal, and rosemary into a food processor and blend to a fine powder. ▶

2 Transfer the crushed dried herbs to a mixing bowl and stir in the baking soda and the cornstarch. ▼

3 Add eight drops each of citronella, lemon, and rosemary essential oils, and 10 drops of pennyroyal essential oil. Stir well in. ▶

Dried pennyroyal

Handy Hint

You will get a finer powder if you remove as many sticks and stalks as possible from the dried herbs first.

4 Put the mixture in a large ziploc bag, shake well, and seal. Leave for a few days for the scents to infuse before use. ▲

All-Purpose Cleaner

There is a high concentration of essential oils in this household cleaner, giving it aromatic as well as antibacterial qualities. Use it to clean any hard surfaces such as kitchen or bathroom tiles or ceramics, thoroughly rinsing away the cleaner with clean water.

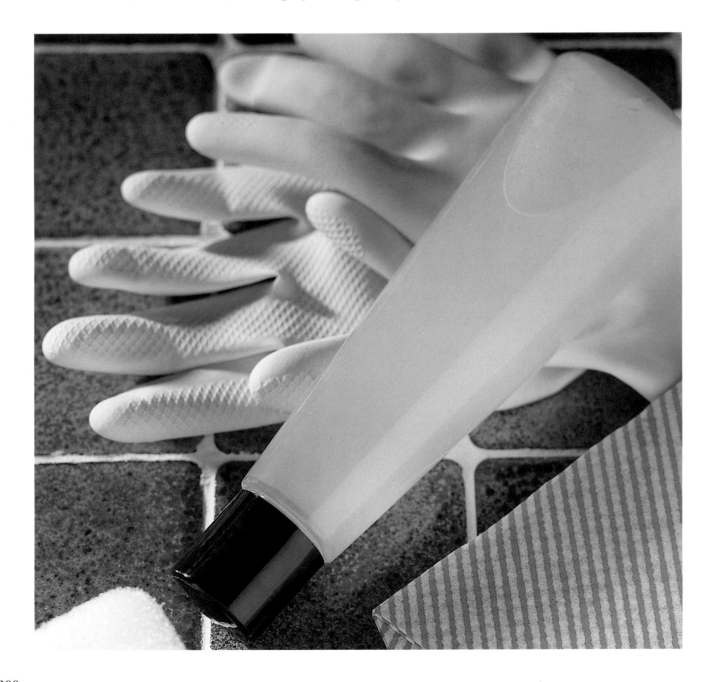

Making the Cleaner

Materials: *Eucalyptus, juniper, lavender, and thyme essential oils • 2 tsp. (10 ml) methylated spirits • 1 tbsp. (15 ml) borax*

Make sure the water is hot, but not boiling, so that it will dissolve the borax but not destroy the power of the essential oils. You can substitute other essential oils, such as citrus-based ones, if you prefer.

2 Measure out the borax and stir into the bowl, ensuring everything is well mixed together. ▲

1 Put the methylated spirits into a small bowl and add 12 drops each of eucalyptus, juniper, lavender, and thyme essential oils. ▲

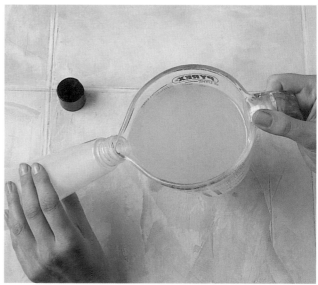

4 Decant the mixture into a plastic bottle, seal, label, and store. Apply with a soft clean cloth. ▲

Essential oils

3 Stir the methylated spirits, essential oil, and borax mixture into 2 cups (500 ml) of warm (not boiling) water. Mix well together. ▲

301

Index